'This is a terrific book! Knafo and Selzer are master clinicians who work with the skill, determination, patience, and grace required to give patients who are in psychological retreat from consensual reality an opportunity to risk re-entering a world they came to find in their past too difficult to bear. The authors present a persuasive case for regarding psychotic symptoms as essential sources of information that provide a foundation for the patient's treatment. They illustrate their approach with many clear and moving clinical examples. They share their intuitions, formulations, and decisions as their work unfolds with individual patients. The book is full of clinical wisdom, important ideas, and practical advice. It is certain to be of value to experienced clinicians and early-career psychotherapists alike.'

**Michael Garrett, M.D.**, *psychiatrist, psychoanalyst, and author of the highly acclaimed book,* Psychotherapy for Psychosis

'While reading *From Breakdown to Breakthrough*, my highlighting pen rarely left my hand, so much was there to note and remember. With crystal clarity and great style, the authors thoroughly refute the despairing deficit model of psychosis by offering a brilliant theoretical synthesis supported with a wealth of references and tied to a potent and practical approach to understanding and responding to the language of the disorder. Their powerful arguments are given felt resonance through many profound and poignant case histories. This book is a victory for the psychoanalytic treatment of psychosis, and I found myself applauding nearly every page. Mental health practitioners of all types, especially early career psychotherapists, will be greatly helped in knowing how to treat those deemed unreachable as they learn to decipher and work with symptoms as forms of communication.'

**Francoise Davoine, Ph.D.**, *psychoanalyst and co-author of* History Beyond Trauma

'*From Breakdown to Breakthrough* is a passionate, responsive, and highly educated exploration and sharing of psychological work with psychosis, emphasizing intricacies of the therapy relationship, its nuances, and possibilities.

Psychoanalytic, psycho-dynamic, and relational perspectives open doors of contact, healing, and growth. This book is a beautiful exposition and affirmation of ways the human spirit connects with difficult, often seemingly intractable, states as it supports and mediates transformative processes.'

**Michael Eigen, Ph.D.,** *psychoanalyst and author of* The Psychotic Core, The Sensitive Self, *and* Contact with the Depths

'This wonderful book, based on extensive knowledge and experience, illustrates effective alternative approaches to the medical model to assist persons who suffer psychosis to achieve a fuller life. Both novice and veteran mental health professionals cannot fail to gain useful insights from any of the chapters as will persons with experience of psychosis and family members. It is written in a style that will readily engage the reader and, in doing so, also demonstrate much better ways of connecting with one's patients.'

**Brian Martindale, M.D.,** *past President of the International Society for the Psychological & Social Approaches to Psychosis (ISPS) and co-editor of* Open Dialogue for Psychosis

# From Breakdown to Breakthrough

As a clear and user-friendly guide for clinicians who work with patients affected by psychosis, this book challenges the false notion that psychosis is untreatable through talk therapy.

The authors contend that since psychotic symptoms are features of survival adaptation, they naturally serve as a valuable source of information, providing clues about the origins of people's psychic derailment along with a path to its cure. The authors advise therapists not only to read and respond to the messages embedded in the symptoms, but also to recognize and utilize the non-psychotic aspects of the patient in facilitating recovery. The overall aim is to recruit the patient as a collaborator in their treatment, thus wresting a meaningful and redemptive narrative from the psychotic experience. All aspects and phases of treatment – from initial encounters through the middle phase to termination, and even supervision – are covered in this volume.

Abundant with clinical examples, theoretical and technical points, and treatment methods, this book is essential reading for all psychotherapists, psychoanalysts, and other mental health clinicians working with psychosis.

**Danielle Knafo, Ph.D.,** is a clinical psychologist and psychoanalyst with expertise in the treatment of psychosis. During her tenure as a professor at LIU's Clinical Psychology Doctoral program for 22 years, she chaired a concentration on serious mental illness. She is a faculty and supervisor at NYU's Postdoctoral Program in Psychoanalysis. She has written and lectured extensively on psychoanalysis, trauma, and psychosis.

**Michael Selzer, M.D.,** is a psychiatrist who directed the Schizophrenia Division at NY Hospital, Westchester Division. He was also a clinical associate professor at NY Downstate Medical Center, where he was director of medical education in psychiatry. He has taught and written about the treatment of psychosis and borderline personality disorder.

PSYCHOANALYSIS IN A NEW KEY BOOK SERIES
DONNEL STERN
Series Editor

When music is played in a new key, the melody does not change, but the notes that make up the composition do: change in the context of continuity, the continuity that perseveres through change. **Psychoanalysis in a New Key** publishes books that share the aims psychoanalysts have always had, but that approach them differently. The books in the series are not expected to advance any particular theoretical agenda, although to this date most have been written by analysts from the Interpersonal and Relational orientations.

The most important contribution of a psychoanalytic book is the communication of something that nudges the reader's grasp of clinical theory and practice in an unexpected direction. **Psychoanalysis in a New Key** creates a deliberate focus on innovative and unsettling clinical thinking. Because that kind of thinking is encouraged by the exploration of the sometimes surprising contributions to psychoanalysis of ideas and findings from other fields, **Psychoanalysis in a New Key** particularly encourages interdisciplinary studies. Books in the series have married psychoanalysis with dissociation, trauma theory, sociology, and criminology. The series is open to the consideration of studies examining the relationship between psychoanalysis and any other field – for instance, biology, literary and art criticism, philosophy, systems theory, anthropology, and political theory.

But innovation also takes place within the boundaries of psychoanalysis, and Psychoanalysis in a New Key therefore also presents work that reformulates thought and practice without leaving the precincts of the field. Books in the series focus, for example, on the significance of personal values in psychoanalytic practice, on the complex interrelationship between the analyst's clinical work and personal life, on the consequences for the clinical situation when patient and analyst are from different cultures, and on the need for psychoanalysts to accept the degree to which they knowingly satisfy their own wishes during treatment hours, often to the patient's detriment.

A full list of all titles in this series is available at:

https://www.routledge.com/Psychoanalysis-in-a-New-Key-Book-Series/book-series/LEAPNKBS

# From Breakdown to Breakthrough

## Psychoanalytic Treatment of Psychosis

## Danielle Knafo and Michael Selzer

Routledge
Taylor & Francis Group

LONDON AND NEW YORK

Designed cover image: Cover art: © Robert Yarber. *Sins of the Scopophiliacs*, 1991.

Cover design: Diana Pepe.

First published 2024
by Routledge
4 Park Square, Milton Park, Abingdon, Oxon OX14 4RN

and by Routledge
605 Third Avenue, New York, NY 10158

*Routledge is an imprint of the Taylor & Francis Group, an informa business*

*British Library Cataloguing-in-Publication Data*
A catalogue record for this book is available from the British Library

*Library of Congress Cataloging-in-Publication Data*
Names: Knafo, Danielle, author. | Selzer, Michael A., 1934- author.
Title: Breakdown to breakthrough: psychoanalytic treatment of psychosis / Danielle Knafo and Michael Selzer.
Description: Abingdon, Oxon; New York, NY: Routledge, 2024. | Series: Psychoanalysis in a new key book series | Includes bibliographical references. |
Identifiers: LCCN 2023024737 (print) | LCCN 2023024738 (ebook) | ISBN 9781032578996 (hardback) | ISBN 9781032579016 (paperback) | ISBN 9781003441519 (ebook)
Subjects: LCSH: Schizophrenia–Treatment. | Psychoanalysis. | Psychodynamic psychotherapy.
Classification: LCC RC514 .K624 2024 (print) | LCC RC514 (ebook) | DDC 616.89/17–dc23/eng/20230830
LC record available at https://lccn.loc.gov/2023024737
LC ebook record available at https://lccn.loc.gov/2023024738

ISBN: 9781032578996 (hbk)
ISBN: 9781032579016 (pbk)
ISBN: 9781003441519 (ebk)

DOI: 10.4324/9781003441519

Typeset in Times New Roman
by Deanta Global Publishing Services, Chennai, India

**To our patients**

# Contents

# Acknowledgments

Our hearty thanks to Donnel Stern for believing in our project and including us in his **Psychoanalysis in a New Key** book series. Thanks, too, to Kate Hawes for her encouragement and Georgina Clutterbuck for her consistent and friendly assistance during production.

Maryellen Lo Bosco, who has edited several of Danielle Knafo's books, was the only person we wanted to edit the present volume. Her editing is superb and always helps clarify the language and lift it to a higher level.

Rocco Lo Bosco, who has been Danielle's writing partner for years, gave generously of his time and made suggestions that improved exposition and style.

Thanks to Orna Ophir for her generous and thoughtful foreward.

Michael Selzer acknowledges Elvin Semrad: "I am grateful to Elvin Semrad, my residency training director who has inspired me through my 50+ years of working with psychosis. Often when I feel stuck, I ask myself, "What would Elvin say or do?" I hear his booming laugh and then his Nebraska accent telling me in no uncertain terms, 'Come on, Selzer. Don't play dumb.'"

Thanks to Danielle's research assistants, Yael Fessel, Ryan Sparks, and Meirong You for their invaluable help researching topics, finding books and articles, and managing the many references. It was important for us to acknowledge that we stand on the shoulders of those who have come before us.

Thanks to Ro'ee Meyer for compiling our index.

Gratitude is due to David Lichtenstein and Peter Merritt who helped us with understanding Lacan's theories on psychosis. Thanks, too, to James Oglive for his assistance in helping us navigate Bion's thinking on psychosis. Thanks to Michael Eigen and Francoise Davoine for sharing with

Danielle their unique views and experiences after decades of work with serious mental illness.

Danielle is thankful to the members of her psychosis peer supervision group for their comments and suggestions on two of the book's chapters and for providing a collegial space in which to share both the excitement and challenges of working with psychosis. They are Michael Garrett, Brian Martindale, Nancy Burke, Nardus Saayman, and Konstantin Lemeshko.

Thanks go to Robert Yarber for allowing us to use his marvelous painting, *Sins of the Scopophiliacs* (1991) on our cover and to Diana Pepe for her beautiful cover design.

Most of all, we are indebted to our patients from whom we learned our craft. We are forever grateful to have had the privilege of working with them.

## Credits List

The authors also acknowledge the permissions granted to republish the following articles:

Knafo, D. (2016). Going blind to see: The role of regression in the psychoanalytic treatment of psychosis. *American Journal of Psychotherapy*, *70*(1), 79–100. *This material was originally published in the* American Journal of Psychotherapy, *Volume 70, Issue 1, and has been modified for this publication.*

Knafo, D. (2020). Alone in a crowded mind: When psychosis masks loneliness. *Psychoanalytic Psychology*, *37*(2), 108–116. https://doi.org/10.1037/pap0000257. © 2020 by American Psychological Association. Reproduced and adapted with permission.

Knafo, D., & Selzer, M. (2015). "Don't step on Tony!" The importance of symptoms when working with psychosis. *Psychoanalytic Psychology*, *32*(1), 159–172. https://doi.org /10.1037/a0038488. © 2020 by American Psychological Association. Reproduced and adapted with permission.

# A Note About Language

Whenever possible, we avoid using the term **schizophrenia**, a much-disputed label that does not refer to one diagnosis and carries a great deal of stigma. Nonetheless, we quote certain authors who refer to schizophrenia in their writings and follow them in using this term ourselves as necessary to explicate their text. The diagnostic label of schizophrenia is being contested in the United States and already has been retired in Japan and South Korea. While some might argue that the term **psychosis** should also be retired, schizophrenia has a much greater stigma attached to it as a medical diagnosis.

For the most part, we eschew the word psychotic as an adjective to describe a person because we do not wish to equate a person with a diagnosis. People are not psychotic: rather, they experience psychosis; they may exhibit psychotic symptoms; and they may have psychotic episodes.

We use plural personal pronouns (they, their, them, themselves) that are gender-neutral to refer to singular nouns that do not have a specific gender. Exceptions to this usage exist where the reader might become confused with the use of multiple personal pronouns in the same sentence. Here is an example of how we might use the plural pronoun: "A psychologist may eschew the term schizophrenia. However, they may choose to use the term psychosis, which has a less fraught history."

All patients mentioned in this text have been given pseudonyms, as have all therapists except for DK (Danielle Knafo) and MS (Michael Selzer).

# Foreword

## by Orna Ophir

*From Breakdown to Breakthrough: Psychodynamic Psychotherapy with Psychosis* is a remarkable, thoroughly researched, and well-argued book that every clinician who works with psychotic patients and every student who is assigned to treat such patients would be advised to read and take to heart. Original in its approach and filling a major lacuna in our literature, this text provides clear guidelines for the treatment of those suffering with psychosis, from the very first session to the termination of symptoms. Knafo and Selzer also provide answers to a wide range of questions about the treatment of patients who are otherwise considered incurable. The "unclassical patients" of psychoanalysis, or those deemed by some analysts as "extremely difficult to reach," do not deter the clinicians and authors of this interesting volume; they firmly believe no one is 100% psychotic. Instead of merely managing people while trying to eliminate their symptoms with medications, therapists ought to see symptoms as signs of their patients' efforts and clues about their major issues. The authors argue that symptoms are efforts to cope, driven by intelligence and logic. Moreover, if therapists would care to listen to patients with psychosis as deeply motivated and driven persons, they could effectively succeed in co-creating a shared world between sanity and madness, where patients and therapists might communicate with greater profit.

The authors offer a comprehensive model of working with psychosis – one that diverges from current practice that is based on the hegemonic medical model. They do not just identify symptoms for the purpose of labelling the patient with a DSM diagnosis; neither do they see symptoms as merely signs of pathology, dis-ease, or dis-ability. Rather, they wisely interpret symptoms as creative attempts on the part of their patients to adapt and survive.

Though many within psychoanalysis have sadly given up on this kind of co-creative work, these seasoned authors – based on their many decades of experience as clinicians, supervisors, and teachers – unapologetically advocate a novel and brave approach to psychoanalytic exploration, which uses traditional Freudian concepts such as the unconscious, transference, countertransference, and regression in the most productive of ways. Their rich account is comprehensive in that it includes history, theory, case materials, and verbatim reports of full sessions documenting the therapist's intervention, as well as the authors' internal musings. Also included is a moving reflection from one of their patients about the method of treatment.

This is a timely volume, as the timeless problem of treating patients with severe mental difficulties has been greatly exacerbated in modern history, not only by methods of deinstitutionalization of the last four decades of the 20th century but also more recently by the effects of the COVID pandemic and the further erosion of mental health care. Many of those who suffer with psychosis end up homeless and in the charge of overburdened social welfare safety nets and law enforcement officials not trained to manage people with psychological difficulties. Although policymakers are recently recognizing the toll of the mental health crisis and our responsibility for individuals who suffer from severe mental conditions, and even though psychiatrists have begun to reconsider the exclusive, reductionist biomedical model for understanding their patients' problems and treating them, most educational programs today are deficient when it comes to training mental health professionals in psychotherapy for those who suffer with psychoses.

This long-awaited book makes for fascinating reading with its rich and moving examples: a patient who warns her therapist not to step on one of her 17 imaginary children; a patient who believes he is going blind; a patient who is afraid he is turning into a vampire; and a patient whose only wish is to be left alone and to live on a deserted island. These cases are taken seriously by the authors, who with great compassion and patience, show how symptoms are in many ways creative, adaptive measures that add up to a comprehensive meaning-making system. The authors demonstrate how, when taken seriously, mental catastrophes can turn into curative narratives and prevent symptoms from becoming chronic. Knafo and Selzer don't believe in the facile adage of "once a schizophrenic always a schizophrenic" and propose a wide array of innovations based on the work of pioneering psychoanalysts in the United States, France, Italy,

Switzerland, the Scandinavian countries, and Israel. The authors provide a rich background on these innovators and exemplify how their theories can be used to treat patients using psychoanalytic methods. As the authors note, psychotic symptoms "signal that a human being is fighting for their life," and the kind of therapy they offer is seen by one of their patients, whose reflection is included in this volume, as nothing short of life-saving.

–Orna Ophir, Ph.D.

New York

# Introduction

## From Breakdown to Breakthrough

In our current era, psychotherapeutic treatment of psychosis is rare and often judged to be inappropriate. For example, Michels (2003) baldly states that "schizophrenia is a relative contra-indication to psychoanalytic treatment" (p. 11). Opposing this view, Bollas (2013) argues that psychoanalysis is the treatment of choice for psychosis. He says, "When the person is at their most vulnerable—and especially in breakdown—they are usually particularly amenable to help, and to the development of insight into the self" (2013, p. 7). Openness to therapy is particularly evident during the first episode and early stages of psychosis. When the psychosis is not addressed immediately, however, defenses and resistances build up, rendering the person more terrified of introspection but nonetheless still able to benefit from psychodynamic psychotherapy.

Diametrically opposed viewpoints are not uncommon when it comes to the treatment of psychosis, the most well-researched yet least understood diagnostic category. Like Bollas, we are seasoned clinicians who have for many decades worked successfully with patients diagnosed with psychosis. As clinicians (with 100 years of experience between us), we have resisted the popular trends discouraging the use of psychodynamic psychotherapy for the treatment of psychosis (Ophir, 2015). In fact, many psychotherapists and psychoanalysts have removed themselves from this work, and psychiatry has nearly ceased training psychiatrists in psychology and psychotherapy (Conan, 2012). Psychiatrist Daniel Carlat (2010) notes that his profession has abandoned the practice of talk therapy for the more lucrative practice of prescribing drugs. The unfortunate consequence of this trend is that when psychosis abruptly enters the treatment room—and it often does—clinicians are ill-prepared to work with it and all too frequently shift their focus to managing symptoms (usually with medication) rather than exploring them. Alternatively, clinicians may rid themselves of such patients altogether by referring or hospitalizing them. One of the reasons for these treatment trends is the therapist's wish to be in control and not have to cope with the unsettling effects of feeling bewildered and/or impotent.

But there is another way. We are writing this book to share our experiences with those who wish to learn how to conduct psychodynamic psychotherapy with individuals diagnosed with psychosis or who are undergoing a psychotic episode. We are also speaking to those professionals who are discouraged by the current standard of treatment for those with serious mental illness. This book is a training guide for mental health professionals interested in obtaining a better understanding of psychosis and ways to work with patients in extreme emotional distress. We present a psychosocial perspective on psychosis with abundant and detailed clinical examples to illustrate theoretical and technical points. All aspects and phases of treatment, from initial encounters through the middle phase to termination, are covered in this volume.

Despite the enormous amount of research that attempts to demonstrate schizophrenics have different brains, most schizophrenic patients have normal brains. Sommer et al. (2013) found that 74.4% of patients versus 73.4% of controls had normal brains and concluded that the basis of psychosis is not necessarily organic. Moncrieff (2007) claims that research concluding that schizophrenic brains are different (i.e., larger ventricles, smaller brain matter) have numerous problems, namely that many of the subjects they used had been institutionalized and/or been on medications for years, and some had undergone ECT, all of which can affect the brain. Meanwhile, the "chemical imbalance theory" has resulted in one in five Americans taking daily psychotropic medications (Medco Health Solutions, 2011), with some clinicians calling the increased use of these drugs a "failed revolution" (Whitaker and Cosgrove, 2015). Instead of the drugs reducing the number of those diagnosed with psychosis, they have increased fivefold (Leader, 2011). Consequently, there exists profound dissatisfaction among both doctors and patients with the current standard of care. Bergner (2022) illustrates, through patients' stories, the heavy price that is paid for the biological view of the mind and the drug-based assumptions that go along with it.

The "incurability" of schizophrenia has turned out to be a myth. The Vermont longitudinal study (Harding et al., 1987) following 269 patients for 32 years found that the common notion of "once a schizophrenic, always a schizophrenic" simply does not hold true. In fact, between 50% and 75% of patients achieved considerable improvement or recovery (Harding et al., 1987). In a longitudinal study lasting 20 years, Harrow and his colleagues (2007, 2017) found that those who had *not* taken antipsychotic medication showed fewer psychotic symptoms and better work histories after 15 years than those who had. In addition, over half of patients on antipsychotic medications stop taking them (Dolder et al., 2002; Morken et al., 2008). The "miracle drugs" clearly do not work for everyone; in fact, they can have serious side effects, including weight gain, cognitive haze, involuntary motor movements, dulling of emotions, and early mortality (Gaebel and Ücok, 2008; Hamer and Meunch, 2010; Kroeze et al., 2003; Lader, 1999). Moreover, dispensing medications all day can quickly make healthcare practitioners feel like they are pill pushers rather than healers.

In the more recent history of psychology, cognitive behavioral therapy (CBT) has become a popular treatment for psychosis (Herz, 2012; Mandor and Kingdon, 2015; Rector and Beck, 2001; Wykes et al., 2008; Zimmermann et al., 2005; Kimhy et al., 2013; Turkington, et al., 2013). CBT's emphasis on cognition, beliefs, and behavior as well as its ease of application make it appealing to clinicians, and they have had some success with symptom reduction (Rector and Beck, 2001; Wykes et al., 2008; Zimmermann et al., 2005). CBT practitioners scrutinize the evidentiary chain that leads to psychotic thinking, with the aim of correcting it by presenting the patient with conventional logic. Garrett (2019), who combines CBT and psychodynamic therapy when working with psychosis, compares the two approaches:

> CBT clinicians tend to focus on the patient's cognitions … [and] examine evidence for and against their maladaptive beliefs to help them alleviate their suffering by changing their beliefs. Psychodynamic therapists pay attention to the ebb and flow of affect, psychological defenses, and the patient's transference to the therapist in sessions with the aim of bringing the unconscious meaning of the patient's thoughts, feelings, and actions to the patient's attention with the expectation that the patient's deepening insight into their mental life will alleviate their suffering. Both approaches acknowledge the importance of early life experiences as antecedents to psychological

disturbances in adulthood. CBT and psychodynamic therapists aim to maintain a positive working alliance with patients, but CBT therapists do not rely on the interpretation of the unconscious meanings of the transference to achieve clinical gains

(Personal communication to DK, December 27, 2022).

Our approach differs from CBT in that we are interested in the *unconscious logic* of the patient—what they are thinking and why. What the patient thinks and believes, much of which remains unconscious, offers us crucial information about both their needs and their solutions. For example, a patient who declares "I am Christ" is unknowingly searching for omnipotence as a way to alleviate feelings of inadequacy. It is illogical to believe one is Christ, yet quite logical to seek a solution for feeling pathetic or bewildered. A benefit of approaching psychotic communication in this way is that it fosters empathy. After all, who hasn't lost a sense of potency at some time in their lives? Empathy is what brings the therapist closer to the patient and, therefore, more able to work with them. Indeed, we believe that those who label psychotic thinking as irrational or illogical are employing too narrow (or too conventional) a lens through which to understand the patient's communication. Our approach encourages acceptance of what initially appears to be irrational until the patient's unconscious logic becomes conscious.

We try to avoid the imposition of a certain worldview or way of thinking that implies the therapist knows what is best for the patient and thereby risks "crushing" the patient's belief system (Leader, 2011). Instead, we work to reach conclusions collaboratively with the patient through a multifactorial process. We understand psychotic symptoms as efforts at adaptation and a need for avoidance, as well as strivings for solutions and attempts at survival. Recent research demonstrates just how much psychotic symptoms are, in fact, ways of dealing with trauma (Bentall and Fernyhough, 2008; Davoine and Gaudilliere, 2004; Kirshner, 2015; Moscovitz et al., 2019; Read, 2004; Read and Ross, 2003; Read et al., 2005; Read et al., 2014; Shevlin et al., 2008; Os and Bentall, 2012). Research is making it evident that childhood adversity and abuse are significant risk factors for the development of psychosis (Krabbendam et al., 2004; Varese et al., 2012). In the chapters that follow we show the strong link that exists between trauma (e.g., sexual abuse, physical abuse, emotional/psychological abuse, neglect, parental death, and bullying) and psychosis. Karon and VandenBos (1981) explain, "In every case we have treated, the individual had lived a life that we could not conceive of living without developing his symptoms" (p. 40).

As Garrett mentions, another limitation of the CBT approach in treating psychosis is that the clinician avoids unconscious communication, which can be of great value in understanding the patient and advancing the treatment. For instance, we believe that much information is communicated unconsciously through a person's symptoms, dreams, and transference; for that reason, rushing to eliminate symptoms or complexity is not helpful. Rather than view a person's derailments negatively, we view them as opportunities—an open door—leading to novel explorations. *Breakdowns can lead to breakthroughs.*

We are proposing an alternative model to the medical model and CBT because we regard both, though possessing certain merits, as ultimately reductionistic. Our model contends that psychotic symptoms are a valuable source of information. We aim to elaborate on the enduring concepts necessary for successful treatment of psychosis: focusing on the nonpsychotic as well as psychotic aspects of the personality; viewing the patient as a whole person rather than a collection of symptoms; establishing safety; prioritizing subjective experience and affect; uncovering traumas; making meaning; working with the transference and countertransference; focusing on the patient as a true collaborator in their own treatment; and creating a treatment alliance that provides the glue for a difficult and challenging journey.

This book is both timely and important because the mental health profession has moved away from therapeutic approaches to treating psychosis, and the results have been abominable. The brouhaha surrounding the publication of DSM-5, the latest iteration of the *Diagnostic and Statistical Manual of Mental Disorders*, is evidence of the widespread unhappiness with the medical model (Dillon et al., 2011; Frances, 2013; Sedler, 2016). Similarly, many lament practitioners' turning to the quick fix of pharmacology rather than simply talking to people (Tasman, 2002). Too many training programs do not even teach residents, fellows, psychologists, and social workers how to work therapeutically with serious mental illness because very few value the efficacy of this approach, much less know how to do it. This book aims to close that gap. We not only show how once psychoanalytic therapy was the *sine qua non* in the treatment of psychosis but also argue for a renewed appreciation of the psychodynamic treatment of psychosis—one that incorporates up-to-date knowledge and treatment modes that are at our disposal today.

## Deficits of the Deficit Model

Since Emil Kraepelin (1919) first coined the term *dementia praecox*, medicine has been seeking an organic basis for schizophrenia. In the mid-20th century, two major scientific advances occurred that drastically influenced the psychiatric treatment of patients exhibiting psychotic symptoms. The first was a series of promising discoveries in the field of psychopharmacology. At first, the only pharmacological treatments were those used to sedate or stimulate people with a variety of psychiatric disorders. Additional treatments were electroconvulsive therapy and, the most drastic treatment of all, neurosurgery. Laboratories had been actively pursuing specific treatments for a mental condition now labeled *schizophrenia* and also investigating the biochemical nature of the disorder. In the 1950s, newly created drugs (e.g., chlorpromazine; haloperidol) appeared to have specific applications for this disorder (Kyziridis, 2005; Lehmann and Ban, 1997). The second major advance affecting treatment occurred in radiology: new technology and techniques allowed for a more precise study of brain activity (Lavretsky, 2008; Kyziridis, 2005), which allowed clinicians to actually "see" the brain in action.

Buoyed by these advances, psychiatrists and other mental health practitioners hoped that the underlying cause of schizophrenia would soon be known. By the 1960s, it seemed that, even though the precise nature of the cause of the "deficit" was yet to be discovered, schizophrenia was indeed a brain disease. New drugs were popping up everywhere, and they seemed to be a perfect fit for the prevailing theory of schizophrenia as a brain disease. Since radiological pictures were unable to pinpoint where the diseased "lesion" might be, available treatments were used to reduce symptoms. In many cases, evidence of the disorder remained, and symptom suppression and return to function became the therapeutic goals until a cure could be found.

MS, a psychiatrist who lived and worked during the era when the medical model gained ascendance as a treatment for mental illness, recalls how his colleagues jumped on the pharmacological bandwagon, partly because they felt marginalized by their peers, the "real" doctors. Embracing the medical model provided them with a new legitimacy with which to join the medical community. Moreover, the medical approach proved to be the most lucrative. Psychiatry's *Diagnostic and Statistical Manual of Mental Disorders*, also called the DSM (American Psychiatric Association, 2013), is the gold standard of diagnosis and serves as the basis for what insurers will pay for when it comes to treatment. Economics played a considerable role in formulating treatments since medical management is less time-consuming and easier to demonstrate to insurance companies than talk therapy. For example, a physician using medical management may see five patients an hour, while the same physician practicing psychotherapy can see only one.

By the 1990s, the "decade of the brain" (Jones & Mendell, 1999), the deficit model was touted as the only way to think about psychosis. Clearly, a paradigm shift had occurred, one that has not been entirely helpful in the treatment of psychosis. While major advances have taken place in the understanding of brain functioning as well as in the fields of genetics, biochemistry, and pharmacology, we argue that the wholesale embrace of psychosis as a brain disorder without including the significant role that conflict and trauma play in this illness is a serious omission.

We maintain that the deficit model imposes restrictions on both the therapist and patient, limits treatment goals, and demoralizes both participants. First and foremost, in the deficit model, the therapist exerts complete responsibility. The patient's role is to provide necessary symptom information so that the practitioner can complete the symptom checklist to determine whether the DSM requirements for the diagnosis of schizophrenia have been met (Beecher, 2009). Then the patient gets a treatment regimen: they must take their medication and report back to the doctor on its efficacy as well as whether they experience any side effects. Compliance with the medication regimen is paramount (Beecher, 2009; Smith and Bartholomew, 2006). Noncompliance in this model is never deemed a reflection of a patient's seeking autonomy but, rather, viewed as the patient's thwarting the therapist's good intentions. One potential result of this imbalanced perspective is that the therapist, lacking a full partner in the therapeutic enterprise, feels isolated. At the same time, the factors that cause such isolation also preserve the therapist's authority. Concurrently, some patients are only too happy to identify with and embrace the deficit model, for it provides them with medically certified permission to opt out of mainstream society and/or opt out of making strenuous efforts to understand themselves and their symptoms. They have a disease, they are told, comparable to diabetes, for which the only remedy is a lifelong dependence on drugs.

The deficit model precludes the patient from being able to legitimately challenge the doctor's authority. The patient's "deficit" prevents them from being held accountable. The therapist must do all they can to either subdue or eliminate the symptoms, at which time the therapist may then have a partner. If the patient does not comply with the treatment, the therapist may choose to interpret the patient's opposition as a manifestation of their illness. Perhaps the therapist has chosen the wrong medication or the wrong dosage, or the drug hasn't had time to work. Whatever the cause, the patient is denied a role in treatment, and the therapist preserves sole authority. Nonetheless, the therapist may be forced to recognize the powerful role a patient can play in the outcome when they claim to be taking their medication, for example, but instead throw their pills away.

Another negative consequence of the medical model, more insidious than the first, is the limited role the deficit model allows the therapist. Once having established that the patient meets the criteria for schizophrenia, the therapist is limited primarily to inquiries about how well the patient is doing on their meds. This limited focus, the repetitive nature of the questions that must be asked to clarify the progress of the medical treatment, and the lack of recognition of patient complexity and paradox, can lead to the therapist's developing a sense of devitalization, preceded by a distressing experience of boredom. Therapists want to feel helpful and needed, especially in a situation where they feel a heavy weight of responsibility. Repeated efforts without results can produce self-blame since the deficit model reinforces the therapist's authority and makes it difficult for them to recognize their own vulnerability. And without vulnerability, there can be no appreciation of countertransference.

It is easy to understand the therapist's quandary when working in this model. If the patient is being controlled by a brain disease and its consequences, then that patient certainly cannot be held responsible for their behavior. But if the patient is not responsible, then who is? On the one hand, the patient can't help having a diseased brain, but on the other, that patient is expected to follow the doctor's orders in taking medication. Based on the medical model, it doesn't make sense for a therapist to be angry with, frightened of, aroused by, or enamored with a patient who is not in full control of themselves and whose personality is masked by their symptoms. "I knew it was the symptoms talking and not the patient; I tried to talk myself out of becoming upset," claimed a psychiatrist struggling to understand his "uncalled-for" reaction to his patient. Yet, if "symptoms talk," one can't help but wonder what happened to the person. If the patient accepts that it is their symptoms talking rather than themselves, then they are dissociated by default. If the patient rejects such a premise, then they are automatically in the wrong, and the therapist will not listen to what they have to say or, at any rate, not give it any credence. From either side of the dyad, this approach to therapy is a no-win situation.

It is common for therapists to experience many "uncalled-for" reactions toward patients undergoing a psychotic episode or other extreme states. They may experience a loss of control, fear that they are losing their mind, or suffer a sense of impotence—feelings that are forbidden to those following the deficit model. Yet these feelings may arise in them anyway, despite their view that it is the patient who is suffering and that it is the therapist's job to alleviate that suffering. Given this view, it is easy to see why the therapist may dismiss their reaction to the patient. But that dismissal may have unfortunate consequences since the reaction to a patient can easily influence the conduct of the therapy. One of MS's supervisees spoke candidly about how annoyed she was by her patient's snoring during their sessions. Further inquiry revealed the patient's snoring was secondary to his being overly sedated by her. As MS questioned the supervisee further, it became apparent that her anger toward the patient was related to her feeling ineffectual about how poorly the treatment was going. She later reported that the patient was no longer snoring after she reduced his medication. However, she continued to insist that it was his snoring that had made her angry. Several sessions later, she confessed to MS that she had in fact oversedated her patient because he had previously yelled in sessions.

The deficit model reduces the patient as well as the therapist, and a patient's content is relevant only insofar as it validates the diagnostic decision-making or treatment plan of the therapist. Thus, the patient becomes a spectator in their own life, waiting for their "real self" to emerge, which would then allow them to partner with the therapist in a new joint effort. This therapeutic stance results in several negative consequences. First and foremost, the therapist and patient end up collaborating on a view of the patient as "split." Second, the content of the patient's delusions and hallucinations are deemed as having no intrinsic value or significance, since they are seen as mere reflections of a disordered brain.

But what if the content reveals important evidence about the patient's struggle to adapt to conventional life, however unsuccessfully? Might the therapist, in eschewing inquiry, miss crucial information about the patient's efforts to keep their sense of self alive? Might the therapist realize the patient has not abandoned their attempt to assign meaning, and instead has organized their experience in a way that provides them with an explanation of what has befallen them, however idiosyncratic those assumptions might seem to the therapist? Such a patient might be more complex, and undoubtedly more perplexing, but also more interesting. For example, Ted, a patient terrified by his aggressive impulses, needed to paralyze himself out of concern not only for himself but for those around him. He was convinced he was being invaded by monsters who put a spell on him, rendering him weak and ineffectual, thus providing a solution to his dilemma. But that was not enough for this tortured soul. His tale cried out for an answer to the question, why me? He needed to provide the monsters with a meaningful basis for their motivation, to construct a reality in which the monsters recognized that Ted was an angry person who needed to be punished.

According to the medical model, if a man sees monsters, he is hallucinating; if he imagines them, he is delusional. Focused on getting rid of these "symptoms," the therapist has not thought of acknowledging that, however misguided, symptoms represent a person's efforts to cope. Measured by conventional standards, the man who sees monsters is a failure. He is unable to live in this world. From this perspective, his trying to live in his own world, a terrifying one for which he has provided himself with a solution, is discounted because it conflicts with conventional reality. Using conventional outcome measurements blinds the therapist to an appreciation of the patient's strengths and the continuity that exists between pre- and post-psychotic states, all of which are often revealed within the context of the patient's pathology. For example, Ted's psychotic symptomatology revealed a struggling individual interested in providing meaning and coherence to his life and demonstrated both organizational capacities and a will to live. Symptoms like Ted's are also dismissed by the medical model as not having any value in predicting outcomes. Rather, the therapist must wait until Ted's symptoms abate before predicting how Ted will react in the future. Such thinking creates a divided person—someone whose past, at least since the onset of his symptoms, is of no significance in either understanding the present or anticipating the future. Alternatively, by not cutting Ted off from his past self, the therapist could help him see that he never lost himself but was, in fact, struggling both then and now to adapt to a difficult world. A patient's ability to integrate psychotic and nonpsychotic parts of the self means that they have developed the capacity to accept their whole self.

Ignoring content has several additional negative consequences. By examining psychotic content, therapists can learn how a patient is likely to protect themselves in their immediate situation in therapy as well as in the world at large. For example, Ted might secretly believe that the medication he has been given is a direct consequence of some malfeasance on his part, and for that reason, he might be compliant. The therapist can then remind Ted of the similarity in his response to the medication and his delusion, in that he welcomes being controlled. Thus, Ted can see the continuity in his current and past self. The therapist doesn't have to wait for the symptoms to abate to learn that Ted is struggling to make sense of the world and is using earlier psychotic tools in his current efforts of adaptation. What is important to see in this example is not the presence or absence of psychosis, but the therapeutic emphasis on coherence and continuity.

Not valuing the content of psychotic symptomatology limits the therapist's ability to form a treatment alliance with their patient. Even if medications have been successful in eliminating symptoms, the therapist should still begin by respecting the patient's concerns, making them a partner, and providing them with a sense of security. If medication succeeds without any patient participation, the patient may experience the process as a kind of magic. The medication may not continue to be effective, and even if it is, the patient will not have discovered anything about why they encountered difficulties in the first place. They may also feel unsure of their own coping abilities and might again feel endangered. Without appreciating the relevance of their past experience, will they be equipped to handle future dangerous situations, or will they again resort to psychotic symptoms or pursue another course of symptom relief?

One additional negative effect of the medical model concerns the therapist's ability to understand the deep sense of failure that preoccupies so many people with psychosis. By dismissing the significance of the content of psychotic symptoms, the therapist fails to appreciate that much of the patient's sense of distress centers on the failure of their own efforts to control the situation they find themselves in. The truth is that most patients have struggled mightily for a long time; they have persistently tried to keep danger at bay. When the patient's efforts are appreciated, they will, on some level, know that they are being respected, even though their defensive structure may not be working to their advantage. By using symptoms solely to guide medication decisions, practitioners miss out on the very tools that can help them to understand the dynamics that created the psychosis. Inviting patients to become collaborative partners in their treatment creates the power of the therapeutic relationship and leads to healing.

Now that we have laid out the scaffolding of our philosophy and treatment approach, we turn to a brief description of the chapters in this text, each of which can be read separately as a coherent exposition. However, we strongly encourage practitioners who pick up this volume to read it through, especially if they are treating seriously ill patients. The information in each of the chapters is interactive, and, as the old adage says, the whole is greater than the sum of its parts.

## Chapter 1: Psychoanalysis Meets Psychosis: Theory and Practice

This chapter introduces the psychodynamic approach to understanding and treating psychosis, beginning with Freud, who, despite his brilliant insights into psychosis, believed the condition was not conducive to psychoanalytic treatment. A number of his followers—Jung, Klein, Bion, Searles, Sullivan, Fromm-Reichmann, Winnicott, Lacan, Eigen, Bollas, and others—disagreed and contributed important guidelines to the treatment of psychosis. We review some of the thinking that created the backbone of psychodynamic work with psychosis and consider the cultural variables that are important to bear in mind when encountering psychotic symptoms. We also discuss some of the research evidence supporting psychodynamic approaches to working with psychosis.

## Chapter 2: Beginnings

Most analysts agree that first meetings set the stage for all that follows. This chapter introduces the reader to what to expect when first encountering a patient experiencing psychosis. We believe that many therapists, even experienced ones, are discouraged in their first encounters and, as a result, may choose not to work with this population. We distinguish between fears about psychosis and a lack of preparedness to engage with extreme emotions and behaviors. We also distinguish between therapeutic work with people whose problems are on the neurotic and psychotic spectrums. We alert therapists to aspects of themselves and the work that, when unrecognized, impede engagement with their patients. Most importantly, we stress that each patient has a unique voice—an individual set of images and stories (including delusions) — that reveals their experience.

## Chapter 3: Establishing a Pre-Alliance

This chapter discusses how to begin treatment with patients who have difficulty with boundaries and self–other differentiation and who show limited capacity for verbalization and reflective capacity. We believe it is best to approach such patients with a preparatory phase during which the therapist's primary function is to see the patient and witness their struggle to become. With these patients, the therapist cannot create an alliance that relies on separateness and relatedness or that uses verbalization and reflection. What the practitioner can do is become a companion who bears witness to the patient's developmental journey, making sure to minimize impingement along the way. Being together rather than doing something is key. Eventually, the patient will feel safe enough to be curious about themselves and ready to explore their inner and outer worlds.

## Chapter 4: Sample First Session: Psychosis and Cannabis

This chapter presents a verbatim initial session with a young man who experienced an acute psychotic episode while at college. David smoked a lot of marijuana since the age of 13, a background that increased the likelihood of a psychotic episode. DK begins by identifying the patient's unique idiom and adjusting herself to it. She shows how David's fundamental message is received with seriousness and interest. The session allows the reader to be present in the session and hear the therapist's interventions and internal musings. Countertransference issues, case conceptualization, and a treatment plan are discussed.

## Chapter 5: Outpatient Treatment with Psychosis: Managing Isolation and Creating Safety

Unfortunately, outpatient treatment for individuals experiencing psychosis is rare due to concerns about isolation, danger, and safety. This chapter details the factors to be considered when deciding the suitability for outpatient treatment (e.g., patient's strengths, expectations, external support, observing ego, level of functioning, capacity for relatedness, and so forth). We compare the advantages and disadvantages of outpatient and inpatient treatment and discuss the role of medication. Most important, transference and countertransference issues are illustrated with case material.

## Chapter 6: "Don't Step on Tony": Working with Psychotic Symptoms

In this chapter, we argue that analyzing symptoms is a crucial inroad to understanding a patient's issues, although symptoms are often disregarded in today's mental health environment. Symptoms provide a vital gateway for a potential working relationship with persons suffering with psychosis. A detailed case illustration is presented—of a woman who hallucinated 17 children and became their caretaker—to demonstrate how working with symptoms gives credence to the patient's reality and aids in creating a working alliance and moving the treatment forward.

## Chapter 7: Anybody Home? Working with Negative Symptoms

Most of the literature on psychosis deals with positive symptoms, yet many patients exhibit negative symptoms—anhedonia, apathy, asociality—generally understood in terms of restricted emotional expression and motivation. We discuss different approaches that can be used when working with patients who resort to defensive withdrawal. First, therapists need to identify the impact such cases have on them, such as feeling attacked or ineffective, before they can help patients cope with their own emotions. Because patients with negative symptoms seem to want nothing from the therapist, the provision of holding and containing helps to create safety from which the patient can emerge from their retreat, thus allowing the therapist to feel useful.

## Chapter 8: Alone in a Crowded Mind: When Psychosis Masks Loneliness

This chapter explores the special nature of psychotic loneliness as an exile from reality. We discuss the relationship between loneliness and psychosis and how the former interacts with the latter, even triggering psychosis in some individuals. We also examine some strategies individuals with psychosis use to cope with loneliness. Paranoid delusions and hallucinations in particular are regarded as defensive coping mechanisms against loneliness. But not every psychosis is defined by such striking symptoms. In fact, many present with what has been called quiet, discreet, or white psychosis (Leader, 2011). We offer a detailed 16-year treatment of a man who fit this description, as he exhibited only negative symptoms: near-complete social withdrawal, lack of motivation, loss of meaning, and abandonment of self-care. We argue that hospitalization and the medicalization of psychosis further isolate a person, increasing loneliness and stigma. Finally, we discuss how therapists who treat this type of psychosis experience a particular kind of loneliness in the countertransference.

## Chapter 9: Coming Undone: Acute Decompensation and Creating a Narrative

The acute psychotic episode, with its experience of fragmentation and disintegration, is the subject of this chapter, along with how to intervene therapeutically to prevent the condition from becoming chronic. Such mental states result in a person's urgent need for protection, which sometimes creates refractoriness during therapeutic interventions. The fear of being overwhelmed by one's emotions may also lead to a fight–flight response. Therefore, establishing a safe space and a collaborative relationship is critical. Creating a trauma narrative with the patient helps overcome their sense of discontinuity while facilitating mourning for what they have lost. We show how some crises emerge from therapists' own insecurities, fears, and confusion, i.e., some therapists have difficulty handling their patients' projections, intense love, anger, aloofness, or clinginess. Replacing the therapist's reactivity with curiosity and discourse helps to advance the therapeutic process.

## Chapter 10: Going Blind to See: A Case Study of Trauma, Regression, and Psychosis

The role of trauma and regression in psychodynamic work is covered in this chapter. We present the analytic treatment of Josh, a highly intelligent man who began therapy proudly claiming to be schizophrenic. He entered treatment on the verge of suicide, convinced of his utter isolation. Josh gradually confronted his lifelong paranoia and learned to trust his analyst and the therapeutic process. Josh experienced three psychotic episodes and one major depressive episode. This case study explores the benefits and risks of allowing psychotic regression in treatment. Regression can offer the repair of a traumatic past in the presence of a safe holding environment. Josh's comments on his psychosis and the analysis are included.

## Chapter 11: Endings

Many believe that to end a treatment, the patient must internalize that treatment as well as the functions of the therapist to be able to go it alone. Termination takes place not simply when psychotic symptoms disappear. When the treatment has been successful, termination with a patient diagnosed with psychosis includes an expansion of their personality, demonstrations of a vaster range of interests, an awareness of inner worth, and an acceptance of reality that no longer contains intense fear and distrust. In such outcomes, the therapeutic relationship has been meaningful and has stood the test of time, and its ending can be mourned externally, even while the work is continued internally.

## Chapter 12: Supervision

Supervision is a complex triangular process that involves the therapist, the patient, and a supervisor in two mutually influencing dyads. Supervision involves being aware of the many transferences, countertransferences, and parallel processes at play. Psychodynamic psychotherapy with psychosis can be challenging and rewarding, scary and informative. Some therapists develop a savior complex, believing they are the only ones who can deliver their patients from madness. But all too often, the therapist finds almost nothing in their patient resembling their own experience, past or present, personal or professional. We regard the central supervisory task as assisting the supervisee in the importance of making a human connection and becoming aware that their patient is struggling with issues, some of which are similar to the therapist's own, with the primary difference being the defenses the patient uses to manage these conflicts. Supervising therapists who work with psychosis often involves addressing their fear that efforts at empathy can come only at the expense of discovering psychotic aspects in themselves.

# Chapter 1

# Psychoanalysis Meets Psychosis

## Theory and Practice

**Emil Kraeplin**, a German physician whom many consider to be the founder of modern psychiatry, was the first to identify the mental state of psychosis, for which he coined the term *dementia praecox*. According to Kraeplin (1919), dementia praecox had an early onset (unlike senile dementia) but nonetheless continued to progress toward a state of dementia, an irreversible deterioration of cognitive functions. He considered the condition endogenous—due to internal causes—and did not see any value in attempting to understand the symptoms he described: hallucinations, delusions, incongruous emotions, impaired attention, negativism, stereotyped behavior, and dilapidation in the presence of a relatively intact sensorium. He first divided the syndrome into three, and later four, types: hebephrenic, catatonic, paranoid, and simple. He also distinguished dementia praecox, an intellectual disorder, from manic depression, which he believed to be a mood disorder. Although Kraeplin eventually came to realize that not all cases of psychosis ended in dementia, and some patients even attained a complete recovery, he nonetheless maintained the view that psychosis is terminal and not amenable to treatment (Arieti, 1974b). Kraeplin's (1919) views proved influential and long-lasting: his interest in patients as a collection of symptoms, rather than humans with stories, led to the DSM's descriptive emphasis on the symptoms of disorders, and his dire characterization of psychosis as incurable also endured, encapsulated in the adage: "Once a schizophrenic, always a schizophrenic."

Swiss psychiatrist, **Eugen Bleuler** (1911/1950), is credited with humanizing the syndrome described by Kraeplin and renaming it *schizophrenia*, to emphasize various splits in psychic functions, which he understood as the illness's defining characteristic. He broadened the inclusion criteria for schizophrenia and added simple schizophrenia as a

DOI: 10.4324/9781003441519-1

subtype of schizophrenia, a designation Kraeplin also adopted. Bleuler noted the continuity between madness and normality. He observed that a clinician can observe schizophrenic symptoms in so-called normal persons and that the largest number of cases are latent and found in people who do not require hospitalization. Lacanian psychoanalysts later elaborate on this idea with their designation of *white psychosis* or "quiet madness" (Leader, 2011). Bleuler (1911/1950) proposed four main symptoms of schizophrenia (the four A's): *loosening of associations* (loss of logical connection between thought and speech), *affect* (incongruence of emotions with regard to the situation at hand), *ambivalence* (conflicted emotions), and *autism* (withdrawal from the external world). Bleuler is credited with introducing the latter two concepts. Unlike Kraeplin, Bleuler considered hallucinations and delusions mere accessory symptoms in schizophrenia, an idea Freud would expand upon. Whereas for Kraeplin, the mad were objects of scientific interest, for Bleuler, they were human subjects engaged in existential struggles not unlike the rest of humanity (Bentall, 2003).

**Carl Gustav Jung** was a student of Bleuler's, and, like his mentor, Jung believed that most symptoms were due to psychical causes and that schizophrenia was the result of splits or dissociations unable to cohere into a central personality due to a combination of ego weakness and a lowered threshold of consciousness that allowed intrusions outside of a person's conscious control. Jung opposed the medical model of psychosis, stating that strange schizophrenic contents "are most emphatically not the result of poisoned brain cells, but are normal constituents of our unconscious minds" (Jung, 1939, p. 1004). He compared such universal contents to those encountered in dreams, stating that "the dreamer is normally insane" (p. 1005) and the phenomenology of dreams and schizophrenia is identical. The schizophrenic, he believed, was unable to withstand a level of panic or extended stress triggered by adverse conditions, which he described as: "the drop that falls into a vessel already full, or of the spark that incidentally lands upon a heap of gunpowder" (p. 1004). Indeed, Jung preferred "conditionalism" to "causality" when speaking of the precipitants of schizophrenia.

According to Jung (1907/1960), dreams and schizophrenic symptoms possessed both personal and collective (archetypal) unconscious material. He believed that psychosis involves the eruption of mythic, symbolic material into the ego consciousness. Images of god-devil, heaven-hell, good-evil, messiah-savior, and death-rebirth are common in psychosis, and they reveal the person's emotional issues as well as their attempts at renewal and healing after trauma.

When Jung lectured on the origins of schizophrenia, he had already been treating cases for 20 years. Unlike Freud and many others, who believed that those with schizophrenia would not be responsive to psychological treatment or psychoanalysis, Jung took his chances and found that many of his patients improved. When Jung spoke of his successes, others insisted the patients had not been schizophrenic (Jung, 1961, p. 128). Emphasizing the importance of therapist engagement and optimism, he wrote, "In psychotherapeutics, enthusiasm is always the secret to success" (Jung, 1939, p. 1010). He even claimed that so-called "hopeless cases" could be improved, saying he learned the most from his most difficult cases, those previously deemed impossible to treat. "I treat such cases as if they were not organic, as if they were psychogenic, and as if one could cure one by purely psychological means," Jung said (p. 1011). He correctly saw himself as a pioneer in this realm and pleaded with the medical establishment to put off theories of medical causation until "the psychical side of schizophrenia has had a fair deal" (1939, p. 1011).

In his memoir, Jung (1961) wrote of a young, mute, catatonic woman who had a traumatic past (abuse by both her brother and a schoolmate), but who also shot a doctor who had tried to molest her. She warned that she'd shoot Jung too if he failed her. Jung slowly established an alliance with this patient until she trusted him enough to share her story. He learned that she lived on the moon, which he interpreted as her having become alienated from the world due to her traumatic experiences. She became attached to Jung but also projected onto him. Jung's patient was initially furious with him for bringing her back into the world. The first time he broke through and she couldn't return to the moon, she had another breakdown. Working with the transference allowed them to reconnect her to the world, return to life, marry, and have children.

**Sigmund Freud**, in contrast to Jung, is known to have said that psychoanalysis was not an appropriate treatment for psychosis, mainly due to his belief that people who experiencing psychosis, because of their narcissistic withdrawal of libido, are unable to develop the necessary transference (Freud, 1911/1958). Yet he also wrote that analyses of those suffering serious mental illness are important for advancing our scientific knowledge (Ophir, 2015). He was interested in the dynamics of psychosis but did not show a strong motivation to have such cases in treatment. Nonetheless, David Lynn (1993), who examined Freud's 133 cases, found among them one patient with paranoia and ten with schizophrenia, and the patient in the Wolf Man case exhibited delusional symptoms. Moreover, many of Freud's cases of hysteria, which he treated with Josef Breuer (Breuer and Freud, 1893-5/1957) would be considered examples of psychosis by today's standards (e.g., Lucy R's olfactory hallucinations and Katherina's visual hallucinations).

Freud first wrote about psychosis in *The Neuro-Psychoses of Defence*, written in two parts (1894/1962a, 1896/1962b). In these treatises, he did not distinguish neurosis from psychosis, except for noting that each employs different defense mechanisms. Both conditions are attempts to deal with traumas, painful emotions, or incompatible ideas; both use defenses to cope and make the afflicted person's reality more bearable. In the first paper, Freud wrote about a condition he called *hallucinatory psychosis* in which reality is foreclosed or repudiated and replaced with a more acceptable reality. Repudiation (*verwerfung*) is a defense mechanism employed by the ego to reject an aspect of reality and behave as if it does not exist. His second treatise discussed a case of paranoia, in which the defense mechanism used is projection. Both cases revealed a patient's reaction to trauma—the first to the trauma of rejection/abandonment, and the second to the trauma of early seduction. In his treatise *Neurosis and Psychosis* (1924/1961), Freud repeated the notion that neuroses and psychoses share a similar etiology—the frustration of childhood wishes—yet he claimed one important difference: "Neurosis is the result of a conflict between the ego and the id, whereas psychosis is the analogous outcome of a similar disturbance in the relations between the ego and the external world" (1924/1961, p. 149).

Clearly, Freud's understanding of psychosis changed over time, and his views often seem contradictory. London (1973a, 1973b) proposed that Freud held two theories of psychosis. The first is a theory of unity because it can apply to all disorders: unconscious conflict exists in everyone and is resolved by enlisting a defense mechanism. London calls Freud's second theory a specific theory because it identifies psychosis as qualitatively different from neurosis. In psychosis, the afflicted person withdraws their libido from objects, which removes their ability to engage in transference. According to London, Freud favored the second theory.

In fact, Freud always considered normality and pathology to exist along a continuum. In his analysis of the Schreber case, he wrote about the "truth" embedded in Schreber's delusion as well as his own doubts about whether his analysis of Schreber made him (Freud) delusional (1911/1958, p. 79). This articulation of the fine line between normality and pathology is one of Freud's trademark insights. He seemed always to be telling clinicians not to get too comfortable when assessing psychopathology as a condition found in the Other. Freud (1938/1964) noted that even a person who is in a state of hallucinatory confusion, seemingly "far removed from the reality of the external world," possesses a hidden normal person "in the corner of their mind...who, watche[s] the hubbub of illness go past him" (p. 202). Freud wrote in his essay on construction: "The transposing of material from a forgotten past on to the present or on to an expectation of the future is indeed a habitual occurrence in neurotics no less than in psychotics" (1937/1964, p. 268). Later in that paper, he wrote that "mankind as a whole … has developed delusions which are inaccessible to logical criticism and which contradict reality" (1937/1964, p. 269).

Freud used the Schreber case (1911/1958) to expound upon his libido theory and thoughts about narcissism. He proposed that persons with psychosis, like Schreber, withdraw their libido from the outside world. In Freud's view, Schreber's end-of-the-world delusion—a common psychotic delusion—was a projection of the internal catastrophe he himself was experiencing. When a person withdraws their love from the world, it becomes a desolate place. As a result, libido becomes narcissistically invested, which leads to megalomania: Schreber believed he was being transformed into a woman who would copulate with God to create a new race. Freud's genius was especially noteworthy in his understanding of psychotic symptoms as attempts at recovery and reconnection to the outside world and its objects. He was careful to caution clinicians not to confuse the symptoms with the illness. Psychotic symptoms, like hallucinations and delusions, were, for Freud, attempts at recovery. The paranoid person is trying to reconnect to others, even though they now view these others as persecutory. The illness is quiet whereas the recovery (symptoms) is loud. Although Freud saw psychotic attempts at recovery and reconnection as hopeful, he did not grasp their potential for analytic work. According to his biographer, in 1928 Freud speculated on his aversion to working with psychosis, opining that it might be due to his privileging intellect over id (Gay, 1988, p. 537). Yet as early as 1905, he claimed that it was "not at all impossible that by suitable changes in the method we may succeed in overcoming this contraindication—and so be able to initiate a psychotherapy of psychosis" (Freud, 1905/1953, p. 264). Freud left this work to his followers; fortunately, some of them met the challenge.

## The Americans

**Harry Stack Sullivan** revolutionized psychiatry and psychotherapy in general and the treatment of psychosis in particular. He was a synthesizer of psychoanalysis and social psychiatry and the originator of *interpersonal psychiatry*, a school holding that interpersonal relationships, not drives, form character and pathology. Therefore, a healing relationship, rather than interpretations, is most curative. The therapeutic alliance is key, and treatment involves the establishment of a "me-you" pattern—that is, a dependable, solid relationship that is new to the patient (Sullivan, 1956, p. 363). The therapist is Sullivan's "participant–observer," a paradoxical juxtaposition that comprises engagement and disengagement, relatedness and standing apart.

Sullivan dedicated his life to helping the severely mentally ill; he worked at Sheppard and Enoch Pratt Hospital in Maryland from 1923 to 1930. During that time and into the present era, his work and writing have influenced many to adopt an interpersonal understanding of the etiology and treatment of psychosis. His was a humane approach, and he believed schizophrenia to be curable, not chronic. In his view, schizophrenia simply is a response to the problems of living and the result of disturbed interpersonal relationships (Sullivan, 1962). Because he considered loneliness to be the most difficult human emotion to bear, he claimed that too much stress and threats from the social environment (when one is sensitive and socially isolated) can be damaging to a person's mental health. Sullivan agreed with psychoanalysts who focused on the early relationship with the patient's mother; however, he added the necessity of considering what takes place in the adolescent period.

Preadolescence and early adolescence, he wrote, are stages of development during which sex, lust, and problems with intimacy gain prominence; failure to deal with these problems can turn into a "social liability" leading to a retreat into psychosis (Sullivan, 1956, p. 347). The repeated assaults on one's self-esteem characteristic of this period can prove too much to endure for extremely sensitive individuals who are not socially and mentally equipped to handle rough treatment (Sullivan, 1972). These assaults lead to a fragmented self-system, which includes "not-me" (dissociated) parts and security operations (transactional mechanisms that cause anxiety because they are not recognizable to the self and because they have not received the interpersonal "imprimatur" needed to be cognized) that reduce the person's anxiety but also their self-awareness (Stern, 1997). The more "not-me" a person is dealing with, the more severe the pathology. Sullivan's treatment involved bringing to light a patient's anxiety received through contagion from their parents' anxiety. Unlike Freud, who understood defenses as intrapsychic mechanisms, Sullivan viewed them as interpersonal at their core. A person deals with the anxiety of others through contagion but not via symbolic representation.

Sullivan believed that schizophrenics are highly anxious individuals and that the therapist needs to attend to their shifts in anxiety and security operations. Since patients suffering from psychosis use language for security purposes rather than communication (Kasanin, 1944), the therapist needs to attend to a patient's motivation, not simply their symptoms. Clear communication was key for Sullivan, and collaboration had a central role in his therapy. He believed that a therapist should formulate an observation in six or seven words or not proffer it at all (Sullivan, 1956, p. 334). Though he thought it important to take a history, he deemed it more important to know what a patient knows (and doesn't know) about themselves (Kvarnes and Parloff, 1976).

Sullivan's deep understanding of schizophrenia may have been in part due to the fact that he had undergone a psychotic episode while attending Cornell University, during which he was hospitalized "under mysterious circumstances" (Hornstein, 2000, p.125). Being gay at a time when homosexuality was deemed socially unacceptable seemed to have heightened his sensitivity to sexual-identity precursors to breakdown. Since Freud's analysis of the Schreber case, paranoid schizophrenia had become incorrectly associated with homosexuality. Sullivan was probably the first to understand that it was not simply a person's sexual identity that created a tendency toward paranoid psychosis; rather the stigma and consequent shame accompanying socially unacceptable desires and behaviors were factors that pushed people into madness (Blechner, 2019).

Perhaps Sullivan's most audacious move was to create a ward for gay male schizophrenics during the years 1925–29. He was the first to use para-professionals in the treatment of these men, and no women were allowed on the ward (Allen, 1995). His sensitivity to the social effects of prejudice against homosexuality and the pressures this prejudice creates in the development of schizophrenia led Sullivan to shelter these men by creating a therapeutic milieu in which they were accepted and not judged so they might emerge from their psychotic solutions. In 1962, he wrote, "It occurred to me ... that if ... we regarded them [schizophrenics] as persons, we attempted to discover what continued to be of interest to them, and we attempted to adjust the environment to which they are exposed in a fashion of harmony ... we might then discover a rather remarkable recovery rate" (Sullivan quoted in Conci, 2010, p. 135). When writing about schizophrenia, Sullivan made his famous statement: "We are all more simply human than otherwise" (Sullivan, 1956, p. 26).

## Chestnut Lodge (Fromm-Reichmann, Searles, Will, and Podvoll)

Istvan Hollos, a patient of Freud's (for a short time) and also of Paul Federn's, (known for his work with psychosis), made one of the first attempts to create a psychoanalytically based hospital, in Hungary, for patients with psychosis. Already in the 1910s, he believed "the 'liberation' of the mentally ill from the chains of their stigmatization will only become possible if society arrives at a psychoanalytic understanding of its own madness, if nurses are taught that there is meaning in psychotic talk, and if caregivers analyze their Unconscious and integrate the 'mad parts' of themselves" (Pestalozzi et al., 1998, p. xx). John Kafka (2010) claims that Hollos gained a broader understanding of treatment possibilities, beginning in 1910, when he visited Chestnut Lodge in Rockville, Maryland, the hospital best known for specializing in the treatment of psychosis. The Lodge was a large experiment in which practitioners were encouraged to be authentic and develop their own ways of working with extreme cases, mostly without medication. Benjamin Weininger, a staff psychiatrist at the Lodge, said, "We assumed that every person in the hospital, no matter how many years he had been ill, had a chance to improve" (Hornstein, 2000, p. 194).

Many psychoanalysts trained and worked at Chestnut Lodge, and much of the interpersonal psychoanalytic movement began there. Perhaps the most influential practitioner was **Frieda Fromm-Reichmann**, who lived and worked at the Lodge for 50 years. Her biographer wrote: "The Lodge was never simply her affiliation: it was who she became"; indeed, she was called 'the queen of Chestnut Lodge'" (Hornstein, 2000, p. 189). Fromm-Reichmann's optimistic approach to psychosis was compatible with Sullivan's, whom she invited to Chestnut Lodge to give seminars to practitioners, twice weekly, from October 1942 through April 1946 (Hornstein, 2000).

Fromm-Reichmann disagreed with Freud's claim that people with psychosis could not develop transference. She wrote: "the schizophrenic is capable of developing strong relationships of love and hatred toward his analyst" (1959, p. 121). Indeed, she believed that the schizophrenic patient's early interpersonal relationships had been traumatic, causing hypersensitivity and distrust, withdrawal, and a weakened sense of security that could be triggered later in life. She is thought to have originated the controversial term *schizophrenogenic mother*, which she used only once (Hornstein, 2000) to indicate the deleterious effect some mothers, who are overprotective yet manipulative and rejecting, have on their offspring (Fromm-Reichmann, 1948).

Fromm-Reichmann proposed certain modifications in the treatment of psychosis. These included eschewing the couch, free association, and interpretation. She believed the patient's silence ought to be accepted rather than challenged. She also recommended a long preparatory period in which therapist and patient establish a working alliance based on trust and acceptance. Only after fear and anxiety dissipate and dependency grows can the treatment weather the intense emotions and regressions that will inevitably emerge. The therapeutic relationship, rather than intellectual insights, is what matters. The only insights she deemed crucial were those that helped the patient understand what led to their psychosis. Like Freud, she believed that the schizophrenic's personality had nonpsychotic parts and an awareness of their delusions, along with the loneliness that accompanies living in a private, delusional world. Fromm-Reichmann also stressed the importance of treating the patient on two levels: the psychotic/regressed level and the adult/in-touch-with-reality level. She argued that the psychotic, though dealing with early trauma, had nonetheless progressed to adulthood and, therefore, possessed adult skills. The therapist should not, she cautioned, relate only to the psychotic parts of the personality. Fromm-Reichmann believed that if the therapist could not communicate with a schizophrenic patient, it was their fault (1952).

During her lifetime, Fromm-Reichmann was known for her successes with patients with psychosis; however, much of her renown came after her death with the publication of Joanne Greenberg's (1964) account of her four-year treatment with Fromm-Reichmann. Greenberg's memoir, *I Never Promised You a Rose Garden*, portrays a creative and intelligent adolescent who nonetheless manifests floridly psychotic symptoms, including hallucinations, body mutilations, and the creation of her own world and language. Fromm-Reichmann patiently worked with Greenberg, gaining her trust and entering her world without judgment, gradually helping her relinquish the security she found in madness. Greenberg learned to face reality and made a full recovery, finished college, married, and became an acclaimed author. With a mixture of pride and humility, Fromm-Reichmann once told colleagues: "It is an intense satisfaction to help that girl grow up to be better endowed than I am" (Hornstein, 2000, p. 237). Not surprisingly, many professionals who heard about Fromm-Reichmann's success argued that Greenberg could not have been schizophrenic (Hornstein, 2000). Any person who successfully treats psychosis regularly hears such skepticism from those who continue to deem psychosis untreatable and incurable.

## Harold Searles

Harold Searles worked at Chestnut Lodge for fifteen years, beginning in 1949 (Stanton, 1992). Although he was influenced by Sullivan and Fromm-Reichmann, he was an original thinker who proposed many new ideas, especially about working with severe mental illness. Many agree that his greatest contribution to psychoanalysis was a better understanding of the mechanisms of transference and countertransference. He admitted to having "narrowly avoided a schizophrenic break" during his college years (Hornstein, 2000, p. 375), which may have sensitized him to psychotic dynamics in himself and others. His papers were often rejected for publication because they proved too radical for his time. Aron and Lieberman (2017) noted that what Searles wrote about transference and countertransference in 1948 and 1949 didn't become central to practitioners' understanding of these mechanisms until late in the 20th century.

Searles's first book, *The Nonhuman Environment* (1960), expanded the concept of transference beyond human objects to the nonhuman environment. He believed that humans go through a developmental stage during which they are indistinguishable from their environment, including its nonhuman aspects, which is why such aspects must be considered, along with human interactions. Searles wrote that we relate to the nonhuman environment on two levels. First, we displace and project meaning onto, say, a cat or a tree. Second, we relate to a cat as being a cat and a tree as being a tree. Searles offered numerous examples of schizophrenics who animate the nonhuman environment, feel themselves to be nonhuman, or react to others as if they are nonhuman—thinking of them as either animals or inanimate objects, like dolls.

Searles was one of the first to recognize that the therapeutic situation is a two-person dynamic with a permeable boundary between patient and therapist (Searles, 1979a). He believed that patients with psychosis can read the therapist's unconscious (Young, 1995) and that they are aware of dissociated aspects of the analyst (Benatar, 2008). The patient's transference, he wrote, no matter how delusional, has a kernel of truth in it, and this is important for the therapist to acknowledge. Searles offered an example of a patient who seemed to randomly say to him in a condescending manner, "You're welcome" at the end of each session. Searles came to realize that the patient was reflecting an element of his own "obnoxious condescension" back to him (Searles, 1965, p. 393).

Searles was exceptionally open in his expression of countertransference feelings, and few practitioners in the psychoanalytic literature can match his honesty. His sensitivity was a highly polished lens he used to peer deeply into conscious experience and communication. Searles confessed to both loving and hating his patients, wanting to marry them, having homosexual desires for them, wanting to merge with them, and so forth. He said, "Our aim should be to remain maximally aware of our changing feelings during the analytic hour, not only because these feelings will be communicated behavioristically to the patient—via variations, no matter how subtle, in our tone, posture, and so on—but also because our feelings are our most sensitive indicators of what is going on in the interpersonal situation (Searles, 1978–79/2017, p. 204). He contended that when the patient is not getting better, it is because the therapist has failed to analyze a part of themselves.

Searles (1979b) argued that all humans are born with a psychotherapeutic striving, and he considered transference and countertransference as interchangeable because each member of the therapeutic dyad tries to change the other. In a paper on the patient as a therapist, he wrote, "I know of no other determinant of psychological illness that compares in etiologic importance with this one" (Searles, 1979b, p. 381). The patient wishes to cure the therapist of their conflicts as much as the therapist wishes to cure the patient. Searles was convinced of the importance of allowing patients to help their therapists in this manner. The extremely lively or colorful inpatient, Searles said, might be attempting to relieve depression in the therapist or the ward (Searles, 1965.

In another paper, Searles (1959) explained how we are driven crazy by others, and this same process takes place in the treatment. The patient with psychosis not only wishes to heal the therapist but also to drive that person crazy the way they were once driven crazy. While healing the therapist and driving him crazy seem to be opposing goals, Searles believed that both desires can be present at different times, or even at the same time.

Working with psychosis is a risky business, and reading Searles's many accounts further reveals this truth. Ogden (2009) wrote about the benefits of reading Searles: "Searles transforms what had been an invisible and yet felt presence, an emotional context, into psychological content about which the patient may be able to think and speak" (p. 134). Perhaps a good example of Ogden's observation is a hebephrenic patient who, in the middle of a session, stopped and said "hello" to Searles. He was at first confused by this communication and asked the patient for an explanation. The man responded, "A friendly hello as we pass on the avenue." Upon reflection, Searles unpacked the patient's deeper meaning: "The metaphorical impact of the whole statement hit me—its implications about the fleetingness of life, the impossibility for us as human beings to overcome our innate separateness from each other, the rarity with which we can enjoy a moment of simple and uncomplicated friendliness with one another" (Searles, 1965, p. 397). The clinical setting is one in which therapist and patient each play multiple roles while engaging one another behaviorally, consciously, and unconsciously (Searles, 1978–79/2017).

Many other psychoanalysts worked and trained at Chestnut Lodge, but we will mention only two more here: Otto Will and Edward Podvoll. **Otto Will** succeeded Fromm-Reichmann as director of psychotherapy at the Lodge and held that job for 20 years. He was in analysis with Sullivan toward the end of his life and was strongly influenced by him. Continuing the Lodge's interpersonal view of psychosis, Will (1958) believed that due to adverse early relations with family and culture, persons with psychosis develop a disturbance in the relational field and in their ability to communicate. They are anxious and sensitive, have low self-esteem, and fear human contact. He, therefore, believed that treatment must emphasize close contact with another person (who could be the analyst, nurse, or even another patient) who would serve as a benign, supportive, stable, and well-defined figure to help alleviate anxiety, loneliness, and the need for dissociation, and distinguish between the patient's inner world and external reality. Will claimed to never have resorted to medicating his patients (Thompson and Thompson, 1998). According to Will, the analyst must be nonintrusive and able to maintain a low level of tension to allow for meaningful communication, and both parties must be willing to be changed by the other and willing to accept the other's needs, including the need to grow and become independent.

**Edward Podvoll,** who was in analysis with Searles, worked at Chestnut Lodge and then at Austen Riggs in Stockbridge, Massachusetts, which also specialized in the psychodynamic (psychoanalytic) treatment of serious mental illness, although Austen Riggs was/is not an inpatient facility. Podvoll was drawn to Buddhism and later developed a contemplative therapy program at Naropa University in Boulder, Colorado, where he and his colleagues founded the Windhorse Project in 1981, and he became its medical director. This home and community-based center worked with treatment teams to help those experiencing extreme states, like psychosis and bipolar disorder. Podvoll (1979) wrote about similarities between psychosis and mystical experiences. In both states, he claimed, there exists a desire to move beyond, renounce, and even destroy the ego self in an attempt to transcend, heal, resurrect, and liberate the true self. It is a mistake, he claimed, to view psychosis as destructive and try to rid the patient of it. Rather, the clinician should recognize the patient's unique journey for continued survival, self-transformation, and renewal and help them guide and channel the psychosis itself into a workable life situation.

In 1990, Podvoll published *Recovering Sanity: A Compassionate Approach to Understanding and Treating Psychosis,* which combines a Buddhist approach with psychotherapy in treatment. Like Sullivan, Podvoll called for a humanistic attitude toward someone experiencing psychosis.

He emphasized taking a history of both sanity and pathology and discovering a patient's islands of clarity. Treatment consists in acknowledging and nurturing these islands: the repulsion toward one's current way of living, the longing to transcend the self, the urge for discipline, compassion, and courage. Podvoll eventually traveled to India and then to a meditation retreat in France, where he remained for twelve years after having renounced his family and possessions. He became known as Lama Sampa Mingyur (Immovable Intention for Enlightenment) (https://windhorseguild .org/legacy-project).

## Self-Psychology

**Heinz Kohut** (1971, 1977), the founder of *self psychology*, named the self as the central agent of the human psyche. In addition, his focus on narcissism as both healthy and unhealthy led the way for his understanding of psychosis as a pathology of self-cohesion. Kohut believed that we are all fragile to some degree and that psychosis is in the eye of the beholder. In other words, a person perceives psychosis in another for whom they lack empathic understanding. Once empathy is achieved, the person is no longer psychotic (Tolpin and Tolpin, 1996).

For Kohut, psychosis emerges in a person who has experienced early rejection, neglect, and/or excessive criticism. Such a person later experiences a crumbling self that manifests heightened vulnerability and hypersensitivity. The traumatized person then attempts to reconstitute the self by any means and may become irritable, easily provoked, or paranoid and may perceive the world as an attacker. Kohut suggested that a therapist approach the patient with empathy, saying something like this: "I think you are feeling quite sensitive, quite injured by something, and it's too much for you to take today; something has gotten to you in an especially hurtful way" (Tolpin and Tolpin, 1996, p. 149). In Kohut's view, empathic understanding creates a bridge between therapist and patient, and interpretation can wait.

**David Garfield and Ira Steinman** (2018), two contemporary self psychologists, described *inter-affectivity*, which they say is needed in the treatment of psychosis to achieve "cross modal attunement" (Garfield and Steinman, 2018, p. xxxiv). Step one involves the therapist's grasping of the patient's feeling state based on their overt behavior. Step two requires the therapist to match the patient's affect, yet to do so in a way that removes aggression. In step three, the therapist contextualizes and interprets the source of the patient's feeling state. Mirroring, idealization, and twinship—Kohut's three types of self–object experiences seen in the transference—are welcomed as entries to the establishment of an alliance that leads to repair and healing. Empathy and attunement are the key psychoanalytic tools.

## Independent Voices

New York analyst **Michael Eigen** has written extensively on the understanding and treatment of psychosis, what he calls "the Cinderella of psychoanalysis" (Eigen, 1986, p. 5). In the preface to his book, *The Psychotic Core*, he states: "My hope is … to relax our gaze" (Eigen, 1986, p. viii). He is intrigued by what psychosis offers, which is to take us to the edge of what it is humanly possible to experience. "We never recover from being human," he says, and considers sanity to be a heroic achievement (personal communication to DK, April 16, 2021). In psychosis, the therapist witnesses a duality that includes detachment and clinging, cynicism and naivete, rigidity (adhesiveness of defenses and delusional thinking) and chaos (dissolving boundaries and a fluid and constantly changing self). Eigen delineated six problem areas that the therapist must contend with when working with psychosis: hallucination (the tension between memory and perception is destroyed when the former is turned into the latter), mindlessness (anesthetizing oneself to pain can slow or nullify the mind), boundaries (interweaving of self and other can result in a sense of dissolution or invasion), hate (one's self and the world are distorted through hatred), epistemology (how one constitutes reality, truth, and the world in a distorted fashion), and reversal (experience is turned into what it is not) (Eigen, 1986).

Eigen noted the importance of acknowledging that working with some patients with psychosis can evoke disgust or anger in the therapist. Rather than disengage because of these feelings, he advises the therapist to cultivate a fascination for the grotesque side of life. Eigen (1993) provides such an example when he writes about working with unwanted patients, such as a woman who experienced herself as feces, was convinced the food she ate was feces, and she was a toilet. Eigen suggested the analyst use their negative reactions to such a patient as cues to the amount of frustration a patient can tolerate to feel alive. He also noted that, by not disengaging from one's feelings when working with a patient with grotesque symptoms, the analyst stays alert, works more cautiously, remembers to keep their distance, and remains aware that closeness is undesirable, even dangerous.

For beginning therapists learning to work with psychosis, Eigen advises clinicians to respect the embryonic nature of our beings; respect the unknown; dialogue with different parts of the mind; deal with self-hatred in one's self and others; learn to be alone together; cultivate the ability to sit—what he calls *creative waiting*— and be persistent; beware of the need to be right/to know; and pour energy into smaller units/doses so as not to overwhelm. In short: less is more (personal communication to DK April 16, 2021).

**Christopher Bollas** said that people become psychotic when they are unable to bear what is being presented to their minds. Bollas (2013, 2015) understood breakdown as an unconscious attempt by the person to present their self to another for transformative understanding. If a person receives such understanding, then a breakdown can turn into a breakthrough. Bollas believes psychoanalysis is the best treatment for psychosis because this is the state in which a person is most vulnerable, amenable to help, and open to the development of insight into their condition. Psychosis creates a rupture with a person's historicity, leaving them without a narrative. Bollas recommended the practitioner to extend sessions when a patient is on the verge of breakdown, and to see that person every day, sometimes all day, until the therapist and patient reach an understanding of what is going on with them. Bollas is not alone in his approach to patients in acute crisis. Rosen (1947) was known to have held four to ten hour sessions, and Knafo sees, or is in contact with, patients every day during acute episodes. This type of treatment can potentially render a breakthrough. Rather than develop a parallel (psychotic) construction to explain what happened to them, with the help of psychoanalysis, a patient can restore a place for the self, guided by the hegemony of the I, within their own past, present, and future narrative.

## The British

Unlike the Americans, who by the late 1970s largely stopped using psychoanalytic methods to treat psychosis (Ophir, 2015), the British never did, thanks to **Melanie Klein** and her followers, who have consistently worked with early psychic processes of children. As a result of her treatment with young children, Klein (1963) postulated that the infant's anxieties in the paranoid-schizoid position (first three months of life) are psychotic in nature. She believed that introjection, projection, splitting, and omnipotent denial are common defenses in both infancy and psychosis and that they represent an attempt to protect oneself from annihilation anxiety and disintegration.

Whereas Freud spoke of the withdrawal of libido in energic terms, Klein added the object-relational lens to explain withdrawal. She always envisioned instinctual forces as attached to objects. Thus, the infant's fear of annihilation (death) takes the form of persecution because the fear is attached to a person who is experienced as "an uncontrollable over-powering object" (Klein, 1975, p. 4). The anxiety is too much to bear for the infant and, when it becomes internalized, the anxiety is experienced as an internal persecutor. According to Klein, defenses are enlisted to deal with this persecution and potential destruction—key among them is splitting the object into good and bad/loved and hated—which is accompanied by a corresponding split in the ego. Whereas such splitting preserves the good object/self, it can also fragment the ego, resulting in a lack of cohesiveness and disintegration characteristic of psychosis. The degree of splitting is key, said Klein, as it can produce a healthy paranoid-schizoid position (good/bad split that can later be integrated into the depressive position) or excessive destructiveness (when the death instinct becomes predominant) leading to fragmentation and confusion in psychotic conditions.

While Klein's emphasis on splitting mechanisms in psychosis recalls Bleuler's, her approach possesses a singular quality. Splitting, for Klein (1975), refers to the division of object relations and human emotions which, under the fear of annihilation, forces the ego to split itself into separate parts. These parts may then be projected onto and into another (projective identification), with the result of a person losing themselves in the other and becoming incapable of discriminating between what comes from inside and what comes from outside—i.e., the person becomes incapable of reality testing. *Projective identification*, which Klein conceived as a prototype of aggressive (hateful and destructive) object relations, reveals the underlying cause of paranoid persecutory anxieties. When the subject reintrojects dangerous parts of the self that have been projected, that person fears being controlled and persecuted from within. Although these early defensive strategies are universal, according to Klein, some people remain stuck in the paranoid-schizoid position or are overtaken by their anxieties and the methods needed to cope with these anxieties.

For Klein (1963), treatment necessitated an attempt at recovery of what has been projected outward as well as a healing of the splits that have taken place. Whereas some analysts (e.g., Federn, 1952) attempted to maintain a positive transference in the treatment of those suffering from psychosis, Klein believed that the therapist needed to address the negative transference with all its destructive qualities. Maintaining the object relationship while interpreting psychotic sadism is one of the greatest challenges in treatment. The analyst must try to experience the patient not as an adversary but, rather, as an ally in the attempt to accept parts of the hated self that the patient has denied, projected, or obliterated (Bott Spillius, 1983). To move from the paranoid-schizoid position to the depressive position, the patient must confront their envy and destructiveness, bring together the good and bad internal objects, and identify the good objects to form a cohesive ego. Together, the patient and analyst then face the pain and losses characteristic of the depressive position.

Klein's followers continued to develop an analytic understanding and treatment for psychosis. We will mention a few here. **Hanna Segal** (1991) distinguished two types of symbol formation and symbolic function. In the first, which she called the *symbolic equation*, the symbol is equated with the object. This type of concrete thinking is typically found in psychosis. The example she used is when a violin becomes a penis; thus, playing the violin equals masturbating and must not be done in public. *Symbolic representation*, on the other hand, represents the object itself rather than the word equated with it. For Segal, symbol formation involves three aspects: the symbol, the object it symbolizes, and the person symbolizing. Without the person, there can be no symbol. Therefore, sufficient separation is needed between the subject and the object, something that does not exist with projective identification. In psychosis, confusion of the symbol with the object results in difficulties in communication, especially when words themselves are treated as objects.

**Wilfred Bion** did much to further thinking about psychosis and its treatment. First, he believed that we all have psychotic and nonpsychotic parts to our personalities (1984b). Second, the ego is never entirely withdrawn from reality; rather, reality is merely masked by omnipotent fantasy, which is aimed at destroying the ego, or at least destroying one's awareness of it. Following Klein, Bion believed that the psychotic person is overendowed with destructiveness—a hatred for emotions, a hatred for life. This destructiveness is aimed at obliterating awareness of psychic and external reality, which is feared and hated because it is felt to be painful, overwhelming, and persecutory (Symington and Symington, 1996). Consequently, splitting extends to attacking the connections within the thought processes themselves (Bion, 1984a). Unlike the neurotic, who uses repression as a defense, the psychotic uses splitting and projective identification to rid themselves of the apparatus (the mind) that carries out repression (Bion, 1984b). The unfortunate result of this coping strategy is that the psychotic is trapped because they have destroyed the very apparatus that can help them become aware of what is happening to them, and thus, cannot fathom a way out.

Fragmented sense impressions are expelled and projected in psychosis, often resulting in what Bion (1962/77) called *bizarre objects*, similar to Segal's symbolic equation. Such objects are often experienced as uncanny and threatening. An example Bion offered of a bizarre object is that of a gramophone endowed with auditory and visual qualities, and therefore, experienced as watching and listening to the person. The power of such objects derives from their combination of external and internal (projected) realities. Whereas the neurotic problem deals with the resolution of conflict, the psychotic problem deals with the repair of the ego, a difficult task to accomplish when the patient is busy destroying the very apparatus that makes them aware of internal and external reality. Bion (1959) called this mechanism *attacks on linking,* a process that obliterates the capacity to distinguish internal and external reality, therefore destroying thinking and curiosity and stunting growth.

Bion (1962/1977) believed that people with psychosis were incapable of dreaming—that is, they could not engage in the psychic work that allows a human being to understand and grow; instead, they see visions while awake. For Bion, dreaming indicates that the mind is working to make its conscious and unconscious material comprehensible. Being unable to dream means the mind can not attend to memory, judgment, association, and so forth. Thinking repairs the splits in the ego by making connections. **Thomas Ogden** (2003) elaborated on Bion's thinking, claiming that dreaming is what makes us human. If one cannot dream, wrote Ogden, one cannot differentiate between conscious and unconscious thought or between waking and sleeping life. Thus, the psychotic lives in a timeless, undreamable panic.

Dreaming, for Bion, represents the beginning of integration. Bion (1992) postulated that *alpha elements*—sensory impressions—are capable of being stored in memory and are usable in dreaming. *Beta elements* consist of impressions that are nameless or lack meaning; they are felt like foreign bodies that cannot be thought about, only evacuated. Therapy helps a person transform beta elements into alpha elements, allowing the formation of connections, memories, and meaning to promote thinking and growth. The therapist accomplishes this task by helping the person with psychosis to gradually confront discomfort, tolerate frustration and pain, develop curiosity, and think about their situation (Bion, 1990).

According to Bion (1967), psychosis attacks the links to thinking and dreaming, and analysis must therefore try to repair what has been attacked by reversing projective identification. One way of accomplishing this daunting task is for the analyst to tolerate the patient's aggression and envy as well as become aware of what has been projected into them as a therapist. The analyst becomes a *container* for the patient's projected elements and detoxifies these elements infused with sadism, returning them to the patient. The patient then reintrojects them in a less threatening and more palatable form (Hamilton, 1990). When the therapist contains the patient's aggression, anger, envy, and confusion, the patient is relieved of the pressure and pain of these feelings. The therapist then links these emotions to his or her own understanding of what is troubling the patient—the drivers and elements of their psychosis—and articulates these elements in the course of dialogue so that the patient can reintegrate them into a new, less toxically felt, narrative framework.

Klein clearly made more use of the death instinct in clinical practice than Freud (Bott Spillius, 1983), and so did several of her followers. **Herbert Rosenfeld** (1971) distinguished between *libidinal narcissism*, in which good objects and parts of the self are idealized, and *destructive narcissism*, a condition in which destructiveness is idealized and pleasure derived from destructive behavior while keeping the good objects and good parts of the self-imprisoned and paralyzed. **Betty Joseph** (1982) described patients who are addicted to near-death and who obtain perverse pleasure from destructive and dependent parts of the self. **John Steiner** (1982) described a continuum, from a healthy self to *malignant narcissism*. In psychosis, he wrote that the destructive self dominates and destroys the healthy parts. In 1993, he formulated *psychic retreats* as highly structured pathological personality organizations that are constructed with defenses aimed at protecting a person from pain and anxiety. Psychic retreats are a safe place in which fantasy and omnipotence reign at the cost of isolation, stagnation, and disconnection from reality. Steiner considered psychosis to be the ultimate psychic retreat.

Clearly, these writers are referring to patients who are difficult to reach and who may enter into a negative therapeutic reaction (Riviere, 1936), patients with whom it is difficult to make meaningful contact and who resist getting better. Understandably, the destructive parts of psychosis can discourage many therapists from engaging in clinical work with patients experiencing psychosis. Yet, Klein and neo-Kleinians have braved the aggression and deadness that arise in the treatment of such cases, leading the way for the rest of us not to give up on them, to tolerate their attacks, and to hold their despair until they can face their buried and frightening need to connect and get help to reintegrate the good parts of themselves and their good objects.

**D.W. Winnicott** (1965, 1975) advanced specific recommendations for the treatment of psychosis. He believed that psychosis is the result of environmental failure/privation during the infant's stage of absolute dependence, resulting in the creation of a defensive, false organization designed to protect the true self. He argued that such a person's fear of breakdown is, in fact, the fear of a breakdown that has already taken place (Winnicott, 1974). The analytic situation invites regression/breakdown, due to its reliability and return to dependence in the therapeutic relationship. Winnicott advocated for regression despite the risk involved, because the analytic situation could provide the ideal arrangement for the patient to reexperience breakdown, this time in a facilitating (holding) environment. In an ideal case, an unfreezing of the early environmental failure takes place, the patient discovers their true self, and anger related to early deprivation is expressed. Moving from regression to dependence and then to independence is facilitated by the analyst's ego support and holding of the patient through their regression. Winnicott believed that it takes courage to regress and to have a breakdown, and he understood it as the patient's striving toward maturation and self-cure.

**Margaret Little** (1990), an analyst herself who was in analysis with Winnicott, wrote a book about his therapeutic approach to her own psychotic regressions. She noted that "the experience of being 'mothered' is truly mutative in that it resolves anxiety concerning survival and identity by providing reassurance and continuity of being" (Little, 1990, p. 90). Winnicott, who was not a woman and did not have children of his own, apparently had the capacity to mother his patients.

## The French

Whereas Klein had the greatest impact on British psychoanalysis, **Jacques Lacan** remains the formidable influence on French psychoanalysis, as well as on analysis in other European countries and Latin America. His own attentiveness to psychosis began early—when he wrote his dissertation (Lacan, 1932/1975) on the treatment of a paranoid patient named Aimée— and lasted throughout his lifetime. The perception of psychosis for Lacan (1981) and Lacanian psychoanalysis is generally considered to be structural rather than diagnostic since Lacan proposed three clinical structures: neurosis, psychosis, and perversion. Rather than focus on surface symptoms, like delusions and hallucinations, by which one commonly diagnoses psychosis, Lacanian analysts concern themselves with how the subject structures his or her self in relation to lack—the tension between demand and desire. Lacan's theory of psychosis involves a breakdown in the use of language, which, in his view, involves the relationship among the *Symbolic, Imaginary*, and *Real* in the use of language so that it loses its symbolic play and becomes too real, concrete, and threatening. The Oedipal myth/ structure/complex, as referred to by Lemaire (1977), involves forming a figurative, symbolic, playful relationship with language by having the father figure function as a metaphor for the mother's desire.

Lacan adopted Freud's (1894/1962b) term of foreclosure (*Verwerfung*) when speaking of the radical defensive repudiation of the signification of reality that characterizes psychosis. Foreclosed parts of reality cannot enter the symbolic realm of speech because they never existed in that place to begin with. Lacan (1981) believed that what is foreclosed in psychosis is the Name-of-the-Father, the paternal metaphor, which refers to the object (parent or parent stand-in) that is the agent of castration and that fundamentally structures our existence, in a similar way in which the law symbolically functions to structure society. Without a structuring object to bind together the imaginary (the realm of fantasy and delusion but also creativity), the symbolic (language), and the real (the unsymbolized), the person must deal with a gap or absence that they try to fill with meaning with imaginary identifications or psychotic solutions—e.g., hallucinations and delusions.

Referring to Freud's famous study on Schreber during one of his first seminars on psychosis in 1955, Lacan illustrated how the individual with psychosis is "the unconscious subject who is literally present, in this hallucinatory discourse. He's present, alluded to—one can't say in a beyond, since the Other is lacking in delusion—but on this side, in a sort of internal beyond" (Lacan, 1981, p. 123). In this quote, Lacan speaks about the breakdown in the language function in psychosis and the failure of the patient to establish the locus of the Other, where the play of language can take place. The delusion is too real: the subject is "literally present" rather than symbolically so. Thus, language becomes too concrete, words and letters are things in themselves rather than signs. The Other is where unconscious symbolization takes place as such and is not a delusion but another scene of fantasy and desire, represented by signs and images (called *Vorstellungrepresentanz,* or the ideational representative, in Freud's writings). In Lacan's view, psychosis is the structural failure to establish a reliable symbolic register or locus (the Other).

Twenty years later, Lacan revised his view of psychosis as a structural failure when, in his annual seminar, he conducted a close study of James Joyce (Lacan, 2005). In this seminar, he introduced the concept of the *sinthome* and inaugurated his late "topological" period, in which he revised his earlier structural viewpoint. As he began questioning the stability of neurotic structures, Lacan placed more emphasis on individual solutions that psychosis allows for. James Joyce's *Finnegan's Wake*, for example, is written in a language characteristic of psychosis, with its jumbled use of words and a plethora of neologisms. Lacan argued that while Joyce was neither psychotic nor schizophrenic, per se, his writing functioned as his *sinthome. Sinthome* or *synthomme* is Lacan's own neologism, in which he uses an archaic spelling of symptom (*sinthoma*) to signify both symptom and synthetic and indicates that the patient artificially crafts his or her being (synthetic + homme, which is French for "man"). Lacan believed that Joyce's writing functioned as his unique *sinthome*, the psychical mechanism that knits together the three registers of the Real, Symbolic, and Imaginary, and as such, keeps the patient—or author—from unraveling into florid psychosis. Lacan was also demonstrating how a creative person can in fact use psychotic mechanisms to save themselves from psychosis.

During the final years of his life, Lacan became increasingly concerned with the categorization of psychosis, believing that many people slip between neurotic and psychotic structures (David Lichtenstein, personal communication with DK, March 14, 2021). Jacques-Alain Miller pursued Lacan's line of thinking on the matter when in 1998 (See Brousse, 2008) he introduced the concept of *ordinary psychosis*. Ordinary psychosis is a term indicating a type of mental illness that falls somewhere between neurosis and psychosis, although some Lacanian therapists (Leader, 2011) say ordinary psychosis belongs firmly within the psychotic structure. These therapists designate a set of contemporary clinical observations of persons who demonstrate tendencies associated with psychosis but who do not necessarily present with its more severe symptoms. For example, an eccentric person who lives an isolated life may have delusional thinking and "blank spots in...[his or her] consciousness but has never had a breakdown and thus manages to stay away from psychiatry and hospitals" (Miller, 2013). It should be noted that even Bleuler (1911) claimed that many schizophrenics do not attract attention, receive treatment, or even know that they are schizophrenic.

Hence, Leader (2011) argued that we must de-emphasize the common association between psychosis and flagrant symptoms and behaviors. If we do, then we may be able to learn what protects some people with psychosis from the more extreme manifestations of the condition. Persons who might be "ordinarily psychotic" manage to function in everyday life, despite gaps in their consciousness and some delusional thinking (Serieux and Capgras, 1909). Leader believes that our current form of treatment encourages people to hide their psychosis and conform to social expectations, but the Lacanian psychoanalyst working with ordinary psychosis can help patients concealing their symptoms to establish a useful form of psychotic identification that allows them to enter into the social bond through their unique psychotic symptoms and craft a solution not unlike that of Joyce's *sinthome* (see Rowan, 2014).

Lacan's theory is difficult to translate into a therapeutic approach. In fact, he is known to have joked, "Clearly I had some psychotic patients in psychoanalysis. I cured some of them; I'm not able to say how" (Davoine and Gaudilliere, 2009, p. 140). Some of Lacan's followers have tried to be more explicit; for example, Leader (2011) created guidelines for the treatment of psychosis. Importantly, he argues that the most common forms of psychosis go unnoticed. Because much of psychiatry focuses on external symptoms and behaviors and pays little attention to a patient's internal world, practitioners may overlook a patient's psychosis. Moreover, distinguishing between being mad and going mad, and between behavior and internal phenomena is important and can be accomplished through dialogue with the patient.

Leader (2011) claims that medication interferes with a person's meaning-making capacity; he considers drugs to be anti-therapeutic and does not recommend them in the treatment of ordinary psychosis. He notes that a distinction should also be made between a patient's collapse and their efforts at recovery (i.e., delusions are solutions). The therapist should try not to interfere with the patient's own resources and creativity in their attempt at self-therapy. Rather, therapists should take the position of what, according to Leader, early 20th-century clinicians called a "*secretary of the alienated subject*" (Leader, 2011, p. 305). Lacan himself referenced this way of working when he used the term *secretaries to the insane* (Lacan, 1981, p. 206). This stance is nonintrusive and nonjudgmental, where the analyst never tells the patient who they are or should be. Rather, like a secretary, the analyst takes notes, asks questions, clarifies, helps organize, and reminds the patient of what has been said. Such a clinician should be sensitive to the patient's speech and the logic of their worldview while helping them map their history and identify the place they hold and the place the therapist occupies. A secretary, explains Leader, is not a boss. Therefore, the analyst–secretary should not fill the empty space, because empty spaces are important; they indicate places where work is needed to build something that is not yet defined.

**Francoise Davoine and Jean-Max Gaudilliere** (2016), who studied with Lacan, explored his thinking on the Real (the unsymbolized) and insisted on the importance of social and historical traumas they believe are at the root of psychosis. Indeed, they compare psychosis with war trauma: in both, (1) there is destruction of the symbolic order, (2) people are dehumanized and treated like things, and (3) there is "an area of death, where time stops, where there is no other, except for a ruthless agency that erases truth and trust" (Davoine and Gaudilliere, 2016, p. 104). These two regularly look for catastrophes in the lives of their patients and their patients' ancestors. Madness, they maintain, is "a war against denial and perverted social links, waged in order to restore the given word and explore historical truths falsified for the sake of power games" (Davoine and Gaudilliere, 2017, p. 98). Rather than attempt to squash a patient's madness or medicate it away, as prescribed by the medical model, these analysts suggest standing alongside the patient at the intersection of the catastrophes each carries. The stoppage of time is to be found in the intergenerational transmission of a trauma that has not been recounted or processed. Therefore, such trauma is passed along through the generations and experienced as desert landscapes replete with catastrophes and surviving images.

Davoine and Gaudilliere (2004) devised their own version of the Salmon principles for treating trauma: (1) *proximity* (carefully moving toward the Real, the uncanny, and the *catastrophic zone*, by listening to the patient's account of details, accidents, and coincidences), (2) *immediacy* (presenting one's therapeutic self during first encounters as "auxiliary and unpretentious" while locating points at which language is unanchored), (3) *expectancy* (inspiring trust and a belief that the analyst can be counted on, thus inspiring hope for the future), and (4) *simplicity* (expressing oneself in clear and jargon-free language). The analyst picks up something from the patient's account that is then expressed in the analyst's unconscious (e.g., via dreams), allowing the patient and the therapist to meet "at the crossroads of their respective stories and history" (Davione and Gaudilliere, 2017, p. 99). In summary, their approach consists of entering the traumatic realm in which time has stopped and language is unavailable, respecting what the patient has done to survive, and gradually accompanying the patient to a place in which language is formed so that he or she can narrate their history and find their place in time and space.

## Italy/Switzerland

**Gaetano Benedetti** was a psychiatrist and psychoanalyst who was born in Italy and lived the latter part of his life in Switzerland. He is known for having worked with psychosis for over 50 years and for having founded the International Symposium for the Psychotherapy of Schizophrenia (ISPS). Benedetti (1987) delineated three ego disturbances in schizophrenia: ego activity (passivity and lack of agency), ego boundaries (permeability of self and other; inside and outside), and multiple splitting ("lacerating of the self" and the persecution of one part of the self by another).

Treatment of psychosis, according to Benedetti, involves the transformation of the patient's self by means of their perception and internalization of the therapist's positive mirroring of parts of the patient that have been denied by psychosis. The analyst also internalizes the patient's self-perception, opens it up to communication, and corrects it via *positivization*. Now the old symptom gains a new context as the patient identifies with the coherent and cohesive aspects of their therapist. This symbolic exchange, or *psychosynthesis*, between therapist and patient creates a *transitional subject* and a *third reality* that exists between the detached observer (therapist) and the irrational (patient). Although Benedetti calls this *autism for two*, he sees it as the first step for the person with psychosis to perceive the other as a separate person (e.g., the patient might begin hearing the voice of their therapist). Because so much of this process is preverbal and irrational, communication is not always verbal and can include pictures and mirror drawings—drawings using tracing paper in which the therapist and the patient contribute, modify, and copy. Important here is Benedetti's insistence that both parties accept each other's perceptions and become involved in the therapeutic process. Benedetti considered interpretations of psychotic experiences as meaningful and open to interpretation only if they aim to stimulate the coming together of split-off fragments or highlight dynamics that exist in the relationship between patient and therapist. Most important is the emphasis on the patient's nonpsychotic, adaptive parts and the mutuality of the treatment. Both therapist and patient are changed by the encounter.

## Scandinavian/Nordic Countries

Scandinavian and Nordic countries have added to our knowledge of psychodynamic approaches to psychosis primarily by focusing on family, group, community, hospital, and milieu therapy. A central feature of these contributions is sensitivity to context both in the creation of psychosis and in its cure, which demonstrates how interpersonal relations are key to the onset of and recovery from psychosis. Importantly, these countries have also provided research documenting their therapeutic work and outcomes.

**Danish** psychoanalyst and researcher **Bent Rosenbaum,** a pioneer in this area, conducted a longitudinal study titled the "Danish National Schizophrenia Project" (Rosenbaum 2012; Rosenbaum et al., 2015), which compared supportive psychodynamic treatment with treatment as usual in 269 first-episode psychotics. Fourteen psychiatric centers participated, and subjects were assigned to different conditions based on locale. Those who were given psychodynamic treatment fared significantly better at two and five-year follow-ups (Rosenbaum et al., 2005, 2006, 2012; Rosenbaum, 2015; Rosenbaum and Harder, 2007). Supportive psychodynamic treatment followed a manualized procedure, with initial, middle, and termination phases. The procedure involved tolerating dependency and slow growth; helping the patient make sense of their symptoms, feelings, and attitudes through focused structuring interventions, especially as they applied to relationships with others, including the therapist; helping the patient cope with losses and develop hope and realistic optimism; and, with the help of clarifications, maximizing adaptation strategies and working on the development of the self.

Finland has become known for its success with first-episode psychosis using the **Open Dialogue** (OD) approach, which has been developed in Western Lapland over the last 35 years.

Although Jukka Aaltonen (Alanen, 1997), a psychoanalyst, was among the first to name the treatment *open dialogue*, most do not attribute its origins to psychoanalytic principles, such as free association, multiple determination, unconscious processes, transference and countertransference, tolerance of uncertainty (Martindale, 2015; Putman and Martindale, 2021) and reflection (Andersen, 1991). Yet, OD's emphasis on dialogue and meaning is akin to the psychoanalytic tradition. OD is known for its quick response to someone in crisis, initiated by a treatment team (of at least two) that continues working with the person and their family and supportive others until the patient shows consistent improvement. Mikhail Bakhtin (1984), a Russian philosopher and literary critic, noticed the multiple narrative voices in Dostoevsky's novels, in which no one point of view dominates. Practitioners of OD have learned from Dostoyevsky, through Bakhtin, and have tried to replicate that experience of polyphony by encouraging dialogue among all participants, in which each voice is deemed equally important (Seikkula, 2011).

Questions about what is happening and the goals of the meetings are addressed with all participants. Because meetings take place in the setting most comfortable for the service user and their family, people remain connected to their environment and significant others, and they begin to entertain multiple perspectives on what is happening. Family members do not feel blamed or excluded from the process but rather enlightened and helpful. OD practitioners consider all resources to be valuable.

Furthermore, the use of mobile crisis intervention teams and home visits prior to considering hospitalization result in much fewer hospitalizations. The OD approach does not consider medication to be the primary treatment modality, although drugs are sometimes used to achieve better sleep and to treat overwhelming anxiety, and neuroleptics are used only in a minority of cases, mainly on a temporary basis.

Multiple outcome studies compared OD to other treatments and evaluated OD service users over time at five and 19-year follow-ups (Seikkula et al., 2006; Bergström et al., 2018). Study findings showed a significant decrease in hospital stays, especially long-term hospital stays, for patients who received OD services. As a result of the improvement shown in most patients, diagnoses for OD patients were changed from schizophrenic disorders to brief psychotic reactions. These findings indicate that psychosis need not be viewed as a long-term condition. Early intervention and social networking are clearly effective in reducing psychosis and have been adopted in many other countries (Putman and Martindale, 2021).

Swedish psychoanalyst **Sverker Belin** wrote extensively about the challenges and benefits of working in a psychiatric hospital unit. He sees treatment as necessarily involving individual therapists and staff members working together. Patients meet with the entire staff, each from different professional backgrounds, at the same time. Group supervision is recommended with professionals who work with the same patient; the input of all involved is valued (Belin, 1993). Belin even asserts that anything emerging in individual therapy should be shared with the rest of the staff. This model assumes that it is difficult to contain the intensity of emotions and the various countertransference reactions that arise when working with psychosis. The message is that clinicians inevitably become the carriers of their patients' emotions as well as enactors of their family dynamics. When the therapist takes on their patients' projections, they induce bodily sensations, emotions, and ambivalence, and they are in turn affected by the surround. One goal, therefore, is to educate all staff members about these processes and strengthen the staff's capacity to deal with projections as they arise in therapy and on the unit.

## Israel

Psychoanalysis is held in high regard in Israel and even has been incorporated into the treatment of serious mental illness in public mental health inpatient units and clinics. The Lechol Nefesh Project (Amir and Shefler, 2020), translated as "for every soul," was begun in 2010 in one unit treating 18 chronic patients deemed untreatable by other means and who were willing to agree to a minimum of three years of three times weekly psychoanalytic treatment. The therapists were supervised by experienced psychoanalysts from the Israel Psychoanalytic Society (IPS) and the Tel Aviv Institute for Contemporary Psychoanalysis who volunteered their time and service.

Project originators **Ilan Amir** and **Gaby Shefler** (2020) coordinated a research study that tracked the progress of the patients in the program compared to a group with similar socio-demographic characteristics who had received treatment as usual. They found that the study group fared significantly better after the second year of treatment than the control group with respect to treatment outcomes as measured by a dramatic reduction of days spent in the hospital, reduced anxiety, fear, suspicion, outbursts of rage, depression, psychosis, obsessivity, and suicidal tendencies. The project's success is evidenced by its growth: it began with one unit treating 20 patients and currently has five units treating 100 patients.

## Summary

We have provided a long tour of a variety of psychoanalytic modalities used in the treatment of psychosis in the 20th and 21st centuries. We have confined ourselves to what has been done in Western countries because that is where psychoanalysis is most prevalent. Based on the similarities and differences among the various theoretical perspectives on psychosis, we propose the following 12 points as insights to guide the understanding and treatment of psychosis.

1. The psychotic state may display symptoms that can include hallucinations, delusions, and bizarre behaviors that indicate the patient is no longer able to clearly distinguish what is real from what is not, what is past from what is present, and what is inside from what is outside. A person makes little sense of their memories of disturbed relationships and destructive events; sometimes even constructive events are not felt to belong to them. Though the patient may appear to be suffering from a deficit, they are likely trying to make sense of a difficult situation, a sense that often defies conventional reality;

2. The outward appearance of psychosis potentially has a countless array of underlying psychological profiles, all of which point to the way in which a patient perceives themselves in relation to their capacity to tolerate affect. Psychosis may appear to be a way of escaping unbearable conflict, avoiding loneliness or feelings of inadequacy, seeking transcendence, taking revenge, expressing overt trauma (e.g., abuse), expressing deprivation (e.g., neglect), attacking others and/or the self, and so forth. Psychosis might even be a way of hiding in plain sight. And each of these motivations can be quite distinct. From this viewpoint, there are many types of psychosis. Like people, each psychosis appears unique. For this reason, it is so important to discover what led to the break from the patient's point of view and to discern what methods they used (symptoms) to manage their plight. Even if they are wrong in telling what they did, what they say will provide clues to their journey;

3. Psychosis is frightening to "sane" people because it reminds them that what they think of as normal and what comprises human reality is quite fragile. Patients with psychosis confront "normal people" with the primitive and irrational components that are part of everyone's psyche. Psychotic symptoms and utterances speak somewhat like dreams about conflicts and threats that severely disrupt a functional frame of selfhood and mind. The more everyone accepts that psychotic communications have value, the more all people become vulnerable to questioning the boundaries of what "normal" does and does not include;

4. An adult mind that can know reality begins as an infant mind that does not. In between knowing and not knowing is a period of childhood in which fantasy, a sense of omnipotence, primary narcissism, and childhood delusion dominate the immature mind—a mind that resembles the psychotic mind, with the caveat that psychotic thinking occurs *after* a person has developed the capacity for "normal" adult thought. This fact lends credence to the notion that no one is 100% psychotic; nonpsychotic parts of the person remain and can be accessed with psychoanalytic techniques. Because the patient has moved to a position resembling that of childhood, we can think of psychosis as a regression to an earlier state of mind, a retreat not merely from reality but from the adult stage of mind that discerns reality. This retreat is due to the person's felt incapacity to bear certain emotions, memories, or aspects of reality;

5. Though a patient may have constitutional tendencies toward psychosis (which are still far from being understood), childhood trauma and the struggles of adolescence, with its psychosexual and identity conflicts and the need to position oneself with respect to adult life and responsibility, usually play a large part in the development of psychosis. Not surprisingly, the most vulnerable ages for the onset of psychosis are adolescence and early adulthood. Trauma often involves early caretakers;

6. Psychosis is a problem of derailment of the ego, which falls off the tracks of the conventional world. But more deeply, psychosis is understood as an estrangement between the unconscious and conscious mind, between processes of memory assimilation and the current situation in which a person finds oneself. Psychosis is related to the threat of being overwhelmed by affect. This threat either has not yet happened or, in Winnicottian terms, has happened too early to have been symbolized. The patient experiencing psychosis is so afraid of future annihilation that they cannot focus on the present, except to try to control their emotions. This is why early intervention and social networking are critical components of the restoration of balance between the unconscious and conscious mind. Sanity is itself a form of resilience, always a struggle not to be overwhelmed by the suffering engendered by human reality. Sanity is a constant struggle against the pandemonium of the unconscious, a type of high-wire act that both the therapist and the patient must perform;

7. The very self of a person becomes overwhelmed by traumatic disturbances, whether those traumata involve discrete events or incremental accumulation, such that conscious selfhood becomes incoherent as it speaks its condition in a language riven with unconscious elements like irrationality, dream, fantasy, and archaic symbolic representation. When a person with psychosis is overwhelmed by what originated outside of themselves and is introjected with terror, confusion, and pain, they often become paranoid, hostile, and even hateful. That reaction should not surprise anybody;

8. There is good reason to believe that even in the throes of florid psychosis, lines to sanity may be obscured, but they are still open. Understanding psychosis as a defense against annihilation and unbearable conscious pain, the therapist can approach its manifestation with the view that

the mind is yet trying to heal itself and, however badly it is failing, it continues to try. Meanwhile, the patient is stranded in a hellish and lonely world of breakdown in which they are unconsciously attempting to present their self to another for transformative understanding. The patient has a desire to communicate and believes, at least on some level, that the therapist has something to offer them;

9.  What is most critical for the successful treatment of psychosis is the therapeutic alliance, which must be built upon authenticity, trust, acceptance, and nonjudgment. This requirement presents the greatest possible challenge for the therapist, who must attune themselves to the unique psychological idiom of the patient, which itself is obscured by the psychosis. The therapist's flexibility is key, as they must do what it takes to maintain contact with someone who may feel threatened by such contact. Ideally, the therapist faces the condition head-on in full acceptance and dialogue with the "unconscious subject," conveying that what may make no sense today may come to make sense tomorrow. Thus, the dyad must be willing to endure regression and frightening enactments during the sessions, in which memory and unconscious conflict are expressed and integrated, affording the opportunity for memory processing and new narrations. To this end, in a situation in which the therapist discerns that the patient may have positive support from some community and/or family members, it behooves the healer to enlist and monitor such outside support. Quickly following a psychotic episode, the therapist should be willing to see the patient as frequently as possible, be in contact with supportive others, and work with that person for as long as it takes;

10. There is no way to do this kind of work with any success without being profoundly affected and changed by every case. Experiencing psychosis is like being in the underworld. Empathy requires that the analyst first experience a sense of bafflement and a lack of certainty; only when the analyst can share with the patient the uncertainty of ever finding their way out can the patient feel met and understood. Supervision helps therapists through challenging times when they themselves are facing the limits of human resiliency;

11. Because the ego is often dissolved in psychotic experience and the unconscious mind is more fully realized, the patient sometimes manifests mystical intimations and may also be exquisitely sensitive to

unconscious fears, affiliations, and identifications of the other. If the therapist is faking it in any way, it is likely the patient will know;

12. All forms of psychosis have some relationship to reality, and determining the nature of that relationship is crucial—and necessitates a multipronged investigation. For example, what is the degree of commitment to obliterating versus engaging reality? What is being substituted for that reality? What specific aspects of reality are too toxic for the patient? How much does the patient need the therapist to accept their reality? These investigations yield important information. First, they open a window to the non-psychotic aspects of the personality. Second, the therapist will learn the patient's degree of distance from reality, which will indicate the depth of work needed to achieve a therapeutic alliance. Third, the areas the patient selects to eliminate from what they are willing and or able to acknowledge frequently help to identify the core conflict. Finally, the initial connection between patient and therapist often depends on the therapist's ability to recognize the degree of threat reality poses for the patient. Conversely, the more the therapist can appreciate the necessity for the patient's denial of reality and /or need to substitute an alternative reality, the more the initial connection will be facilitated.

# Chapter 2

# Beginnings

This chapter discusses what to expect in the first sessions with persons diagnosed with psychosis. As we have mentioned, many therapists, even experienced ones, are discouraged in their initial encounters with psychosis and for that reason may choose not to work with this population. What is it about these encounters that gives a therapist so much pause? Is it because many new therapists have been told that psychiatrists and psychopharmacologists are the primary treaters of psychosis (Ophir, 2017)? Is it due to fear of individuals who exhibit symptoms of psychosis? Or is it a lack of preparedness to engage with psychological and behavioral extremes? We believe all three reasons are relevant, but the most important one is that therapists lack preparation. We hope that by better understanding the challenges presented early in the treatment, more of our colleagues can overcome what seem like insurmountable hurdles and establish a treatment alliance that allows for the successful continuation of therapeutic work.

We do not mean to imply that, at the end of the initial period, treatment will proceed smoothly, at full speed. Nor do we intend to idealize beginnings. To do so would only result in a disappointing outcome for both the therapist and patient or in both feeling betrayed or at least disillusioned. Rather, both participants in the initial period have the opportunity to consider what each brings to the table in the way of expectations, fears, and desires, and how they might be gratified. Moreover, both participants have the opportunity to establish early on in treatment their requirements for feeling safe. These themes will continue to resonate throughout the treatment, but the initial period focuses on how best to allow the therapeutic process to unfold. In the discussion that follows, we give particular attention to the therapist's becoming aware of those aspects in themselves which, when unrecognized, impede engagement. Identifying those obstacles is crucial if the work is to progress.

DOI: 10.4324/9781003441519-2

## Differences between Psychosis and Nonpsychosis

We believe that everyone's personality has both psychotic and nonpsychotic parts in varying degrees, although most people present as nonpsychotic. However, we'd like to point out how many patients who are exhibiting psychosis differ from nonpsychotic patients and must be approached differently when beginning therapeutic work with them. Specifically, when a therapist meets a patient who is nonpsychotic for the first time, they can safely rely on a few basic and shared assumptions. First, such a patient identifies themselves, however ambivalently, as someone seeking help from the therapist. Second, to varying degrees, both parties agree that the therapist is there to help the patient and possesses a body of expertise the therapist will use to aid the troubled person. These assumptions are rooted in the notion that the patient has some ability to engage in reality testing and self–other differentiation and has an observing ego.

When working with a patient with psychosis, a therapist still seeks points of agreement to provide a base from which to explore differences between them. However, when the patient is in the throes of psychosis, the therapist is far less likely to find common ground about either the goal of the treatment or how each of them will contribute to its outcome. Patients with serious mental illness approach reality and interpersonal relationships with defenses that are primarily psychotic, and if the therapist is unable to find areas of consensus, he or she will lack the steadying influence of a shared reality. Therapists are likely to learn about this lack of consensus the hard way. We believe it is of utmost importance for therapists to be aware of the threat to their equilibrium and the difficulty they will face in attempting to find solid ground from which to launch the therapeutic journey of exploration.

For example, a therapist and their nonpsychotic patient may discuss a play that both have seen and might disagree about aspects of the play, but their differences would be anchored in a shared consensus. They have watched the same play, and their differing perceptions are a function of differences in their preconceptions, personalities, and tastes. "I see where you're coming from," is a statement that captures consensus and registers empathic recognition of the other's comprehensible point of view. A neurotic patient might describe how much they enjoyed the play because it was funny while complaining how much they were tired of plays with messages. The patient's response demonstrates that they recognize some theatergoers enjoy message plays, and people can differ in what they enjoy. The patient with psychosis is often unable to accommodate other views and believes that "You're either with me or against me." Only one interpretation of the play exists—theirs—and their interpretation *is* reality.

A neurotic patient may believe that the lead actress misinterpreted the playwright's intent. By contrast, an individual with psychosis might believe that the same actress is controlled by a propaganda machine that puts words in her mouth. The patient dismisses the fact that a script exists or that there is an actual play. Yes, the patient has seen something resembling a play, but they weren't fooled by that charade. The so-called actors are victims of a propaganda machine. The patient does not explain their reasoning but simply declares, "I know propaganda when I see it!" The therapist in such a situation may not understand that the patient is referring to an interpretation of a play they've seen; unfortunately, patients with psychosis often omit context and may leave the therapist bewildered. Further, patients experiencing psychosis often deny therapists the information they need to empathize.

There are many reasons such patients fail to provide context. The patient may be suspicious about what the therapist will do with any information provided—in the patient's view, the less the therapist knows, the better, which makes the patient feel safe. Often the patient is confused about how they have arrived at their conclusions and does not want to know or be shown the illogicality of their assumptions.

After many years of treatment, Ben told his therapist (MS) that when he put into words how he arrived at his conclusions, MS made Ben realize how crazy he was. "But better you than me," he added. "I at least trusted that you were doing it to help me. If I [was the one who had] made myself aware of how my mind works, I would hate myself for what I did to me."

Less often, the patient believes that the therapist already knows the information, either because they have read the patient's mind or have been tipped off in some way. Regardless of why context has been omitted by the patient, the therapist, especially in the early sessions, must be prepared to live with ambiguity. A common error is for the therapist, already fearing they are in over their head and wishing to appear confident to conceal their bewilderment with a veneer of understanding when what is called for is: "I don't get it. What made you conclude that?" The patient may initially react to feeling mocked, intruded upon, doubted, or challenged. However, over time, the patient will come to see the therapist's actions as an expression of genuine interest in getting to know the patient's world.

Sometimes the therapist asks a question or offers an alternative perspective, and the patient smirks in a dismissing manner. After repeated efforts to engage prove futile, the therapist might withdraw. What may be unknown to the therapist, however, is that the patient has a tightly organized delusional system centered on a belief that they are a genius of such proportions that anyone meeting them, including the therapist, inevitably becomes envious. The patient believes that the therapist will devalue them due to the therapist's own anger and envy. Thus, the patient does not see that the therapist is offering an alternative view on an external object, person, situation, or idea, but instead believes that the therapist is attempting to humiliate them (the patient). People are always envious, the patient thinks, and he or she has lots of practice thwarting the haters.

Another way of looking at the patient's predicament is to see that they are stuck in a kind of loop, a very specific loop that is like a Mobius strip, in which it is impossible to pinpoint what is inside and what is outside. A Mobius strip is created with a long strip of paper: one side of the strip is twisted and then attached to the other side to create a loop. The twisted loop now has a surface without a definite orientation. However, if a person draws a continuous line down the center of the Mobius, the line will connect to itself. The therapist's task is to find a way to help the patient cut the loop and regain access to what is inside and what is outside—to distinguish the internal world of fantasy from the external world of consensual reality.

Therapy with a psychotic patient must begin with authentic exploration. Once the clinician understands that he or she and the patient do not have a common ground of conventional reality, the therapist can then be motivated to turn to the patient to see if, together, they can find a path back toward each other. The therapist's resistance to discovering who the patient is—rather than whom they need them to be—poses a significant obstacle to making that journey. In the previous example, the therapist could ask the patient if they are talking about a play and actress who the patient believes is controlled by outside forces. Asking for enlightenment means that the therapist takes nothing for granted and remains in a state of constant curiosity and uncertainty. Meanwhile, the patient with psychosis can ill afford to consider the possibility of an alternative interpretation of the actress's behavior. The patient feels they must defend their psychotic stance at all costs because usually, on some level, perhaps deeply buried, the patient suspects that their psychotic stance cannot pass scrutiny.

In summary, a therapist cannot assume that they share a reality with a person with psychosis, and the therapist must instead begin with an inquiry into the patient's reality. With a nonpsychotic patient, describing and reifying a shared frame of reference allows the therapist to understand the context within which the therapeutic interaction is occurring. Absent that information when working with people with serious mental illness, the therapist must tolerate a great deal of uncertainty. The therapist who fears they are about to exceed their tolerance level is likely to seek certainty by inventing a hypothetical reality or giving up and retreating.

A variety of strategies may be employed by the therapist to seek certainty and stability. For example, the therapist may assure themselves that their previous clinical work can be applied to their current experience, regardless of whether it can or cannot. Convincing oneself that "I have seen the likes of this patient before" is an attempt to restore a sense of confidence. This strategy won't work, however. Instead, the therapist needs to see that a patient in psychosis has a different way of thinking and that, rather than being affectively related to the therapist, they are often struggling to defend themselves against both the fear of and a wish for merger and prefer to see the therapist's efforts as having magical properties.

Psychotic symptomatology makes it difficult for a person to accept traditional role definitions. The therapist believes their role is to help the patient, but the patient may believe the person sitting across from them is a messenger sent by God to punish him or her. God has sent lesser messengers to punish them in the past, but this new one seems more dangerous. A neurotic patient may also enter treatment with a wish to be punished, unconsciously assigning the therapist the role of punisher. But while the latter example is transference, the former represents a systematized delusional system. Even though there are transferential elements in the patient's delusion, efforts to explore the genesis of the psychotic need for punishment are likely to be futile. The patient's explanation has already been baked into the delusion itself. They have inserted the therapist into their system and have defined the therapist's role. Much as the therapist struggles to reclaim the role of therapist, the patient has cast the clinician as a participant in a complex and perhaps unknowable universe. Worse, the clinician's position may appear fixed and refractory to examination, at least for the time being. The therapist, who is unable to ply their analyzing craft, may doubt that the patient can really mean what they seem to be saying, or, if the therapist accepts that they do, they may feel caught in the patient's web from which they must escape. Dismissing the patient or fleeing from them are not good options. The patient needs a therapist who will not retreat, even if they can make almost no sense of what is taking place. The patient needs to know that they are not too much for the therapist (unless the patient is). This therapeutic stance is a step in the right direction, even if it does not secure the attainment of object constancy. The example that follows demonstrates how the therapy can be moved along.

Sam fears he's being turned into a vampire, and he tells his therapist. Following this disclosure, he notices that Dr. Olsen turns her head away from him. He immediately links the two events, based on his psychotic belief: she must have turned her head out of fear that he would fatally bite her.

When Sam tells Dr. Olsen what he's thinking, she confirms his observation that she turned away. However, she tells Sam his explanation is wrong, and she is not afraid of him. Instead, she heard his statement as an expression of profound isolation, which moved her to tears. She turned her head to conceal her tears from him. If the patient were neurotic, the therapist might respond by simply asking, "What makes you think I turned away?" In that instance, the therapist would understand the patient's use of the word "vampire" as a metaphor rather than a literal identification of himself. The neurotic position favors inquiry as the therapist's response. For the patient with psychosis, clarification is the first step; inquiry comes much later. A common error in this scenario might be for Dr. Olsen, already fearing she is in over her head and wishing to appear confident, to conceal her grief from Sam and perhaps inadvertently confirm his delusion—that she is afraid he will bite her.

## Clinical Illustrations

Upon meeting his therapist for the first time, Tom announces that all Dr. Miller needs to know about him is that he is dead. He laughs derisively when Dr. Miller asks why that is all she needs to know. Requests for further clarification fall on deaf ears, and when Tom does speak, he taunts his therapist, accusing her of not being able to face the truth of what he has told her. "It's not true that dead men tell no tales," Tom says.

There's something uncanny about this man. He ends the session prematurely, informing Dr. Miller that he will give her one more chance at the next session, which, he adds, may be their last. Dr. Miller has been unnerved by the session and tries to find similarities between this session and her previous clinical experiences. With a sense of relief, she is able to recall patients who have said they *feel* dead as a way of describing their depression. The next step is to assure herself that she can directly apply her previous clinical work to her current situation. Might "one more chance" and "one last session" refer to thoughts of suicide? She is relieved by finally being able to place her patient within the context of previous clinical experiences. She resolves to dedicate their next meeting to clarifying the suicide issue and making clear she understands that Tom is depressed. However, without realizing it, Dr. Miller has not taken into consideration most of what has unnerved her, including her patient's bizarre affect and the assertion that dead men do tell tales.

Dr. Miller begins the next session by asking a series of questions to assess suicidal intent. Does Tom have a plan, a method? What does he imagine people's reaction to his death will be?

Expecting him to be reassured that she finally appreciates his dilemma, she is confused when he says she is confirming what he said in the first meeting: "You're not hearing me!" Tom issues an ultimatum: the only way he will stay in the room is if she first acknowledges he is dead and that she is speaking to a ghost.

Dr. Miller feels thrown by his demand. She complains to her supervisor, MS: "I can't tell him I believe he's a ghost. That's too crazy!"

MS explains to Dr. Miller that the psychotic relationship to reality can be so far outside the range of an "average expectable environment" that her previous clinical experience simply does not apply. Appeals to objective reality, evidence that has been culturally or scientifically agreed upon, can be of no consequence to someone experiencing psychosis because they not only deny conventional reality but also resist any attempt to introduce an alternative perspective.

Dr. Miller now understands that she was misinterpreting Tom's reality, but it is too late. Tom failed to return and lost a potential ally. And Dr. Miller is left both defeated and relieved.

What might Dr. Miller have done to prevent the therapy from imploding? First, she did not have to accept that the only response to Tom's challenge was to accept his terms: appeasement or therapy will end. That moment of introspection—asking herself why she has boxed herself in—brings her back to being a therapist rather than a hostage. She could have thought about her patient as separate from herself, in both his effort to move her in a particular direction, even more important, in her ability to arrive at a separate conclusion. A hostage feels trapped and tries to escape; a therapist reflects on their sense of being trapped and applies that information to understand the interaction. To explore what Tom meant when he said he was dead requires openness, not self-protection. Dr. Miller first needed to identify that she was afraid and to examine how her fear was impacting her ability to reflect.

Next, Dr. Miller could have asked her patient what it's like to be a ghost. That would have made him feel heard and that she was taking an interest in him. Over time, a picture would have emerged, allowing the therapist to link her patient's delusional system to his past history. Tom's life, one of constant physical abuse, drove him to find a path to immunity. Being dead offered that protection. To believe he was truly safe, Tom not only needed to embrace his psychotic solution (Bollas, 2015) but had to get his therapist to agree as well. There could be no chinks in his armor, either inside or out. His solution was derived from his experience.

Early sessions with patients who are experiencing psychosis are often marked by bizarre declarations about who they are and an insistence that the therapist hold the same perception: "I am Christ, and only your jealousy prevents you from acknowledging me as your savior."

The therapist is often uncertain about how to address such a challenge, fearful that dismissing the patient's assertion will cause a breach that cannot be repaired. On the other hand, agreeing with the patient's assertion compromises the therapist's authenticity. The therapist, though doubting the objective truth of the patient's assertions, has a greater chance of being heard if they first appreciate how the patient's perception of themselves shapes the way that person wants to be experienced by the therapist. "Only if you see me through my eyes will I know you understand me," they demand.

The therapist does not need to accept the challenge and can replace either/or thinking with curiosity and exploration: "When did you know you were Christ?" the therapist can ask. "What makes you think I am envious of you?"

A patient who believes they have been inaccurately accused of being insane might insist the therapist recognize the error and its impact on the patient's life. The more the therapist links the way the world reacts to the patient, the more the patient is likely to believe the therapist understands them. For example, the therapist may say, "You've made it clear that you don't belong in the hospital. I'm interested in why you think so. That information can help me understand what you're up against. Since you feel that you need to get away from the false accusations being spread in your neighborhood, do you think talking with me could help with that?" Alternatively, the therapist may ask, "Do you believe I'm working with your enemies? If that is the case, would you feel safer if I stop talking?" Additionally, the therapist might offer, "What if you taped our sessions and kept the tapes yourself in case you later needed proof of what was actually said?"

## Turning Fear and Confusion into Analytic Work

By initially focusing on the way a patient understands their world, the therapist avoids an immediate struggle, laying the groundwork for exploring the patient's assertions later. When the therapist asks the patient whether they see the therapist as "one of them" (i.e., the patient's enemies), the clinician signals an understanding of the patient's narrative. Applying that understanding as the basis for taking action (e.g., the taping suggestion) reinforces that the therapist recognizes who the patient believes themselves to be and how they wish to be treated. The therapist has heard the patient's plea: "Understand me and you will know what I need."

At no point has the therapist indicated agreement with the patient's perception of themselves. Curiosity and empathy do not equal agreement, and to think otherwise would make articulating empathy dangerous. Frequently therapists confuse communicating understanding with indicating agreement. When the therapist lets the patient know that their feelings of endangerment are understood and their experiences of stress are appreciated, it does not mean the therapist is endorsing the idea that people are spreading false rumors about the patient.

Sometimes the therapist fears becoming too close to the patient who exhibits psychosis. Burnham et al. (1969) identified the "need/fear dilemma," referring to the wish to be close versus the fear of being swallowed up. No doubt, the wish to connect and belong can pose a terrifying dilemma for the therapist who encounters psychosis and probably reflects how the person with psychosis feels in encountering the therapist. Frightened by finding the patient incomprehensible and feeling therapeutically deficient, the therapist may make their priority self-protection and seek to limit feelings of helplessness by reducing engagement with the patient. Understanding what the patient's psychotic solution consists of means the therapist must shift from insisting they need to find a common basis before they can proceed to acknowledging they don't know who the patient is, but as a therapist, they know how to go about finding out.

Psychotic thought and action, rather than constituting a barrier between patient and therapist, is a potential gold mine of information about the patient and their world. What so often appears as an obstruction is in fact a doorway through which a therapist can walk and encounter a much more comprehensible person. The key to opening the door is making sense of the patient's psychotic defenses and symptoms (Knafo and Selzer, 2015). Understanding the patient provides access to both the danger that person is trying to protect themselves from as well as the tools they have chosen to use to feel safe (See Chapter 6).

Understanding what the patient finds dangerous and how they protect themselves are necessary but not sufficient steps on the path to mastery. The previously mentioned patient who insisted he was a ghost, as a precondition for relinquishing his ghost identity, would have to be able to tolerate the pain of being alive. Dr. Miller's ability to help Tom make the leap from psychotically-based safety to vulnerability would depend on more than appreciating the role being dead has played in his life. The therapist would also need to be relatively certain that *she* could endure the affective storm that would follow upon his return to life and that she could provide a safe enough harbor for him. The degree to which Tom can proceed depends on his experience of the strength of the relationship. Feeling understood helps. Even more important is whether Dr. Miller is communicating that she, and they, can contain the fallout from Tom's surrender of his protective armor.

As therapists develop a greater understanding of the patient, they will want to know even more about the contours of the patient's experience. What begins with the therapist's acknowledging the conundrum of their seeming misalliance can ultimately lead to a shared experience. Along the way, therapists are sure to discover things about themselves, especially the limits of their capacity to remain open to patients despite their fears and the patient's resistance. These last comments anticipate the course therapy follows over time and, strictly speaking, is not the purview of early meetings. They are mentioned here to demonstrate how what will follow depends on what has or has not occurred in the first meetings (Knafo, 2018).

## Countertransference and Psychosis

Working with psychosis can be distressing not only because of the psychosis itself but also because of how these patients "deconstruct the defenses crucial to our [therapists'] peace of mind" (Bollas, 2015, p. 36). Bollas believed that to be "normal" means to deny certain realities and to live with certain illusions. The person with psychosis breaks down these illusions and forces us to do so as well. Many therapists who have chosen this line of work state that their patients who are diagnosed with psychosis are able to see through the therapist's defenses, challenging them to confront themselves (Stierlin, 1959). Perhaps this is what Searles (1965) meant when he wrote that we learn the most about ourselves when we work with psychosis.

Bion (1970) has described the ideal listening attitude as one devoid of memory or desire. Yet, in preparation for their first encounter, therapists are likely to anticipate the meeting. Anticipation is protective and has a "fill in the blanks before we meet" component. The greater the possibility of unfamiliarity, the greater the likelihood of superimposing prior experience onto the situation about to unfold, like a projective test. Since working with psychosis is fraught with uncertainty, the therapist will be more likely to rely on the past to navigate the present than to apply Bion's dictum. Attitudes such as "I know what to do because I've been there before," and "I'm never going to let that happen to me again" exemplify resistance to an open and curious stance in the present.

To move past one's resistance, the therapist should first understand its origins. Prior to meeting the patient, the therapist might consider the ways in which his or her assumptions about each of them could affect their work together. Psychosis creates a situation in which both patient and therapist are likely to be riddled with biases, many of which have not risen to consciousness. In the patient's case, they may either keep them out of consciousness, or, to the extent they allow themselves to be aware, deem them too dangerous to acknowledge to the stranger sitting across from them. The therapist may not trust themselves to know the biases they bring to the situation, fearing those biases might lead to erecting protective barriers rather than engaging with the patient. But to the contrary, the therapist who becomes aware of their assumptions becomes freer to work with their patient (see Chapter 8).

Reflecting on certain questions prior to the first meeting can circumvent the therapist's unrealistic expectations of themselves or their patient. Examples include:

- What do I expect from my patient?
- What if the patient doesn't provide what I expect?
- What do I require to freely roam inside my own head?
- Is it instructive for me to periodically review my questions?
- If the answers to my questions change, what might be responsible for the shift?

As already noted, a therapist working with psychosis should be mindful that a shared reality may not exist or may appear only later in the treatment. There may be no agreement about who the patient is or who the therapist is, let alone the role each is to play in the other's life. The previously mentioned Ben suffered from the delusion that he was a world-famous psychiatrist, and that MS was his patient. He further believed his "patient," (MS) would accept his help only if Ben pretended to be the patient. Therefore, he claimed he had to act the part of a disturbed individual. During his sessions, he would shout, as if responding to voices. MS felt the patient needed medication for his auditory hallucinations and made that a condition for continuing the treatment. Ben, fearful of the medication's side effects, told MS that he had only pretended to be the patient to help him, but that suffering the medication's side effects was a bridge too far.

Knowing how patients experience themselves facilitates the therapist's ability to make contact with them. The therapist working for the first time with psychosis may be surprised at how quickly the patient wishes to declare who they are: Christ; a dead man; the target of unbelievable envy; omniscient. The rapidity with which a patient introduces themselves to the therapist may be a way to test the clinician's willingness to accept the patient. Whatever the reason, the patient is providing the therapist with a way to see the world through the patient's eyes. The therapist can then use the information to shape their interventions.

When therapists inform the patient of the link between their interventions and what the patient has revealed about himself or herself, the patient feels respected and known, and that enhances trust. For example, a young male patient in the first session informs his female therapist that he has barely escaped his persecutors who are intent on discrediting him. These evil people, he says, are masters at using benign information to craft malevolent accusations against him. The therapist is mindful that her patient is likely to perceive her questions as data that can be used against him by his persecutors.

Not surprisingly, the patient becomes upset when his therapist asks for his name and address. Should the therapist ask the patient about his reaction or explain why she asked for this information? The patient's prior declaration of who he is shapes her response. If she prefaces her request with, "We've just met, so you have no way of knowing whether I can be trusted and why I need the information I'm requesting, so let me tell you." The therapist, without saying she believes the facts of his predicament, makes clear she appreciates the effect those facts have on him. She understands that the patient believes himself to live in a world out to get him. His suspiciousness is comprehensible and merits the therapist's providing him with a detailed description of why she is asking questions and what she will do with his answers. She might show him the form she is required to fill out and explain how that information will be used. She could inquire whether the patient would like input into the procedure, an opportunity to demonstrate that therapy is a collaborative process, albeit within certain parameters. If this exchange occurs in an outpatient setting, the therapist might say, "I'm taking down this information, so I'll know how to contact you. If you feel that means that I might have too much access to you without warning, then we will have to work out another system. If I have your email address, I could warn you in advance that I want to speak with you. I also need your address to send you a bill."

By responding to the patient's suspicions, the therapist is both providing and collecting information: she provides enough detail to make the rationale for her questions as clear as possible, offering an alternative explanation to his psychotic distortion. The more detail, the less ambiguous the situation will be, decreasing the likelihood of projection. In addition, her intervention provides the first estimation of the degree to which her patient adheres to his psychotic world. Does the patient sneer when he thinks his therapist is trying to cover up that she is working with his persecutors, or does he listen quietly, reflect on her alternative explanation, and then reject it? The less explanation the patient requires to counter his distortions, the less extreme his adherence to his psychotic world. This encounter is also a barometer for gauging the therapeutic alliance. The greater the trust between them, the more the therapist will be able to inquire about the patient's perceptions rather than provide information about her own activities. The extent to which the patient believes he has been heard will affect his ability to find his therapist credible.

Unlike psychotic patients who insist on immediately telling the therapist who they are, there are those who feel threatened by being known (Steiner, 1993). In both instances, the therapist's aim remains the same—seeking a better understanding of the patient's sense of themselves in the world—but the initial focus will differ. With patients for whom concealment is paramount, the therapist must first understand their wish *not* to be known. Therefore, the therapist does not ask, "Can you tell me about yourself?" Accepting the patient as they present themselves reveals more about what they are hiding from than who is behind the mask. The analysis begins with the therapist communicating their appreciation that the patient is hiding to feel safe. By accepting that the patient sees the world as a dangerous place from which the only protection is camouflage, the therapist sees the patient as they see themselves and can more effectively help that person feel safe. However, the therapist believes the patient's wish to reveal themselves will ultimately emerge. Loewald (1960) remarked that the patient identifies not only with the person the therapist sees but also with the person the therapist sees the patient as capable of becoming.

Irrespective of what has triggered a particular content, it provides the matrix within which the therapeutic process occurs. Given the tendency for many experiencing psychosis to find relatedness challenging, the therapist should anchor exploration in the dyad. The previously mentioned patient who wished to conceal his address might simply declare, "I keep my own counsel."

The therapist could respond, "I see my question threatens you." Similarly, the therapist who feels confused might say, "I'm having trouble thinking right now. Can you help me?" Exploring the process serves multiple functions. First, it emphasizes that what is transpiring in either person impacts the other. By articulating that inevitability, the therapist underscores the impossibility for either participant to completely withdraw from the other. Furthermore, what goes on in therapy can never be written off as either incidental or meaningless. Next, even when the therapist's focus is predominately on themselves, there will always be an impact on the patient, and vice versa. Even when either member of the dyad believes they are alone, the other bears that impact. Finally, exploring the process speaks to the therapist's steadfast determination to follow up which leads to further clarification of who each is to the other, and thus who we are to ourselves.

Bizarre behaviors can represent the patient's efforts to signal to the therapist their most terrifying beliefs, albeit in a confusing, disguised manner. Karon and VandenBos (1981) claimed that the only thing one can know for certain about a person experiencing psychosis is that they are afraid. Such patients tend to make their needs known either clumsily or not at all. Either stance signals their conflict with expressing their needs and knowing what they feel. A therapist who is comfortable expressing their own desires can serve as a positive model for the patient. The more the therapist makes explicit who they are, how they think, and why they do what they do, the more the therapist is clarifying their role and giving the patient an opportunity to consider alternative motivations to those based on the patient's projections. The greater the patient's confusion or distortion of each participant's role, the more structure is needed. Detailed information about the therapist's motivation encourages the patient to reveal their perception of whom each of them is to the other.

In a nutshell, successful therapy depends on the therapist and the patient becoming credible to one another. Rather than taking a history, which is common with nonpsychotic patients, the therapist focuses on what it will take for the pair to meet again. The therapist leads the way by attempting to see the world through the patient's eyes and keeping their vision unclouded by whether the patient's story resonates with objective reality. The therapist who appreciates the crucial role the patient's perception of themselves plays in shaping their experience—and then incorporates this perception into interventions—enhances the chances of being heard. If the therapist thinks they have been lumped together with the patient's persecutors, the clinician might stop asking questions to see if the patient becomes less anxious.

## Nonpsychotic Parts of the Person with Psychosis

The therapist who can find the nonpsychotic parts of the person and align with them in the earliest sessions has found a partner who recognizes that exploration can lead to liberation. Nonpsychotic parts of the person are revealed in the patient's ability to have an observing ego, test reality, differentiate between self and other and inside and outside, and enter into a relationship, even if that relationship possesses delusional qualities. Podvoll (2003) named five indications of nonpsychosis, which he called *islands of clarity* or *marks of sanity*. Being repulsed by one's symptoms can be a sign that one is ready to do therapeutic work. This idea is akin to the motto of Alcoholics Anonymous: "I'm sick and tired of being sick and tired." Expressing a desire to go beyond the self—to discard the psychotic self— can be a sign of health. Displaying an urge for discipline in any form (writing, gardening, cooking, and so forth) without becoming compulsive can be a harbinger of what is possible for doing psychological work and engaging in other types of activites. Compassion for other sentient beings, human or animal, shows a positive and generative connection toward the outside world. Finally, courage points to the ability to face difficult emotions necessary for recovery.

Lawrence presented in an acute psychotic state, believing he had special powers and perhaps was a prophet. To cope with the loss of his sense of reality, he was in the process of creating a narrative to match his symptoms. Along with his delusions of grandeur, Lawrence complained of high anxiety, intense confusion, and a devastating feeling of failure. Despite Lawrence's being in the throes of a psychotic episode, DK noted that he had the discipline to search online for a therapist who specializes in psychosis, the courage to ask for help and expose his vulnerabilities, the ability and discipline to continue his college classes and maintain his friendships, and the willingness to drive one hour each way for his therapy appointments.

Finally, Lawrence said, "perhaps" he was a prophet, leaving room for the possibility that he might be wrong. These significant islands of clarity contributed to Lawrence's positive prognosis for therapeutic work.

Psychotic symptomatology naturally dominates the patient's expectations of the therapeutic process. Whereas all patients (and therapists as well), bring prejudices to the start of therapy, the degree to which the patient with psychosis perseveres in their position can unnerve the therapist. If the therapist who encountered the patient who insisted he was dead had asked, "Might there be another way of looking at this?" the patient's response would likely have ranged from bewilderment to downright dismissal.

Another patient believed a purple light circled his forehead. He believed his aura signaled that he was extraordinary. When, in the first meeting, his therapist asked him to say more about his claim of superiority, he replied, "You must be blind," and refused to say more. The more tenuous the patient's hold on reality, the greater the need to cling to their convictions.

However, the nonpsychotic aspect of the personality can entertain more than one perspective. If someone is seen early on in their psychotic process, the nonpsychotic part is more evident. The patient may be confused and question what is happening to them. They seem different from themselves (depersonalization). Reality is no longer the same (derealization). When a person is feeling that their sanity is slipping away, it is easy to align with the nonpsychotic part that is clinging to a past way of being. "I don't know what's happening to me. Life doesn't seem the same lately," the patient may say. With patients who have passed the initial phase or who are not experiencing their first psychotic episode, the psychotic explanation of their symptoms is more ego-syntonic, dispplaying what Arieti (1974b) termed *psychotic insight*. In such cases, the therapist explores the meaning of their symptoms and defense mechanisms and slowly, within a trusting relationship, questions their logic. The word "slowly" is critical here because the symptoms are the patient's protection from experiences of fragmentation and annihilation; the symptoms are the patient's attempts at recovery and need to be recognized as such. Leader (2011) distinguishes between being mad and going mad. Going mad represents the collapse of the self and one's reality. Being mad is the attempt to recover via psychotic solutions.

It is important and helpful to keep in mind that psychosis is never 100% of the person. The nonpsychotic part of the person "knows" that their psychotic manifestations are defensive. For example, a patient of DK told her he saw himself as a "man whose life has blown up and, as a result, has become hypervigilant." The fact that this patient could step outside of himself for a moment and observe what was happening to him, including his defensiveness, was a mark of sanity. DK and her patient were able to discuss the reasons her patient thought he was losing his mind. Even the most regressed individual at times shows some ability to observe themselves, test reality, and distinguish themselves from their environment, and, therefore, possesses the rudimentary tools for forming a therapeutic alliance and doing therapeutic work.

There are several reasons the person in the midst of a psychotic episode is reluctant to know what they know (the *unthought known*; Bollas, 1987).

Even the nonpsychotic aspect of a person is uncertain of how much they can accept the truth behind their psychotic beliefs since to do so may mean they are crazy. In addition, the person in the midst of a breakdown cannot afford to give up their defenses until they feel able to face whatever they have been defending against.

Before he took his seat at the start of his first session, Bob, one of DK's patients, demanded, "Don't ask me any questions that begin with who, what, where, why, when, or how!"

It is easy to feel controlled by such a patient and to wish to regain one's professional authority. However, DK knew her patient was frightened and defensive and that she needed to make him feel safe and empathize with how dangerous the world was for him before expecting him to be open with her.

Patients usually straddle the psychotic and the nonpsychotic worlds, insisting on the validity of their psychotic world, while at the same time hinting that they are struggling with uncertainty. The first clue might be the appearance of an inconsistency between a person's avowed experience and their behavior.

In MS's initial encounter with Greg, he asked him why, since he was "certain" that a listening device had been implanted in his brain, he had never explored whether the device could be removed? He had failed to get an MRI of his brain, which could have revealed the anatomical location of the device. Perhaps it was close enough to the surface to be easily removed?

Greg interrupted MS's investigation of this discrepancy to ask if he was willing to help him. MS responded that he was confused by his request, since MS was not a neurosurgeon and, in fact, had been quite clumsy when he was on a surgical rotation.

Greg's response represented an opening into the nonpsychotic part of his personality. He considered, "Maybe it's not a bug at all."

The patient may reveal their nonpsychotic part by projecting it onto the therapist. In a first meeting, Karl described in detail the "evidence" that a foreign power was out to get him. At one point, he looked up at MS, smiled, and said, "I bet you don't believe me."

When MS asked if Karl was as doubtful of his therapist's believing him as he was of the evidence that the government was intent on destroying him, he shouted, "That's enough for now! Next topic!" Indeed, Karl's need for MS to validate him at all costs revealed his doubts about the reality of his perceptions.

Several weeks later, when he was covering similar ground about the foreign government's malevolent interest in him, MS said that his facts appeared convincing, but would he be even more certain if he had more information? Might it help to look more deeply into what seemed to be the evidence for the foreign government's evil intent? The effect of these questions was to enhance collaboration between the therapist and the patient and to raise doubts regarding his psychotic solutions. They became co-investigators in the search for the truth of the situation. This part of the work is similar to what is done in cognitive behavioral therapy (CBT) when these therapists work with psychosis. Garrett (2019), for example, employs CBT methods to examine the evidence of his patients' delusional claims. Eighteen months into the treatment with MS, Karl began to talk about a "slight doubt" he had about the "evidence," but he warned MS not to get any "wrong ideas," insisting he continued to believe he was in danger.

## Safety of the Patient and Therapist

Securing the safety of both patient and therapist begins in the earliest sessions. Bolstering the patient's sense of safety necessitates understanding the patient's needs and the ways in which he or she makes it difficult for the therapist to meet those needs and why. The therapist also must think about what they can and cannot do to make the patient feel safe. Because the therapist is unknown to the patient, the patient might be at the mercy of their own projections. Therefore, the first step is to understand what signifies danger to the patient. This isn't always simple or straightforward because reading that riddle can be quite complicated, and the solution can shift rapidly. At one moment, the patient may signal their wish to be left alone, and, in the next, demand that the therapist rescue them. Needing to be seen can be rapidly replaced by wishing to remain invisible. To make matters worse, especially at the beginning, the patient is more likely to communicate through actions than in words. Putting their fears and wishes into words requires the patient to have self-awareness and want to share information with the therapist, a dubious proposition.

Even if the therapist assumes that the patient wishes to know themselves, it is doubtful the patient will believe the therapist is capable of understanding them in the way they insist on being understood. A patient might declare, "If I say I am Jesus Christ, it is because I am Jesus Christ." There is nothing to interpret or understand here beyond the literal meaning of the statement. Because fear is this patient's overwhelming dynamic, they are more likely to signal what they wish to avoid than what they seek. Desire must take a back seat to protection.

For example, Daniel shut his eyes when MS spoke of certain topics. Months later, he explained that MS's words cut his eyeballs. He was closing his eyes to protect himself from becoming blind. Two years later, now in a relationship, he told MS that when his girlfriend spoke, he kept his eyes wide open. Prior to meeting his girlfriend, his life revolved around avoiding being blinded. Nothing else mattered. Near the end of the treatment, he confessed that it had taken him years to figure out that what he really wanted was to keep his eyes open. Vision—having it or losing it—is especially significant in psychotic conditions and often takes on a concrete manifestation.

Chapter 10 describes one of DK's cases in which the patient was convinced he was going blind as he was losing his capacity for insight. Similarly, Nathan, a second patient of DK, removed his glasses and put them back on, depending on what he could tolerate hearing/seeing.

The patient who hides their longings makes it difficult for the therapist to maintain their therapeutic zeal. Especially at the start of treatment, concealment can be the patient's primary way of creating a safe place for themselves. When that is the case, the patient feels that the therapist's wish to know them threatens their safety. Steiner (1993) has written about *psychic retreats,* omnipotent places of safety to which some patients withdraw to protect themselves from anxiety and psychic/relational pain. Steiner believes that psychosis is the ultimate psychic retreat since it protects a person from other people and reality. Patients in psychic retreats are understandably difficult to reach, due to their powerful system of defenses that result in isolation, withdrawal, and stagnation. According to Steiner, the therapist must hold the patient's despair and need to connect until the patient can emerge from their retreat. During that time, the therapeutic atmosphere may be one of deadness or isolation. The patient who clings to a psychic retreat may avoid dealing with their problems, leaving the full responsibility to the therapist, who must, especially at the beginning, respect the patient's need to feel more secure by not pushing. Rather, the therapist's role is primarily one of containment, and the therapist's patience becomes the patient's security. To be comfortable with this therapeutic milieu requires the therapist to believe that listening today makes exploration possible tomorrow (For more, see Chapter 6).

The therapist also promotes trust by letting the patient know when the information they provide enables the therapist to circumvent a dangerous situation. "If you hadn't alerted me to X, I would have done Y," the therapist might say. By showing the patient that their communications have influenced the therapist's actions, the therapist challenges the patient's belief that expressing their needs leads to exploitation rather than protection. On the other hand, the patient may fear that they have been too open about their vulnerabilities and have exposed themselves to greater danger. To counter this belief, the therapist might say, "It took courage to tell me that. You might have thought I'd use it against you."

Successful therapy depends on both participants feeling safe. Initially, the therapist is the primary guardian of the process. It is important for the therapist to first ensure their own safety to be able to reflect on what they are experiencing with their patients as well as within themselves. They need to protect their ability to maintain free-floating attention, including the freedom to observe and learn what is causing an inhibition when they are unable to freely observe.

When the patient is first seen in a hospital setting, the therapist will either observe the patient in an acute state of a psychotic episode or a chronic state of psychosis, usually medicated (and often overmedicated). A patient is in a hospital because they are assumed to be dangerous to themselves or others, or they are considered too much for a single person to handle and require a team effort and round-the-clock behavioral observation. The holding environment is provided by the hospital milieu, and in this setting, the therapist works with the staff to prepare the patient for exploratory work (Selzer, 1983). The therapist should note a patient's object-seeking behaviors, which can inform the strategies the therapist can later use to develop alternative interactions.

## Summary

While we have focused in this chapter on issues dominating the beginning of treatment with individuals who struggle with psychotic features, these threads run through the entire treatment process. Giving and taking is one such thread. To be sure, from the therapist's perspective, giving is more dominant in the beginning phase. However, for many patients, merely showing up is experienced as having something taken away from them, be it their anonymity or grandiosity, or simply having their psychotic processes exposed.

What the therapist gives is structure, containment, understanding, witnessing, acceptance, alternate points of view, and parts of themselves to identify with. How the therapist gives involves reassurance, empathy, validation, curiosity, and authenticity. The more the therapist gives, the more the therapist will expect the patient to go into his or her pain—more than the patient imagines is bearable. Interpretation is rarely used in the early sessions. The art of therapy is providing the correct balance of giving and taking from both participants. We have emphasized what might get in the therapist's way of giving what the patient needs, by focusing on the clinician's own dynamics as the primary source of fear, lack of understanding, or resistance.

Taking involves the therapist upping the ante by raising expectations and challenging the patient. Taking depends on prior effective giving but is always a risky venture. When the therapist can realistically expect the patient to give involves an exquisite sense of timing, a talent that perhaps relies largely on intuition. Besides becoming aware of a more open atmosphere in the therapy room, the therapist carefully attends to the cues the patient offers, invitations to enter their world at the precise point they locate themselves.

Beginning sessions are of the utmost importance. This is the time when therapist and patient are introduced to one another and to the possibilities of working together. Hopes and fears on both sides inevitably emerge. In beginning encounters, the therapist takes note of psychotic and nonpsychotic parts of the personality, cautionary tales, and islands of clarity. This is the time to create a safe, nonjudgmental space and a therapeutic alliance that will enhance future work. Most of all, it is a time for the therapist to gauge how they are feeling and why, and to use these feelings to guide interactions with the patient. Working with psychosis is as rewarding as it is challenging. Being well-prepared for what to expect and how to handle unusual behaviors is the key to success.

# Chapter 3

# Establishing a Pre-Alliance

Most patients experiencing psychosis will have moved beyond the earliest stages of psychological development, which means that the therapist can play a familiar role from the outset: making use of the patient's subjectivity, feeling free to interpret, and moving in and out of serving as a primary object. This chapter explains how the therapist can establish a pre-alliance with patients who have not attained these milestones.

Human development can be viewed as a slog toward autonomy. Nothing except survival takes precedence over the quest to individuate (and sometimes that quest even takes precedence over physical survival). Psychosis, however, turns the usual developmental process on its head. In psychosis, many patients believe they cannot exist without their primary object, and their lives have become a testament to their need to remain undifferentiated from their objects. One seeks fusion to gain safety, even at the cost of losing one's self, and to preserve infantile omnipotence. Since boundaries are incompatible with fusion, the distinction between inside and outside or internal and external reality becomes impossible. A somewhat similar situation occurs when the patient, appearing to separate, remains bound to the object via appeasement, in the form of the emergence of a false self (Winnicott, 1965). Developmentally, the false self is less of an obstacle to treatment since it suggests a partial recognition of self: "I will keep her close by ceasing to exist except as a being whom she wishes me to be." Those who remain fused and undifferentiated or who present a false self (Winnicott, 1965) share a fear that a separate existence is dangerous; however, the ensuing symptomatology is quite different.

Psychoanalytic psychotherapists who write about psychosis generally describe people with a common initial presentation, whose major feature is an outsized need and fear of dependency (Burnham et al., 1969). These

DOI: 10.4324/9781003441519-3

patients' crises are viewed as remediable if the therapist can provide sufficient support for the patients' exploration of themselves. The therapist who can provide such a holding environment will enable the patient's pursuit of selfhood (Winnicott, 1965). According to this formulation, the patient possesses at least a rudimentary awareness of a desire for a self that, however conflictual, wishes to engage in further development. The wish is concealed by psychotic symptomatology that paradoxically also provides information for the uncovering of the desire. In other words, psychotic symptomatology reveals the path to a therapeutic alliance while also defensively protecting the patient from self-discovery.

Of course, some persons experiencing psychosis are more difficult to reach than others. Their developmental arcs are interrupted at different stages, attributable to many factors, not the least of which is the unreliability of the holding environment and/or relational impingement. Thus, it is no surprise that therapists must alter their approach for each patient, including the amount of support they provide; the degree to which they avoid interpretation; the choice of involvement versus accompaniment; the use of verbal versus nonverbal interventions, and so forth. As patients progress—especially with regard to boundary formation, the need to cling, and the ability to distinguish help from submission, self from other, and inner from outer reality—therapists can alter their interventions accordingly.

A small but significant subgroup of patients experiencing psychosis have yet to reach the state of development described above. Patients in this subgroup are seriously deficient in boundary formation, which results in difficulties in self–object differentiation; they are also limited in their capacity to verbalize and self-reflect. Some may have achieved sufficient differentiation earlier, only to have regressed to a point of nondifferentiation. Those patients who had achieved a degree of internal cohesion earlier, which may be possible to resurrect, have a better prognosis.

## Challenges of Fragmentation

Selzer (1983) and Selzer et al. (1984) wrote about the challenges of beginning therapy with patients who are fragmented to the degree that they recognize neither a self to which they belong nor a coherent other. As long as they remain undifferentiated and immersed in their fusion, these patients are impervious to the existence of an external world. Instead, infantile omnipotence confers upon them the power of creating and/or abolishing the world. The therapist may be indistinguishable from a piece of furniture or several scattered pieces of furniture, or even more accurately, have no presence at all. Scattered and seemingly aimless, the patient appears to be meandering purposelessly with no discernible method to their madness. Ron Unger, a psychologist who himself had experienced psychosis, likened this state to wandering in the wilderness (personal communication with DK, September 8, 2022). Patients with psychosis have no words for their experience, nor can they make room for anyone else's insight or speculation. Any effort by the therapist to make sense of what they see in the treatment room may be experienced by the patient as an effort to swallow them up.

Boundarylessness, or the absence of self–object differentiation, poses a formidable obstacle to the goal of establishing an alliance with the part of the patient seeking autonomy (Bion, 1957). Moreover, the patients being discussed here often display little conflict about remaining undifferentiated. Attempting to create a therapeutic alliance, as well as use interventions that address separateness and relatedness, must await further development. Instead, the therapist needs to remain steadfastly present as these patients give full rein to their fragmented, undigested, and not-yet-symbolized selves.

The therapist's presence is nonetheless important, and he or she is more than a spectator. Therapists share the patient's experience, accompanying but not interpreting, participating without comment about what is going on—bearing witness. Gradually, bearing witness without intruding facilitates the patient's internal cohesion and aids in the dawning recognition of the therapist as a *companion* on the patient's developmental journey. Grossmark (2016) has written about the therapist becoming a psychoanalytic companion to patients who are unable to engage in mutuality. How transformation occurs is less the result of what the therapist does than what they do not do. What must be avoided is anything the patient might experience as impingement, which would remind them of unbearable separateness. An extreme example would be offering interpretations or directives, such as, "Don't do this," or "I hope you don't do that." Far less direct statements could be equally provocative and send the patient into hiding, so that they miss sessions, remain silent, or attempt to appease the therapist by giving them what the patient assumes they want.

For example, MS once thanked his patient, Oliver, for showing an aspect of himself that allowed MS to understand him better. This patient responded by retreating into silence for weeks. When MS let Oliver know that his statement had value for the therapist, Oliver felt taken over, and his efforts to become himself were destroyed.

Similarly, Frank, a talented new therapist whom DK was supervising was nonetheless overly confident in his skills. Upon returning from vacation, Frank overenthusiastically greeted Jeffrey, one of his beloved patients. Jeffrey punched Frank in the face and broke his nose. Frank had wrongly assumed object constancy in his patient and thought that Jeffrey could pick up where they had left off.

What becomes clear from these examples is how much patience and caution therapists need in conducting themselves in ways that avoid being perceived as impinging on their patients. When therapists can keep in mind that the purpose of the first phase is to facilitate the patient's eventual engagement in mutuality, they will better be able to wait patiently and not intrude until they reach the goal. The patient's autonomy is not being sacrificed. Rather, the therapist is doing everything to not stand in the way of the patient's own unique self-definition. Things need to happen *in the presence of the therapist*, not necessarily *between* the patient and the therapist. An excellent illustration of this concept is how Frieda Fromm-Reichmann worked with a man who refused to emerge from his room or even recognize her. Fromm-Reichman did not abandon this patient due to his lack of participation. Rather, she brought a chair and sat quietly outside his room day after day until one day, he looked at her and asked what she was doing there. He was ready for a dialogue to begin (Hornstein, 2000).

DK saw Charles, a man who had experienced severe childhood abuse and neglect, in twice-weekly therapy for six years. Charles began every session in an identical fashion, tentatively trembling on the corner of the chair and announcing each time, as if for the first time, "I'm OK. I'm hangin' in there."

DK heard these words as laden with meaning. She noted that Charles reassured her first ("I'm OK"), after which he announced that he was "hangin' in." She wondered whether Charles meant he was at the end of his rope, having thoughts of suicide (i.e., hanging), or simply holding on. Nonetheless, she was assured by his "OK" that he was not in danger of harming himself, so she did not inquire or interpret, as she felt Charles was not yet ready to have her probing thoughts interfere with his need to lead the way.

After several years of this ritualistic beginning to each session, Charles entered the room, sat down in his usual fashion, and said matter-of-factly, "I'm hangin' in there." DK was just about to ask about the repeated refrain when Charles wondered aloud, "Why do I always say that?" DK knew he was finally ready to explore the meanings of his signifier. The work could now move from being fellow travelers to working as collaborators, each capable of reflecting on why things happened to him as a child and how to understand his current relationship with DK. The emergence of curiosity and the reflective function meant Charles and his therapist could cautiously move beyond the pre-alliance phase of treatment.

## Other Voices

We are not the first to suggest a revised form of treatment for those who require a pre-alliance phase. Joseph Lichtenberg (1963) defined *untreating* as "Finding some way of spending time with the patient in which both the therapist and particularly the patient can actively share and communicate. … The usual psychotherapy situation must be replaced by an informal means of being together" (p. 315). Untreating, wrote Lichtenberg, is especially necessary for those patients who manifest strong distrust, narcissism, and regressive modes of functioning. He recommended creating an informal atmosphere with flexible location and time arrangements and focusing on the here and now. Lichtenberg emphasized that mutual trust must be developed before any investigative therapeutic work can be done. He wrote as if speaking to such a patient: "First we have to work to restore your faith that you and another human being, who is a trained therapist, can understand your basic needs. We must do this slowly and patiently without allowing either of us to exploit the other by unrealistic demands and within a context that at all times maintains a therapeutic objective regardless of the formal means employed" (p. 317).

Winnicott (1965) believed that psychosis is due to environmental failure at early stages of development. This failure is overcome only by a special therapeutic setting Winnicott called a *holding environment*, similar to what a good enough mother provides. In therapy, the holding environment consists of reliability, predictability, consistency, and the therapist's ability to survive a patient's aggression. Winnicott described "primitive emotional development" as including a hefty dose of illusion and omnipotent control. A patient who is in such a state experiences "the object … according to magical laws, i.e. it exists when desired, it approaches when approached, it hurts when hurt. Lastly it vanishes when not wanted" (Winnicott, 1975, p. 153). Therapists, Winnicott believed, must allow themselves to be *used* by their patients.

Michael Balint (1968) also wrote about patients who develop a *basic fault*, usually due to childhood trauma or deficiency, which results in a developmental deficit. Like a geological fault, psychological stresses could cause strain and disruption in personality structure and relationships. Balint suggested that such patients need their therapist to relinquish interpretation in favor of being utilized as a primary object—that is, the therapist must perform *psychological mothering*— even allowing regression when necessary.

Sheldon Bach (1985) spoke about therapy with the *unclassical patient*; however, he objected to calling what he did a preparatory phase. "This *is* the analysis," he stated, "conducted in another way" (p. 224). Bach wrote about the importance of allowing the patient to own the treatment and feel like it belongs to them. He likened treatment to a mother who allows the child to play in her presence. So too must the therapist allow the patient to treat themselves in the therapist's presence. The patient can create any world they need, and it is the therapist's role to share that world, even if it lasts for a very long time.

Robert Grossmark has written about the *unobtrusive analyst* (2012) and *psychoanalytic companioning* (2016), an approach he views as instrumental with persons who do not possess self–other differentiation and therefore cannot engage in mutuality. Grossmark (2016) wrote: "The analyst companions the patient into the dark, 'archaic' areas of functioning and regressed object relations that are not available for discursive interaction or mutual study, rather than seeking to foster greater relatedness and mutuality in the session" (p. 699). Though the therapist is unobtrusive, he or she is still engaged with their patients. The therapist does not withhold their subjectivity; rather, they engage in a different register of subjectivity, one in which the therapist speaks from within the patient's own images and illusions.

## Working with an Undeveloped Self

What we perceive as a patient's purely intrapsychic experience can be, for the patient, an interpersonal event. We become privy to therapeutic encounters which, at the time, appear to have no direct impact on the patient's interpersonal development. Yet, months later, the patient might refer to one of these encounters as having been meaningful as an interpersonal occurrence.

A patient of MS violently pounded on the office wall one day. In recalling this event six months later, he said he had only now realized that: "Had you tried to stop me, I would've been aware of your presence and wouldn't even have started to bang on the wall. What the hell is the matter with me that I always fear that my 'me' will be smashed, so I hide?"

For two years, Don, a patient of DK regularly walked into her office and turned the heat up before he took his seat. She never asked about this behavior or interpreted it, since she understood it as a way for Don to control the setting to make himself feel comfortable, to turn it into a womblike space. This went on for over a year until, one day, he approached the thermostat, suddenly turned to look at DK, and exclaimed incredulously: "I never asked you if you felt too hot or too cold." That session ushered in a new phase of treatment that involved interpersonal recognition and mutuality.

The path that therapists take can be unfamiliar and challenging, leading to considerable self-doubt. They may wonder about what they are doing and feel foolish, unskilled, and unable to apply their prior training. Their professionalism may feel challenged. The rare therapist feels delight in their freedom to extemporize. To counter their sense of being thrown off balance and deprived of tried-and-true analytic tools, therapists may seek some common point of reference—a touchstone that makes their out-of-contact patient feel less alien and that provides the therapist with a greater opportunity to empathize. But even using the word "alien" may assume more than may be present. Alien implies there is a "someone," albeit a not-like-me self, whereas the patient may not feel themselves to be a "someone" at all—neither friend, nor enemy, nor alien—which makes the therapist's empathy suspect.

We liken the therapist's encounter with the strangeness of psychosis and other extreme states to the experience of a traveler who, when voyaging to a new, unfamiliar place, searches for familiar signs of their own place of origin. What is this new country? What resembles home and what is different? Unfortunately, such a search for familiarity superimposes a structure on a structureless situation, giving rise to an illusion that something is already known and that what is seen can be appropriately measured against what one already knows. Instead, what is required for this novel experience is a willingness to accompany the patient on their own unchartered journey, where there are no precedents that can be communicated. Without a clear thrust toward autonomy, the journey can seem to have no goal, unless remaining undifferentiated is its goal. Rather, the path is composed of accidental exposures, bumping into something rather than purposefully moving toward a destination, as most tourists do.

Davoine and Gaudilliere (2004) referred to the importance of *strange interferences*, which most try to normalize, silence, or move away from. "Coincidence" in such treatments, they wrote, should instead be paid attention to and made use of. The French term *flaneur*, referring to an urban explorer who strolls or idles with no specific destination in mind, is apt here. For the poet and essayist Charles Baudelaire (1863/1995), one could remain anonymous and autonomous even amid the ebb and flow of city movement. Essayist Nissim Taleb (2012) emphasized the differences between a *flaneur* and a tourist. The tourist has a plan, places to visit, and sights to see. The *flaneur*, on the other hand, seeks "optionality," remaining fluid and ready to change plans at every step. In establishing a pre-alliance while working with psychosis, the therapist might think of themselves as a *flaneur*, which can be helpful and also add a sense of adventure and the possibility for creativity.

Thus, when we speak of the patient on their own journey, we mean that the therapist goes together with the patient while in no way impinging on the patient's choice of destination or lack of destination. Eshel (2013) refers to this as *withness* and *presencing*. The patient feels free to leave the therapist unattended, hoping there will be no untoward consequences, or free to test the water to be sure it is safe and that they will not be abandoned.

Patients should be the primary source of information about themselves. The therapist is present to bear witness both to the patient and the patient's experience of self, no matter how shadowy or insubstantial, fragile, or undeveloped. The therapist's reassurance is only that they will be there, whether the self presents in pieces or as a void. The patient's self-determination is inseparable from and dependent on their ability to develop a capacity for separateness, a task that requires the relinquishment of infantile omnipotence. Conversely, holding on to omnipotence means the patient insists they can either create the world to suit their wishes and needs or that its existence is a result of their wishes and needs. Being the Creator means that one's universe cannot be taken away or destroyed by outside forces. The patient can choose to abandon their universe, however, should they so desire.

In an optimal scenario, freeing oneself from the yoke of omnipotence should open the door to the possibility of connectedness. However, a more likely scenario is that the patient's wish and/or fear of engulfment will sabotage this process. When the pursuit of selfhood becomes synonymous with the loss of safety and the threat of annihilation, surrendering to an all-protective environment becomes an effective solution. The patient's fear of being taken over implies an awareness of possessing something that can be lost or taken away, even if that something is not a fully formed identity. This might be the first hint that Bion (1957) is correct in asserting that people with psychosis have nonpsychotic aspects to their personalities. But what is most important is the recognition that the threat of impingement means the patient is anticipating total obliteration (Hurvich, 2003). The therapist must bear witness to the patient's precarious position and avoid interventions that might be interpreted as the therapist's wish to incorporate the patient into themselves.

When therapy is successful with fragmented and undifferentiated patients, coherence eventually replaces fragmentation. The process is neither smooth nor linear, and the patient must be able to assure themselves that regression is acceptable, should they feel the need to regress. The therapist supports the patient through their regression when it appears, neither encouraging nor discouraging it, but being there alongside the patient so they know that they are not alone. When the patient knows that regression is an option, they are less likely to use it. The patient constantly tests the waters, often less interested in progressing than being accepted when they feel the need to move backward. Safety is the priority. In this initial phase, the challenge for the therapist is to remain aware of how fragile the patient's movement toward integration is and to not get ahead of the patient's momentary pacing and needs.

For years, and during three psychotic regressions, Josh, a patient in analysis with DK, compared his personality structure to an upside-down pyramid. He felt himself to be so much on precarious ground that only the tip of the pyramid touched land. One by one, the bricks from the top were (in his mind) moved to the bottom, as he gradually built a foundation of strength and a sense of groundedness. At that time, Josh also began to feel the emergence of a self, which he compared to a budding plant growing out of the concrete. These developments took years to achieve. (See Chapter 10 for a complete description of this case and its treatment.)

As we have already mentioned, the therapist working with patients with serious mental illness must be able to postpone using their own subjectivity, a vital component of the therapeutic tool kit with nonpsychotic patients. Yet, the therapist remains present as a keen, non-directive, and nonintrusive observer, a fellow traveler in the patient's private quest for self-definition. Self-definition implies at least a modicum of awareness that a world exists outside of, or apart from, oneself. Yet the awareness, which can be seen in reference to both the animate and inanimate world, may be transient and easily obliterated by the appearance of anything unpredictable.

Relinquishing omnipotence is an essential precursor to symbol formation. Once a patient is no longer omnipotent, they must reach out to the world to survive. Symbols become the means of contact. Without symbols—without words and the naming of things—nothing exists beyond needs, fears, and desires that demand attention, and the patient is in a world analogous to an infant for whom a breast does not exist independently (Klein, 1963). Rather, the breast, if recognized at all, exists to sate the infant's hunger. The implications for the therapist are both obvious and difficult to negotiate. The therapist must avoid the temptation to describe the patient's experience to them or, worse, provide them with an explanation or solution to their problems.

The patient's lack of impulse control and need for immediate gratification will be on prominent display, but it behooves the therapist to remember to do nothing to interfere with the patient's own struggle. The form and content of the struggle is the patient's most basic communication about where they are now. Psychodynamic therapists are excessively attached to verbal communication and tend to undervalue what happens without words. As the patient progresses, they will have less of a need to cling and a greater ability to receive help rather than experience it as an act of submission. At that point, the therapist can gradually shift their interventions to more familiar territory.

## Clinical Illustration (Narrated by MS)

The following clinical example concerns a patient who was extremely difficult to reach. Joe, age 17, was his mother's last child. Mother was obsessed with youth and beauty; she clung to Joe "for dear life." She often declared that her last chance to remain young depended on her son remaining "my baby." Mother said that Joe was incapable of sleeping in a room apart from his parents. He screamed and put up such a fuss that Father finally moved out of the parental bedroom, ceding it to Joe and his mother and turning him into an Oedipal winner (Lasky, 1984).

Mother had insisted that Joe be tutored at home lest he fall into "bad habits" by interacting with his male peers. She reasoned, "You know how boys can be. They are always trying to break away from home." Not surprisingly, Joe became increasingly homebound and uninterested in venturing out into the world. At age nine, Joe moved into his own room, often refusing to participate in family activities, such as eating together at mealtimes. He frequently had tantrums, breaking things by throwing them against the wall. He was seen by a psychiatrist who prescribed medication that Joe often refused to take. When he came to see me, he spent his days sequestered in his room, playing video games by himself.

My first encounter with Joe was when he was brought to my office by a therapeutic aide hired by his wealthy parents "to keep him out of one of those dreadful hospitals." The aide informed me that she had been instructed to bring Joe to the session, after which she was free to leave my office for the 45 minutes Joe and I spent together. She was instructed to return promptly to pick him up after the session. This was his third scheduled first appointment; he refused to leave home, so the aide had been unable to bring him to the first two sessions. Father then hired a male aide to help bring Joe to my office, and that seemed to work.

I invited the aide to join us in the office, explaining that I wished to clarify my position about Joe's attendance. The sessions were voluntary, I said. Joe could stay as long as he wished, but he would have to leave when the 45 minutes allotted for the session were over. That was the only rule I expected him to follow. But the session was his time to do whatever he wished. Thus, since the session was his time, he would have to bring himself to my office if he wished to be there. He could call a taxi, just as his aide had done today.

During the meeting, Joe said nothing, alternatively rocking or squirming and making no eye contact. His lack of any recognition of me did not appear to be an act of avoidance. It was more chilling than that. I felt as if no matter where his gaze fell, Joe took no notice of me.

That initial intervention was tricky. On the one hand, it was necessary to make it as clear as possible that I had no interest in controlling Joe. He was free to come and go. On the other hand, I was concerned that by acting in this powerful fashion, overriding the parental instructions to the aide, I might be feeding into Joe's fear of being taken over, even though my aim was the opposite. My goal was to ensure the safety of a transitional space where Joe, over time, could feel safe to explore the possibility of something beyond himself without losing himself. As the therapy evolved, he sometimes did not show up at all, but at other times he remained for the full session. He always left at the 45-minute endpoint. One difficulty early on was my desire to interpret Joe's management of the schedule, to figure out what was behind his no-shows or, alternatively, his punctuality. I was restless, wanting to move things along and be a "real" therapist doing the psychodynamic things that defined my professional identity. What helped me remain silent was remembering that my current role was to honor the primacy of developing a shared experience with Joe. Subjective musings were postponed to a later date.

Joe and I had meetings scheduled for three times per week. When he showed up, Joe might be silent though, most often, he would interrupt his silence by making loud noises and then laughing aloud. For the first several sessions he seemed to show no interest in my being there. Gradually, seemingly related to his noisy outbursts, he would peer over his shoulder to look at me. I had initially smiled at him whenever it appeared that there was a possibility that he was seeing me. Now, in reaction to his own recent behavior, his eyes scrutinized me after his outbursts.

I indicated with upturned palms and a quizzical facial expression that I was puzzled. I did not ask for an explanation nor make any effort to interrupt his actions. One day, he mimicked my gestures, resulting in our uproarious laughing together. The next session followed the usual pattern, with no apparent recognition of me.

A turning point took place about the third month into the therapy. I had routinely left several bowls of Hershey's Kisses in the office, which Joe enjoyed. He did not view the candy as something given to him. The Kisses were there because he wanted them. This was a display of omnipotence in its rawest form. He was hungry. He needed them. That was all it took for them to exist.

On the day under discussion, I had forgotten to fill the bowls. Upon finding them empty, Joe had a tantrum. I responded with similar behavior, and we were soon laughing at our shared experience. Then things changed. Again, through facial and hand gestures, I reflected puzzlement as to why the bowls were empty. To emphasize my point, I went around the room looking for the Kisses. Joe followed suit, interested in what might have happened. We continued to search the office. Joe seemed bewildered. How could this have happened to him? His bewilderment seemed to be a departure from his usual sense of omnipotence. He was considering the possibility of a world unrelated to his desires. Until this moment, a governing principle had been that I do nothing to challenge his illusion of omnipotence.

I decided that it might be time to test the waters. In the following session, I filled the bowls with Hershey's Kisses in front of Joe.

At first, he seemed incredulous, not believing his eyes. He quickly became enraged, selectively pounding the two tables holding the chocolates. Interestingly, he remained for the entire session. From that point forward, Joe came to his sessions regularly, continuing the table pounding and not eating the chocolate.

At the end of each session, with Joe still in the room, I picked up all the Kisses that had fallen to the ground and placed them back in the bowls. His anger did not seem personal (i.e., directed at me); rather, it seemed to be a way for him to present himself to me. It was as if he were trying to solve an important mystery and was frustrated by his inability to do so. His hunger hadn't been enough to make the Hershey's Kisses magically appear. How could that be? Yes, I had withheld the chocolates from him, but he seemed more stymied by the discovery that the appearance or disappearance of the chocolates might be the product of something other than his own needs. After all, hadn't the chocolates been created by his needs? Joe was struggling to connect the dots.

Winnicott (1971) wrote about the role aggression plays in developing an appreciation of an external world. Joe had displayed his anger, and I had not retaliated. I withstood his assault, even providing Joe with more chocolates. I was beyond his omnipotent control, therefore separate, hence capable of being used by him in whatever way he chose (Winnicott, 1971). Until that point, I had been waiting in the wings, bearing witness but not available in any capacity beyond his seeing me seeing him. This marked the beginning of Joe's ability to distinguish the inside from the outside.

After several weeks, Joe once again began to eat the chocolates, initially devouring them as if he couldn't get enough, then gradually eating them more casually, as he had in the beginning. As I watched him devour the chocolates, my thinking began to change. I wondered whether he might be attacking (devouring) the chocolates to punish them for demonstrating that they existed independently of him, thus shattering his illusion. More importantly, I began to speculate about what made Joe tick. I was returning to my more familiar role, reflecting on who Joe and I were and could become to each other. I resumed my therapeutic role.

I began to allow myself to appreciate what I had given up. I had played "follow the leader" for three months, during which time I felt as if Joe had hardly seen me. Nor had I shown much of myself to him. On the other hand, how much had I accepted my companioning role? I considered that I was fearful of not being able to return to my former therapeutic self. What I had failed to appreciate was that I was adding new therapeutic skills and increasing my flexibility, the opposite of reducing my competence.

I had accepted my companioning role, trusting that pursuing therapy in this way would eventually lead to traditional psychodynamic psychotherapy of psychosis. My initial doubt and discouragement were born of several factors. I felt that having to "follow the leader" dampened my creativity, and as a result, I could not use my subjectivity and the impact of the patient on me in the service of the treatment. I had unwittingly separated myself from important aspects of my therapist's identity, perhaps as an attempt to identify with Joe: he felt fragmented, and I felt cut off from my familiar therapist self.

But I wasn't just thinking about Joe. I also wondered how my grievances might have affected my own actions. Was my forgetting to fill the bowls the "accident" I told myself it was? I had also feigned surprise about what happened to the chocolates, and Joe had joined me in searching for them. In the very next session, I filled the chocolates in front of Joe, challenging his omnipotence rather than waiting for him to give me a signal that he was ready to relinquish it. Perhaps my behavior was an expression of anger at having to put up with these restrictions for so long. I thought that my primary motivation was my belief that the time had arrived to challenge Joe's illusion that it was he who made the chocolates appear. I wished to clear the way for his further development. I say "primary" motivation because I am unable to rule out the possibility that other factors did play a role as well, though on a less conscious level. Joe himself had contributed to my thinking that it was time to move on.

Especially telling was his asking, "I finished the chocolates in both bowls. Got any more?" This was a first indication of his ability to, in Winnicott's words, "use the object" (1971).

Even prior to the interactions concerning the missing chocolates, on rare occasions, Joe had shown an interest, albeit indirectly, in what I thought and how I might even play a role in his life. For example, one day he had arrived early enough to see a couple who were my patients leaving my office, which prompted him to say, "I don't want to spend much time with people." Then, seeming to sing rather than speak, Joe declared, "Everything keeps changing for me." He paused and whispered so softly I could barely make out the words, a task made even more difficult by his turning his back to me. If things stood still for a while, he wondered whether that would help. Maybe then, he pondered, he might want to be around people more? I had a strong feeling that Joe was asking me to help him.

We had reached the point referred to earlier where more traditional psychoanalytic psychotherapy of psychosis could take place. Joe had achieved sufficient self–object differentiation so we could begin to examine the world, both internal and external, that, due to a combination of fear of intrusion and omnipotent control, had remained exiled from his awareness. There would be regressions along the way, limited in scope and number, as the therapeutic alliance took hold. My role expanded but continued to include the provision of a holding environment in which development unfolded over time.

## Further Analysis of Joe's Case

When Joe didn't show up or his attendance was especially erratic, MS felt a mixture of relief at not having to deal with him as well as futility related to this question: "Can we ever get to a point of collaboration?" Much later it occurred to MS to consider his unconscious communication as related to the interaction between them. One can imagine a therapist who cannot tolerate the frustration of dealing with their patient's non-presence and who may be tempted to tell the patient who they are—i.e., to interpret. For example, the therapist might say, "You're hiding from me," which would be entirely counterproductive. In such a case, the patient might well pick up the therapist's unconscious communication, namely that they are having difficulty tolerating the patient's lack of presence. To reduce their own anxiety, the therapist may feel a need to define the patient. The patient may then feel invaded and may want to prevent the therapist from overwhelming them.

What kept MS going in this treatment that for months reaped little reward? To a large extent, it was his conviction that avoiding intrusion and all that it implied are the *sine qua non* of the earliest part of the work with such a patient. He felt mandated to avoid anything hinting at invasion and remained steadfast in the face of the patient's nonemergence. While MS was perfectly willing to wholeheartedly endorse the necessity of tolerating uncertainty when working with individuals like Joe, at the same time he was unwilling to reflect on the fact that he himself had embraced certainty by adhering to the injunction that Joe should, under no circumstance, be defined. Ironically, MS was doing the very thing he had resolved not to do: defining Joe as someone who should not be defined. In some sense, there is an inevitability at work in any approach to therapy. Specifically, unless the therapist him or herself descends into a psychotic state, they cannot help but name the reality in front of them, even if they name it as undefinable.

## Summary

This chapter examined the challenges of working with patients who do not have a strong sense of self or self–other boundaries. We believe it is advisable to approach such patients with a preparatory phase during which the therapist's primary function is to see the patient and to witness their struggle to become. The dawn of the patient's curiosity begins with their nascent ability to see themselves. Only then can they begin to explore what lies beyond as well as what lies within. *Seeing oneself begins with being seen*, which is why the therapist bearing witness is a priority.

We have emphasized that during the pre-alliance phase, therapists should avoid making interpretations. Ultimately, all interpretation derives from being able to recognize that which already exists within the patient, though they resist acknowledging it. In that sense, therapists should not get ahead of their patients. Indeed, most people resist acknowledging aspects of themselves, and a premature interpretation is often received negatively, whether it is correct or incorrect. The person reacts to the content of the interpretation, not the process of being interpreted. For example, they may say: "You couldn't be more wrong," "You're just jealous," or "I'm hanging on by a thread. This isn't the time for that." But the patients we discussed here did not respond to content and were likely to hear the therapist's musings as efforts to take them over. What they needed was for the therapist to be present, watching them fumble toward self-discovery, not telling them who they are or how they got that way. These patients had no demarcated self, capable of acknowledging or refuting what was said about them.

Offering an interpretation only has the potential to increase confusion. Therefore, we advise therapists to accompany their patients and allow them to own and direct their treatment: to be with a patient in any way that person finds useful until they can distinguish themselves from others and reflect on the inner workings of their minds. Working in the way we have described eventually pays off. Contrary to what many might believe, this approach is not anti-psychoanalytic. Rather, it is a way of expanding psychoanalytic understanding to accommodate certain types of patient presentations and needs.

# Chapter 4

# Sample First Session
## Psychosis and Cannabis

The connection between cannabis and psychosis is well documented in the medical literature, even if the public at large is unaware of this information. Most studies conclude that daily use of cannabis (especially high-potency cannabis) puts the user at high risk of developing psychosis, particularly if they are vulnerable to psychosis and/or have a family predisposition (Gerlach et al., 2019). One longitudinal study concluded: "Cannabis use increases the risk of both the incidence of psychosis in psychosis-free persons and a poor prognosis for those with an established vulnerability to psychotic disorder" (van Os et al., 2002, p. 319). Cannabis was shown to exacerbate the symptoms of those already diagnosed with schizophrenia (Hamilton, 2017). Whereas cannabis use disorders are known to affect 4–8% of North American adults, youth in First Episode Programs (FEP) have rates between 33–51% (Ghelani, Armstrong, and Haywood, 2023).

Cannabis products have greater potency and higher levels of tetrahydrocannabinol (THC) than ever before, regularly exceeding 20%—and even much more in "dabs," potent products that isolate the active ingredient in the marijuana plant, creating ultra-high concentrations of THC (Rossi and Beck, 2020). It's been found that high doses of THC can trigger temporary psychotic symptoms in nonpsychotic individuals and develop psychotic disorders in vulnerable populations (George and Vaccarino, 2015). Concerned by this trend, coexisting alongside increased decriminalization and legalization of marijuana, Berenson (2019) wrote a controversially received book warning parents about the hazards of cannabis titled, *Tell your Children: The Truth about Marijuana, Mental Illness, and Violence.* He cites evidence that shows an increase in psychiatric hospitalizations in locations where there has also been an increase in marijuana use. After perusing the research on this topic, Berenson concluded that marijuana

DOI: 10.4324/9781003441519-4

does not cause psychosis but raises the risk of psychosis between two and sixfold.

DK has treated at least half a dozen young men who present with first-episode psychosis correlated with high cannabis use. The following is a first session representing all the men DK has treated, who are collectively called David. This composite case is primarily meant to offer an illustration of an initial session with first-episode psychosis; we also wish to raise awareness of the strong connection between cannabis and psychosis as one some of us who work with psychosis are increasingly encountering in the clinic. As we have already noted, the primary goal of a first session is to establish an alliance and create a safe enough space for the patient to want to come back. DK's thoughts and feelings are indicated in italics. The narration is DK's.

David's mother called me to make an appointment for her son, David. She told me he had been "kicked out" of college in the second semester of his freshman year because he had a psychotic break. She was concerned that his college career might be over and was desperate to get him help. I reassured her about the likelihood that he could recover, and we made an appointment for David to come in to see me.

David—a very attractive 19-year-old male sporting a two-day beard and dressed casually in jeans, a T-shirt, hoodie, and baseball cap—walked into my office, appearing somewhat anxious, and looked intently at me. He sat down in the farthest seat from mine and glanced around the office, taking everything in. He seemed simultaneously relieved and frightened to be there. David sat in silence, facing me with his legs spread wide and arms crossed, clearly waiting for me to begin.

*I noted David's tense body language and his spread legs. Was he communicating that he was partially open to me and partially closed? Was his body language telling me where the problem might originate—between his legs (his genitals)?*

*He appeared younger than 19, indicating that he might be less mature than expected for his age. I felt a strong need to make him feel safe and comfortable. Of course, these were only my first impressions, and I waited for further confirmation and/or refutation of these original assumptions. The key was to remain open while remaining skeptical about my own conclusions so that I could gain more information about David. For example, my reaction to wanting him to feel safe and comfortable alerted me to ask myself how that had happened. What was it about David that I was responding to, and how might my response contribute to a bias in reflecting on what he was trying to tell me?*

DK: So tell me what brings you here today.

David: I was in college, and things began getting weird.

*I've heard versions of this story before. Not surprisingly, college is where many first psychotic episodes occur. Being away from home, family, and friends, in addition to having new responsibilities and freedom, can put a lot of pressure on late teens. This period can be a time of great stress, as young people suffer the strain of making new friends and consolidating their gender identity and sexual orientation while learning to be adults. I am always happy to see someone soon after their first episode because I've found that intervening early offers the best chance of turning things around quickly and preventing the slide into a chronic situation. I wonder to myself whether cannabis might have been part of David's breakdown. At the same time, I am mindful of my wish to have this be a first break. I can be most effective if this is the case and, therefore, have to guard against overlooking evidence of an earlier disturbance.*

DK: Hmm…

*I don't want to jump in too soon with a question that David might receive as invasive. So I wait to see if he will tell me more on his own. He doesn't appear to be made more defensive by my presence.*

David: The school told me I had to withdraw and get help.

DK: Do you know what went into their decision?

*I know that something extreme must have taken place for the school to ask him to withdraw. I want him to tell me.*

David: School was tougher than it was in high school. Other students seemed to be having an easier time. In the end, I stopped going to classes. I was staying in my room more and more.

DK: Do you feel comfortable sharing with me what you were doing in your room all day?

*I leave him the option of not telling me if he feels uncomfortable or feels it's too soon to tell me. Respect for a person's autonomy is paramount.*

David: Not much. I just didn't want to be around people. I lived in a fraternity.

DK: A fraternity? How did you manage not to be around people?

*I note the seeming paradox of wanting to be left alone yet living in a fraternity, the last place one would go to find solitude.*

David: I had my own room. The guys pretty much left me alone. But I felt they were talking about me, and I could hear them sometimes, even though the doors were closed.

*I wonder whether he is telling me he hears voices or whether the fraternity brothers were speaking loudly. I suspect it is the former.*

DK: What kinds of things were they saying?

*If he is hearing voices, knowing what the voices are saying can help me understand the issues he needs to externalize rather than face as his own.*

David: They were saying that I'm strange … that I'm gay. They wanted me to move out. I didn't belong. I was different. Not like them.

*He's afraid of being labeled gay. He seems to be experiencing conflict about his sexuality. I choose not to open this up in the first session unless he does. My primary goal is to establish a therapeutic alliance and a sense of safety and comfort for him so he'll want to come back.*

DK: How long did that go on?

David: A few months, but it seemed like forever. It got worse over time.

DK: Do you still hear the voices?

David: Yes. Only now it's my family's voices.

DK: And are they saying the same or different things?

David: Pretty much the same.

*So he is hearing voices, and their message is the same.*

David: (*takes a deep breath*) Sometimes I see things … sexual things…
(*He stares at me to see my reaction*).

DK: Yes… (*I nod for him to continue.*)

David: I see images of me having sex with my brother … with my dog. (*He contorts his face into a grimace*).

*I know he is telling me about the hallucinations he is having. Are they based on anything that happened? I was correct to think that his spread legs were alerting me to something sexual. His grimace tells me he needs to see that I am OK hearing these things.*

*Asking David a question about the story he is unfolding rather than focusing on "What is it that you're thinking?" underscores the need to learn when to probe and when to remain silent. My intervention is guided by the patient; I allow the story to flow as best it can without making the patient feel challenged, or insisting he go deeper than he has signaled he is ready for. Silence is, among other things, a test of the therapist. A question to consider is: "Whose needs take priority?" The zealous therapist who needs to reach the patient's "true" motivation or the patient who needs to feel safe enough to remain in the room?*

*DK:* I see that this upsets you.

*David:* Yes. (*He begins to cry silently.*)

*We sit in silence for a few minutes.*

*DK:* How often do you see these images?

*David:* I don't know. A lot. I imagine nearly everyone I see as a potential sex partner.

*I imagine I am included when he says "everyone." I don't ask about this so soon because I want him to feel comfortable in the room with me.*

*DK:* So when did all this begin?

*I present myself as someone who wants to know rather than someone who wants to correct or guide.*

*David:* After a concert I attended with friends.

*DK:* Did anything unusual take place at the concert?

*David:* I smoked a ton of super strong weed … started in the morning and kept going all day. I was seeing things. I got so deep into the music that I could **see** the notes floating past me in a stream of color. It was amazing. I am pretty sure I took off my clothes and danced naked. I'm not sure if I did that or only imagined I did. But either way, I was having a blast. I never felt anything like that in my life. Everything shattered into tiny pieces inside a river of sound. Then, at some point, I looked around and couldn't find my friends. I got scared, really scared. It felt like something terrible was about to happen to me. The shadows on the floor started to stand up. That freaked me out. I don't remember much after that. I woke up in a hospital. They put me in a psych ward and pumped me up with drugs. I've been a mess ever since. I thought hospitals were supposed to help!

*DK:* You've been through a lot in a short time.

*I am going along with: "I'd like to hear your story as long as you're able to tell it and interested in doing so." Giving permission to talk as well as permission not to reveal is important. I make no promises that I will help him.*

*David:* I'm definitely not the person I was before. Something's happening to me. I've been changed. I don't know this guy, but I know damn sure I'm not him.

*This is very common with psychosis. There is a strong sense of a before and after. There is a loss of a sense of continuity in oneself and one's sense of reality. Anti-psychotics don't help in this regard.*

*David:* No one understands me. I don't understand me.

*DK:* Well, that's why you're here. We can work together to understand you and what happened to you and why.

*David:* I'd like that.

*DK:* Can you tell me about your drug use?

*David:* It goes back to junior high school. I've been smoking weed since I was 13.

*DK:* How much did you smoke?

*David:* At first it was only on the weekends. But it got to be more and more until I was smoking every day.

*DK:* What did the weed do for you?

*I want to know the positive as well as the negative functions of his cannabis use.*

*David:* It made me feel good. I got high. After a while, I used it to go to sleep. Then I started to wake and bake. I basically used it to get through my day. It helped me get through my life—my family, school.

*DK:* Can you tell me what high school was like?

*David:* I hated it, even though I got good grades. Don't ask me how. I guess I'm smart. At least that's what I've been told my whole life. My father forced me to do sports. The only one I took to was fencing. I didn't care much about anything. I was high and in my room most of the time. The only reason I got into college was because I did well on my SATs and was good at fencing.

*DK:* So you did well in your SATs and excelled in fencing? That's pretty impressive.

*I am pleased to hear that David was able to excel in academics even though he was high much of the time. Engaging in a sport indicates that he has the discipline to practice and compete. These are two islands that bode well for therapy. He has a natural intellectual ability and can persevere when challenged.*

*David:* (*Smiles.*)

*He needs some positive feedback and responds to it.*

DK: Can you tell me about your family?

David: I don't like talking about them. My mother is crazy.

DK: What do you mean, your mother's crazy?

David: (menacingly) Are you saying *I'm* crazy?!

DK: That's not what I was saying, but is that something you're worried about?
*I reassure him and then see if he is aware that he is using projection as a defense.*

David: I *am* worried that I'm like my mother. We're the "sensitive" ones in the family. We're the "emotional" ones. She has her own problems. I think she's an alcoholic, though she would never admit it. My father's drug of choice is work. I don't know if he works all the time because he likes it or whether he just wants to avoid my mom. And me. When he is home, nothing changes. He keeps to himself. He's only interested in my accomplishments. He really doesn't know who I am. But then again, neither do I. My younger brother lives at home and I have one sister who's out of the house. Lucky her.

DK: So you thought you'd get away too, but now you're back.

David: What do you mean by that?
*He again shows hypersensitivity to my question. Family is clearly a fraught topic. We'll have to move slowly and gently when addressing it.*

DK: I mean that you wanted to get away from home, like your sister, but here you are back home again. What did you think I meant?
*I first clarify what he has asked me, respectful of the priority of his wish to know what I'm after. Only after I've answered his question do I then ask him about his assumption. Had I simply followed up on his question with a question about him, such as, "What do you think I might have meant by that?" I could have indicated to him an evasiveness or a priority of addressing my question over his need to know. I wanted to see if he could work with me.*

David: I don't know. I'm confused. Everything gets to me these days. I think everyone is implying something negative about me. You probably think I'm paranoid.
*At least a part of him knows he overreacts. At least a part of him knows he is being paranoid, even though he attributes this thought to me. This is a good start. More importantly, he has stayed in the room, volunteered information, and even feels safe enough to have just denounced me.*

*I found David's response advanced for someone in the midst of psychosis. I would have expected him to not answer, deflect, or denounce my question, as in, "You sound like every shrink. I saw plenty of them in the hospital."*

*DK:* Did you smoke weed today?

*I want to know if I am seeing him under the influence.*

*David:* Why do you ask?

*DK:* Well, weed can make some people feel suspicious. I wonder if you can imagine a day when you'll smoke less—or even no weed?

*I avoid the word paranoid. Too charged and too diagnostic. I try to avoid professional jargon when speaking to patients. At least for now, I must resist my desire to ask him to stop smoking weed, to educate him about its negative effects, especially about its connection with psychosis.*

*David:* I'd like to, but I'm not sure I can. I've been doing it for so long.

*DK:* Do you feel that smoking weed has any effect on your emotional states?

*I slow down.*

*David:* Yes. I do. I used to enjoy it. Not so much anymore. It *does* make me more paranoid. I'll try to stop using, but I can't promise.

*In a way, David's response begs the question. He asserts that he knows weed makes him more paranoid, and I assume he knew that before he came to see me. He has some insight. I suspect that his main fear is that he is crazy. The questions for this initial meeting are: "What does he think is going on? Is he beyond help? Is he crazy?" These lines of exploration will take time to develop. My goal right now is to have him come back so that we will be able to explore his questions over time.*

*DK:* I understand. Your experience at college and its aftermath have left you with a lot of unanswered questions. You know the weed isn't helping your state of mind, but it's what you do to avoid things that make you uncomfortable.

*David:* Exactly!

*He feels understood, and he seems to understand the dilemma he's in.*

*DK:* Can we go back to what happened at college?

*David:* Yeah. I don't know. I just became more and more afraid to go out.

*DK:* Did you seek help while there?

*David:* They hospitalized me. I've got schizophrenia, they said. They said it's a disease, like diabetes. They said I'll have it for life, that there's no cure, and that I'll need drugs from now on to keep it under control. The meds make me feel like a zombie, like my brain is in a washing machine.

*I've heard this story so many times. Telling someone they have a disease for life! Putting them on powerful medications and clearly overmedicating them! Destroying their sense of hope at such a young age! I feel called to undo these negative interventions that can be as traumatic for young people as the psychosis itself. I am aware of my bias. I need to be careful not to go on a rescue mission.*

*DK:* I appreciate how difficult it is for you to have been in such distress and found so little help for it. I'm glad that, despite what you went through, you were able to come in to see me today. What meds are you taking?

*David:* Benadryl, Haloperidol, and Lorazepam. They call it a cocktail. Ha!! There might be one or two more. I can't remember. I don't feel human. Do I need to take them?

*DK:* I'll refer you to a psychiatrist who can take another look at your meds.

*David:* Really? That might help. I want to get back to school next year.

*DK:* Well, we can work toward making that happen, but first, I need you to help me understand what took place when you did go to college, so I can do my best to help you.

*I want him to know that we are in this together. I need him as much as he needs me. This is not a one-sided relationship.*

*DK:* How long were you in the hospital?

*David:* A week.

*DK:* Did anyone talk to you while you were in there? Did you get therapy?

*David:* No. I wish I had. I saw a psychiatrist who delivered the message that I have a disease and must take the meds he prescribed.

*DK:* And after you were discharged?

*David:* I went to the college counseling center. But eventually, they told me I'd have to take a leave of absence.

*DK:* What was the counseling like?

*David:* OK. But after a while, I felt my therapist was thinking that I'm gay. *This is a cautionary tale for me. If he begins to think that I believe he's gay, he may quit precipitously. He clearly has an issue with it.*

*DK:* Did you tell your therapist what you thought at the time?

*David:* No.

*Another cautionary tale. He chose to leave rather than discuss.*

*DK:* Well, if you feel uncomfortable with me, or think that I am having negative thoughts about you, I hope you will be able to share them with me. It is likely to happen, so let's talk about it when it does.

*I put the cautionary tale on the table. "This will probably happen here too." But by saying we can talk about it, I'm letting David know that I am interested in how he feels I perceive him and that I can handle it. This is part of the work.*

*David:* I'll try.

*DK:* So, I can see you've been through a lot these last few months.

*David:* That's an understatement!

*DK:* Well, I am glad you are here so that we can begin turning things around for you.

Let's talk a little about therapy, OK?

*David:* OK.

*DK:* Any thoughts about what you'd like to happen here?

*David:* Yes. I want to get a job and go back to school.

*DK:* Those are fine goals. Let's see if we can figure out how things fell apart first. Then we can try to get you back to meeting your goals, but this time from a stronger and more self-aware place. What do you think?

*David:* Sounds good to me. (*He pauses.*) What are you writing?

*DK:* I'm writing some of the things we're talking about, so I don't forget them. Does it bother you?

*David:* No. It's OK.

*DK:* If you'd like to read what I write, you are welcome to. You can also ask me anything you like. I will not keep secrets from you.

*David becomes paranoid when he feels inadequate or vulnerable. It is important for him to see that I am open and transparent.*

*David:* OK.

*DK:* OK. I think it is very important for us to meet regularly to figure out what happened at school. From what you tell me, it sounds like things weren't going too well even before you went away to college. Smoking weed doesn't seem to have helped matters much. Let's see if we can understand how things got derailed, and, hopefully, get you back to school. It may take a while though. How does that sound to you?

*David:* That sounds good.

*DK:* OK. (*We set up twice-weekly sessions.*)

*David:* OK. Thanks. Bye.

    *I'm glad to see David leaving the room more relaxed and hopeful than the way he came in.*

## Case Conceptualization

Some may wonder why DK was not more active in this session, and why she didn't offer any interpretations. The reason for her rather minimalist approach was meant to let David know that he was the author of his own story and that she was there as a witness to listen and authenticate that story without judgment. Beginning to form an alliance was the foremost goal of this session, best exemplified by the patient returning for a follow-up session. DK's nonintrusive stance involved simply asking him to elaborate, without commentary from the therapist (apart from mirroring and offering empathy). This approach allowed DK to learn about David while keeping an eye on making sure he felt safe enough to come back.

It was clear that David was anxious and feeling lost. He didn't have much insight into what had happened to him at school. But he did know that he had undergone an extreme experience after which nothing seemed the same. He also showed self-awareness when he described himself as sensitive and reactive, even using the word "paranoid."

David went to college hoping to get away from his family: an alcoholic mother and a workaholic father. At college, he discovered that he couldn't get by on his natural intelligence, the way he had in high school, without putting in the work. He compared himself to others and didn't feel he measured up to the academic challenge before him. He skipped classes and increased his use of marijuana to avoid dealing with this reality.

David also seemed to have some sexual conflicts. His auditory and visual hallucinations point to sexual preoccupation and formed the crux of his psychosis. Fraternity brothers were talking about him, accusing him of being gay; he saw visions of himself having sex with his younger brother and his dog. Understandably, these hallucinations caused him much consternation. With time, therapy could explore the origin of these hallucinations, their connection to reality, and the meaning they hold in David's psyche.

David smoked a lot of cannabis from a young age because he liked the way it made him feel, and he believed the drug helped him cope with his life. Little did he know that the combination of heavy marijuana use and a sensitive disposition could result in psychosis. He said he is like his mother: both are sensitive, and both turn to substances to deal with their sensitivity.

## DK's Countertransference

DK felt many emotions before, during, and after the initial session with David. He was clearly suffering, which made her want to help him in any way she could. DK's main countertransference to David was that she had "been here, done that" before. She had to resist not placing him in a familiar box: a sensitive young male with family problems and a heavy drug habit (marijuana) goes to college and has a psychotic episode. Each person has their own story, and, as therapists, we need to be careful not to jump to conclusions. DK would have to cultivate patience and listen to David tell his story with its own peculiar nuances.

As a child of the 1960s, DK had known several friends who went over the edge, never to recover because of their drug use. She fought her worry that this might be the case with David. But she saw several signs that indicated David's would be a relatively brief psychotic episode. David was intelligent, insightful, and capable of self-observation, and he seemed to respond to DK as someone who might be able to help him.

Finally, David's preoccupation with sex made DK a little uncomfortable, especially when he said he imagined everyone as a sexual partner. DK did not want to be seen in that way, but she knew she would need to feel more relaxed and secure exploring the subject with David since it was so important to him. Also, if he were to express an attraction to DK, it might be reassuring for him, since it might mean he was not gay, his greatest fear. Thus, DK would need to become comfortable with David's expressions of sexual desire for both of their sakes.

## David's Treatment Plan

As already mentioned, the first and most important objective of therapy with David was to create a space in which he could feel comfortable and safe enough to share his most troubling thoughts and experiences. DK was pleased that she was able to see him so soon after his first psychotic episode. He had questions. He was confused. He had not yet had time to establish a psychotic delusional system to explain what had happened to him. This is the perfect time to step in and make sense of what he found enigmatic, bizarre, and beyond the pale.

After establishing an alliance with David, DK planned to explore the antecedents that led up to his psychotic episode. She wanted to learn more about his family and social network. Was he able to make friends? Did he have a love life? How did he feel about his sexuality? She wanted to get more specifics about his marijuana usage. Was there trauma in his background? These questions whirled around in her head, but they had to wait for the right time; she preferred that David be the one to bring them up.

If all went well, David would develop more self-awareness, learn that marijuana was not advisable in his case, and feel less conflicted around matters of sexuality. He would gradually be weaned off his psychotropic medications, and he would eventually go back to school stronger and more ready to face its challenges.

# Chapter 5

# Outpatient Treatment with Psychosis

## Managing Isolation and Creating Safety

A significant amount of the literature on context reminds us that where and when an event occurs plays a crucial role in shaping a person's experience of that occurrence (Balsam and Tomie, 2014; Robinson and Rollings, 2011; Smith, 1979; Smith and Vela, 2001). The results of these studies are somewhat generalizable to the treatment of patients experiencing psychosis, who are often hypersensitive to environmental clues and may rely on outer structure to contain their inner chaos (Bayley, 1996; Kallert and Leisse, 2000). The absence of structure can be challenging, yet such individuals are often conflicted about routine and predictability (Falloon et al., 1998; Hendrick, 2014). Outpatient therapy most closely resembles the reality the patient needs to adapt to, but both patient and therapist find themselves with additional burdens when they work outside the context of a uniform, less personal institutional setting.

Understanding the historical context for the treatment of psychosis is important for understanding current dilemmas related to outpatient treatment. Therefore, we will briefly consider that historical context and then return to our discussion of the ways in which the outpatient setting affects the patient, the therapist, and the conduct of therapy. Finally, we consider the pros and cons of outpatient therapy with people experiencing psychosis.

Arieti (1974b) points out that Kraeplin developed his ideas about dementia praecox in a hospital setting, which led to the equation of psychosis = hospital. This equation has had some negative outcomes because not all persons with psychosis need to be hospitalized or benefit from hospitalization. Hospitalizing persons experiencing psychosis promotes what Arieti called "hospitalism" and "a passive life without challenges" that can lead to chronicity. Deinstitutionalization, a name given to the policy of moving

DOI: 10.4324/9781003441519-5

severely mentally ill people out of large state institutions and closing part, or all, of those institutions, was meant to address this problem and, as such, qualifies as one of the largest social experiments in history. Integral to this bold effort was improving and expanding the range of services and supports in the community. In effect, approximately 96.5% of people who would have been living in public psychiatric hospitals in 1955 were not living in institutional settings in 2010. Per capita, the state psychiatric bed population by 2010 plunged to 1850 levels (Fuller et al., 2012). Deinstitutionalization was based on the principle that serious mental illness should be treated in the *least restrictive setting*. Of course, what constitutes the "least restrictive setting" is a matter of debate.

Nevertheless, because very few people live in psychiatric institutions today, one might expect an increase in individual outpatient therapy for psychosis. Yet this has not been the case. Fewer therapists work with psychosis on an outpatient basis than ever before (Hammersley et al., 2008; Lazar, 2010; Moffic and Kinzie, 1996). There are several reasons for this dearth of therapy, with the most important one being the growing reliance on psychotropic drugs (Clarkson and Pokorny, 1994; Valenstein, 2004) as the sole treatment for psychosis. However, many people given drug treatment often stop taking their medications for several reasons, one of which is the severity of side effects (Fleischhacker, 2004; Fleischhacker et al., 1994; Olfson et al., 2000; Perkins, 2002; Rettenbacher et al., 2004; Young et al., 1986). Another reason for the lack of therapy is that many training programs have ceased educating mental health professionals in outpatient therapy with psychosis (Whitaker, 2007). Therefore, although medication regimens allow for briefer hospitalizations, a revolving door system is created with patients in and out of hospitals because people fail to take their medications and there are few psychotherapists available to treat psychosis.

Although many psychoanalysts and psychodynamic psychotherapists have handed over much of the treatment of psychosis to psychiatry and psychopharmacology (Ophir, 2015; Grotstein, 2001), we agree with Karon and VanderBos (1981a) and Bollas (2013) that psychoanalytically informed psychotherapy is often the treatment of choice for many who suffer from psychotic disorders. Addressing defenses, the meaning (conscious and unconscious) of symptoms, affect, trauma, and relationships (including the therapeutic relationship) all help in treating psychotic conditions.

Clearly, there is a need for more clinicians to work with psychosis in an outpatient setting. However, not every patient is suitable for outpatient therapy, at least not initially. Below, we address the questions one needs to consider during the initial evaluation with someone exhibiting psychosis, for the purposes of determining where the treatment will take place.

## Initial Evaluation

In his impressive tome on schizophrenia, Arieti (1974b) devoted only two pages to the topic of hospitalization vs. outpatient therapy. All the considerations he mentioned relate exclusively to patient concerns. We believe that equal, if not greater, importance should be put on the therapist's suitability for this type of work. Most important, the therapist needs to feel safe. Harold Searles, an analyst known for his work with psychosis, once said that the "therapist sits in the most comfortable chair" (personal communication to MS). Clearly, the therapist's discomfort may hamper the treatment, as may the therapist's unconscious assumptions about patients who present with psychosis. Questions to ask oneself prior to taking on a patient in an outpatient setting are:

- How do I feel being alone with this person?
- Have I paid sufficient attention to the patient's history of aggression?
- Have I referred to this history in my initial interviews? If I was not able to bring it up, is that a clear warning sign?
- Can I imagine what it would take for me to be comfortable with the patient in an outpatient setting?
- If I have felt threatened by a potential encounter but have been reassured by the history, which describes the patient as being able to control themselves with the aid (if necessary) of a mild or moderate dose of medication, am I comfortable in insisting on medication as a condition of the outpatient therapy? Thus, the therapist might say: "In the past, when you've taken Abilify, you've been able to control yourself in session. I need to know that you will take it for as long as we meet unless we both agree it is no longer necessary. Otherwise, I'm not comfortable seeing you as an outpatient."
- Alternatively, is the patient so distant that I will feel too lonely or push too hard to engage them or retreat into my own fantasy life?

- Is the patient too confusing for my orderly mind, resulting perhaps in my prematurely "organizing" the patient's productions?
- I will also need to assess my own attitude toward hospitalization and medication. When and under what conditions do I feel them to be necessary?

We now turn to the factors related to patients that need to be considered when deciding on suitability for outpatient treatment. Most significant to remember is that if a therapist is conducting a true evaluation, the outcome can go either way. We agree with Alanen's (1997) "needs-adaptive" approach, which is case-specific in determining what is appropriate for a patient at a specific time.

1. No one is 100% psychotic. Therefore, assessing the nonpsychotic and conflict-free parts of the individual's personality is crucial. Freud (1924/1961), Bion (1967), and Eigen (1986) wrote about psychotic and nonpsychotic components in everyone's personality. Buddhist psycho-analyst Edward Podvoll (2003) wrote about the "islands of clarity" that each psychotic person displays. It is important to assess not only pathology but also strengths and talents because those parts of the person will become allies in the therapeutic process.

   Furthermore, having an "inventory" of previous patient activities, assets, or conflict-free spheres provides the therapist with information that may apply later in the treatment. After a year of treatment, Jack, a moderately well-functioning individual, acutely decompensated and claimed he had "no weapons" to fight off his demons. MS reminded him that, during the intake, he had described moments of calm and gaining perspective in which he put his experiences into the frame of a story. MS said, "What if you were to read to me what you said and then try it?" This incident shows how the therapist had a reservoir of patient assets to consider when the patient felt bereft of coping capacity.

2. Some important questions to ask about the patient include: What are this person's expectations? What is known about any previous treatments and, especially, how were they ended—i.e., mutually, or one-sided, and by whom? How does the patient perceive their history and prior treatment? What are their cautionary tales? Ogden (1989) refers to when a patient warns the therapist about why the therapist should be wary about taking them on in treatment. Failure to heed these warnings

early on may indicate omnipotent countertransference. It is essential for the therapist to be prepared for the possibility of failure. Phillip arrived at his first session late due to a car accident (his fault). DK asked if he might be having mixed feelings about starting therapy. He denied the proposition and stated how excited he was to begin exploring his life. After 20 minutes, Phillip was no longer agitated. He informed DK that he always began new projects enthusiastically but that his excitement quickly diminishes. Noting Phillip's cautionary tale, DK asked Phillip to let her know in the future if he began to feel his engagement in therapy waning.

3. Both therapist and patient need external support for outpatient therapy. Are there family members, a spouse or partner, children, or groups? Since working on an outpatient basis does not include the supportive staff found in inpatient work, it is very important to determine who can be counted on in the patient's milieu. The therapist's attitude toward identifying and then accepting help from the patient's environment can provide crucial information regarding the countertransference. The attitude of "I don't need them. Just the two of us are enough" is a flashing red signal that the therapist will soon be in over their head.

4. Patients may have some no-nos or things they refuse to do. For example, does the patient refuse to take medication under any circumstance? Can the therapist accept those terms? Has the therapist explored how the patient's "conditions" intersect with their own need for safety? Is there evidence of flexibility on the patient's part? The therapist's caveats must also be considered in conjunction with those of the patient. If the therapist is unwilling to consider that they have requirements— let alone if they are unaware of what might be on the list—they are signaling to themselves something that needs immediate attention so that they do not prematurely sabotage the work.

5. It is important to assess the patient's capacity for an observing ego. One might see this in the patient's conflict over their symptoms or in their sense of humor. If the patient seems unable to look at themselves, can they "borrow" the therapist's observations—i.e., an auxiliary ego that can be internalized at a future date?

6. Does the patient possess some ability to empathize? This is especially important when it comes to empathizing with the therapist in regard to how the patient's expectations might be received. A reliable way to

assess the patient's capacity for empathy is to ask them some pertinent questions. For example: "I know you fear that bathing will destroy your visionary powers, but is there any way you can reduce the smell in here because it's hard for me to take?" Patients with psychosis may empathize in odd ways. For example, Anne, during the initial consult with DK, said she didn't feel safe. When DK questioned her about what might help her to feel safe, she responded, "If you had an Uzi." Initially, such a comment might shock and scare a therapist. Yet this patient's desire for her therapist to have an Israeli submachine gun expressed her wish to protect the therapist and her realization that the therapist has needs too. If the therapist employs only conventional diagnostic criteria with psychotic patients, they are liable to miss out on important information.

7. What is the patient's highest level of functioning? How independent a life can they lead? How does the therapist imagine the patient's life outside of the office? One man arrived to his initial session carrying two suitcases. Clearly, he was envisioning the therapy office as a new home base.

8. The therapist needs to know the patient's capacity for relatedness, engagement, and curiosity. Freud (1911/1958) mistakenly thought patients with psychosis could not be analyzed because he believed they were unable to form a transference. This idea has since been disproved (Arieti, 1974b; Karon and VandenBos, 1981b; Lucas, 2009; Searles, 1963). One must at times look for a disguised capacity for relatedness manifesting in the symptoms. There are patients whom the therapist will experience as wholly unrelatable: they appear devoid of curiosity or concern about the therapist's person. The interpersonal environment is frigid, and the patient's responses are mechanical. Often, such patients' personal histories reveal no evidence of sufficient attachments since, or even before, the acute phase of decompensation. In such circumstances, the therapist is likely to feel stymied and wish to withdraw. Yet symptoms sometimes contain information that challenges the patient's apparent lack of connectedness.

Tom was MS's 19-year-old patient who was unable to continue college due to his inability to concentrate. He felt he would never be close to anyone and that his fate was sealed: he would live in chilling isolation. Tom developed a complex delusional system in which he was locked in a specially equipped spaceship. The ship required no fuel and thus could remain airborne forever. It was equipped with a high-tech device that picked up the sights and sounds of the earthlings below him. Tom desperately tried to shut down this device. Unsuccessful in his efforts to destroy it, he called it "my tormenting machine." Like all his communications, Tom told this story in a voice drained of affect, but MS saw the opening he needed. Why would Tom detail his experiences if there was nothing he wanted from MS? His communications appeared to increasingly question what was happening to him. For the next several sessions, MS explored the sensations Tom was experiencing in his "so near yet so far" communications with people on Earth. Early on, Tom declared, "Don't get your hopes up about me having anything to do with people. Impossible! What I didn't tell you about the tormenting device is that it can also do simulations of me being in contact with others. You just think I'm here. I'm actually still in the spaceship." Despite Tom's adamant protests, the exploration with MS continued.

9. Is there evidence of a *negative therapeutic reaction* (Riviere, 1936) to the therapist and/or the therapy? In some people, psychosis is dedicated to destruction. One of DK's patients compared himself to a suicide bomber, determined to destroy himself, the analyst, and the treatment. (See Chapter 10 for a detailed description of this case and its treatment.)

10. There are some clear contraindications to taking on a patient with psychosis for outpatient therapy. These include danger and unreliability (which would translate into the inability to show up and/or pay for sessions). We do not believe that the presence of hallucinations or suicidality is contraindicatory in and of itself because process is more important than content. How does the patient speak of their suicidal thoughts? How do they experience their delusions? Are they curious about them? Has the patient developed strategies to combat their negative thoughts? If the patient engages in a dialogue with themselves and with the therapist about their symptoms, then there exists a greater potential to engage in psychodynamic work. If the therapist cannot imagine the patient ever reaching their reported prior level of functioning, that could be an early sign of therapeutic despair (Farber, 1958). Conversely, if the therapist's insistence that the patient can do "anything they set their mind to do" is at odds with the patient's history,

the therapist may be exhibiting an omnipotent fantasy coupled with a defense against therapeutic despair.

## Pros and Cons of Hospital Treatment vs. Outpatient Therapy with Psychosis

### Advantages of Hospital Treatment

In working with psychosis in a hospital setting, the therapist can more safely experiment with the type and dosage of medication while the patient is being supervised for extreme or adverse reactions. Hospitals help to diminish omnipotent fantasies in the therapist by not allowing them to take on more than they can handle. Because there are many professionals involved in milieu treatment (e.g., psychiatrists, psychologists, social workers, nurses, attendants, and occupational and art therapists), multiple perspectives are available. One practitioner might regard the patient as aggressive and unapproachable while another might have a different view.

Ominous psychotic transferences can be better controlled in inpatient settings because there are other staff members to remind the therapist what is real/unreal, and the transference tends to be distributed among several staff members. In a hospital setting, there is less danger that the therapist will fall prey to a sense of undiluted specialness vis-à-vis the patient, which can morph into a rescue fantasy or a chilling sense of aloneness.

Patients with psychosis are known to be a greater danger to themselves than others; therefore, concerns about suicide are sometimes present (Palmer et al., 2005). Consequently, the outpatient therapist can feel burdened with enormous responsibility, which can be quite frightening. In addition, treatment with regressed states and primitive processes can be intense and demanding. Many practitioners do not wish to embark on such taxing work by themselves. The isolation of therapists is well known (see Chapter 8). Working with severe psychopathology can burden the therapist beyond normal limits; treating patients in a hospital milieu lifts that weight to some degree.

The foremost concern practitioners have about working with psychosis on an outpatient basis involves the element of *danger*. Although they are statistically *not* more dangerous than the general population, people undergoing a psychotic episode are often feared as dangerous or experienced as "other"—unfamiliar, intense, not in touch or in control of themselves or their lives (Magliano, 2014; Rüsch et al., 2011).

Since unease begets unease, a therapist who feels unsafe can launch an already unsettled patient into a state of desperation. Thus, if a therapist feels unable to cope alone with the "otherness" of psychosis, they may feel more comfortable treating such patients in a hospital setting or not at all. The need for an individual with psychosis to be assured that their therapist feels comfortable in their presence is illustrated by the following exchange from an initial interview by DK with a psychotic patient, Marjorie.

*Marjorie:* (*anxious*) What if I throw up on your rug?
*DK:* Well, then, we'll just have to clean it up, won't we?
*Marjorie:* (*relaxed*) Yes ... *we'll* clean it up.

Marjorie was asking a question about what would happen when and if she brings her negative emotions and experiences to the treatment. She was questioning whether the therapist could tolerate and handle these states and what the therapist would do. DK's response emphasized acceptance and collaboration, both of which instantly put Marjorie at ease.

Considering the advantages of inpatient treatment with psychosis, one might wonder about the advisability of outpatient psychotherapy. We now present several reasons for engaging in such work.

## Advantages of Outpatient Treatment

Since most hospital stays are very brief and offer little or no psychotherapy, they may not be ideal environments for someone in a regressive state to reconstitute themselves. Too often inpatients are overmedicated and frequently told they suffer from a disease for which they must remain on medication indefinitely. Such "news" does not provide much hope for someone in acute distress. The goals of hospitalization are keeping the patient safe, reducing anxiety, and suppressing regression. To achieve these goals, the hospital most often creates a state of sedation. Unfortunately, these goals focus on adjustment to and within a hospital setting but run counter to what it takes to return to life in the outside world. Marsha Linehan, the originator of the Dialectical Behavioral Therapy (DBT) approach, has often claimed that hospitalizations make many patients more suicidal rather than less so (DK's personal communication with Linehan protégé, Jill Rathus, December 3, 2022). Also, many inpatient units cut off a patient's ties with their outpatient therapist, which destroys the patient's sense of continuity and care, thus potentially worsening their mental health.

In outpatient treatment, safety is the responsibility of both partners, albeit disproportionally the therapist's responsibility at the beginning of treatment. Moreover, outpatient treatment requires that both therapist and patient accept that they will experience anxiety while they are making progress. There will be periods when anxiety increases as the patient seeks new ways of being. Treatment often follows the pattern of "two steps forward and one step back," or even "two steps forward, two steps back." Thus, binding anxiety and tolerating a degree of regression are ego skills initially demonstrated by the therapist and later adopted by the patient. Here we are describing an active process—the opposite of sedation. By not hospitalizing a patient, the therapist conveys *faith* in the patient's capacity to get better and in the therapy's ability to progress without resorting to drastic measures. Patients are less likely to feel they have been abandoned or given up on. They also internalize the faith their therapists have in their ability to work outside of an institutional setting.

Many individuals with psychosis are highly sensitive to their surroundings—for example, light, temperature, space, and privacy—and their ability to have some *control* over these elements can have a positive impact. Naturally, choices for patients are more possible in an outpatient setting. Those undergoing an acute break can even be adversely affected by being in the presence of others in a group setting who are behaving in a regressive or chaotic manner (Bollas, 2013; Seikkula et al., 2003). Rather than help a patient regroup and pull themselves together, an inpatient setting can present a contagion for regressive behavior.

Outpatient therapy carries less stigma than inpatient hospitalization. In addition, it is easier to maintain a person's optimal level of functioning in an outpatient milieu. Hospitals are known to control every detail of patients' lives, thus removing their autonomy and freedom. One patient, when asked why he behaved in a regressive manner while in the hospital replied, "I did it because I could."

Remaining an outpatient, by contrast, taps the patient's highest level of functioning, which has many benefits. A patient can continue to work, see their therapist, and live in their home environment—all of which contribute to the person's stability, continuity, sense of competence, and self-esteem. Since an outpatient is functioning in multiple contexts already, they do not need to transition from the hospital environment to an outpatient environment and/or their life in the outside world. Not being always supervised invites the patient to "pull it together" and function between appointments. The patient is encouraged by their own abilities, and their behavior becomes self-reinforcing.

Having additional environments can provide opportunities to interact in normative contexts, which helps to challenge some psychotic mechanisms. For instance, Josh, who had a case of delusional blindness, reported to DK that he went shopping and played tennis over a weekend, clearly two activities that would be difficult to perform if one were in fact blind. Showing him the discrepancy between his claims of blindness in the session and his level of functioning outside forced him to question his delusion. (See Chapter 10 for more on Josh's case) Inpatient settings do not provide an opportunity to use comparative environments in this manner.

The transference is less diluted in outpatient therapy. Each participant in the therapy dyad needs the other and must work with the other, which results in the patient feeling relevant as a critical collaborator in their own treatment. The "scarcity" effect in outpatient treatment can also produce inventiveness. The fact that the therapist meets with a patient only a few hours per week forces the use of imagination to find ways to "stretch" the effect of therapy over time, paving the road toward greater autonomy. "In the office" and "out of the office" exist on a continuum that has a semipermeable barrier. What takes place in the office is an interim episode sandwiched between times spent in the world.

In the hospital, one must play by the institution's rules, but in the office, the therapist and patient can make up the rules. In outpatient work, the therapist can retain autonomy during the treatment and is less scrutinized than he or she would be in an inpatient unit, which allows the possibility of experimentation. This freedom is essential when working with psychosis because so many patients do not respond to formulaic interventions.

We will now address the two primary reasons given in arguing against outpatient work with psychosis: isolation and safety. We believe that when these aspects of therapy are better understood, anticipated, and prepared for, more therapists will feel encouraged to work with psychosis in outpatient settings.

## Two Sides of Isolation

Psychosis is an extremely isolating experience. According to Klein (1963), the individual with psychosis does not internalize the mother as a good object and therefore cannot rely on their own self, which leaves them feeling lonely. Working with psychosis on an outpatient basis can be isolating for the therapist as well as the patient but has the potential to help the therapist better understand and identify with the patient's isolation. (See Chapter 8 for more on loneliness in patients and therapists.) In the hospital setting, one can check in with other staff for protection, feedback, perspective, and support. In outpatient work, one assumes absolute responsibility for the case and its outcome. In such a situation, it is critical to appreciate one's limits (omnipotent fantasies are common in the counteretrransference), patient limitations, and fear of failure.

One way the dyad comes together in an outpatient setting is through its shared perception of the outside world as dangerous, misunderstanding, or even hostile. Therapists and patients can feel that they are alone, pitted against the rest of the world. Solidarity forms and emptiness dissipates, which can serve as the basis for a therapeutic alliance. If it is "just the two of us," then each member of the dyad needs each other even more. At the same time, it is important to recognize that there is more chance of the therapist forgetting to acknowledge their limits and finitude in an outpatient setting.

Scott, a patient of MS, was told prior to seeing him that he was the only therapist who could help Scott, and the patient concurred with this assessment. "I knew before I sat down, just by looking around [while waiting in the outer office], that you had the strength to face down the monsters who are trying to take over my brain," he told MS. When asked what would happen if MS lacked those powers, Scott moved the question aside, insisting, "I know I'm right about you." As the treatment progressed, MS found himself repeatedly reviewing the patient's lengthy inpatient chart, slowly developing the impression that the previous doctors had failed to appreciate the severity of the deprivations Scott had suffered. It was only when MS mentioned to a colleague that "they [the hospital] got it all wrong," and the colleague replied, "All?" that MS became aware he had succumbed to the belief that he alone could and must save Scott.

Yet, some patients may not be able to cope with the intensity of interdependence and may ask to be hospitalized to defend against the intimacy of individual therapy. Likewise, the therapist can say to themselves, "I can always send the patient to the hospital if ... things get too tough." If the therapist finds they are constantly reassuring themselves about the hospital option, that mantra is a sure sign of their fear of involvement. Thus, even though the therapeutic dyad is meeting in an outpatient setting, the meaning of the hospital always needs to be addressed and understood by both participants and can change depending on the current state of affairs.

Unlike a therapist working in a hospital setting, an outpatient therapist lacks colleagues to inform them about the patient's behavior in other situations. Thus, the outpatient therapist must inquire about the patient's life outside the treatment room. For example, the therapist might ask, "What is a typical day for you?" By relying on the patient for this information and perspective, the therapist shows the patient that they have something valuable to contribute to the treatment and that the treatment is a preparation for the next step—being in the world.

Hisoka, a very secluded young man, began seeing DK after two hospitalizations and brief outpatient therapy. He told DK that he slept during the day and remained awake at night. He spent 8-12 hours per day playing video games. DK allowed herself to imagine Hisoka's daily life and appreciate the extent to which it was devoid of human contact. He was a young man of few words, but he responded to DK's request to teach her about the video games he played, which made him feel important to know something his therapist didn't and to be in the position to teach her what he knew. The knowledge of Hisoka's life outside the treatment room also informed some of DK's interventions, one of which was to have Hisoka begin to sleep at night and stay awake during the day so that he could begin to feel that he was part of the world. (See Chapter 8 for more on Hisoka and his therapy.)

## Safety in Hospital vs. Outpatient Treatment Settings

Josh entered DK's office for the first time and looked around guardedly as if assessing its dimensions.

"Is everything OK?" she asked him.

Josh replied cautiously: "Will these walls be able to hold my anger?"

Here was a case that from the start placed the issue of safety at the center of the treatment. However, we believe that safety is always a major concern when working with psychosis on an outpatient basis—the safety of both the patient and therapist. As we said earlier, the best way to work with this issue is to listen to the patient's cautionary tale (Ogden, 1989), which is often presented at the outset of treatment, as in the example above, and address it head-on. But the safety theme involves shared responsibility.

The patient who wanted DK to have an Uzi to feel safer in the room with her asked, after six months of therapy, why the screen had disappeared.

"What screen?" questioned DK.

"You know, the screen that was here between us."

DK asked Amy to describe the screen and she did so in minute detail. It was a beautiful, translucent Japanese screen with flowery patterns. DK realized that it took Amy six months to feel safe enough to dismantle the imaginary construction she had placed between them. Once her trust grew, Amy was prepared to face her analyst in a less guarded manner.

To address the issue of safety the therapist might say, "We meet today as strangers. One of our goals is to become less strange to each other." Together therapist and patient can, on an ongoing basis, examine what each participant needs from the other and the extent to which those needs are being met. Bob, a paranoid patient, began his therapy by warning DK not to ask him any questions. After two months of treatment, she said: "It used to be that you felt endangered if I asked you any questions. You needed to feel in control of the topics of conversation. Today you've permitted me to ask you about school. What allowed that to happen, and how can we build on this?" Five months into the therapy, she said: "Today you asked me about why I picked a particular picture for my office. Since you originally told me I had to be a 'machine' for you to be able to talk to me, and since machines can't choose pictures, you might be feeling safer about my being a person."

One way to address safety concerns is to acknowledge that, like any therapy, psychodynamic psychotherapy can be a dangerous undertaking, and each of us has the capacity to scare and even harm the other. Patients often up the ante when they feel therapists do not acknowledge their own fear or the danger in the room. Thus, we advocate putting the issue on the table, especially in an outpatient setting, by openly questioning what makes us feel safe/unsafe, and what we can and cannot do about it. That there are limits to what the therapy can tolerate is illustrated by the following example.

Steve, a patient of MS, recognized the previous patient leaving his office—who happened to be a prominent TV journalist. He then became obsessed with the belief that this man would discuss him on television. So fearful was Steve of the "public exposure" that he decided to "strike first" by going to the network and discrediting the journalist by revealing that he was "seeing Dr. Selzer." MS spoke of Steve's sense of endangerment from the journalist, but he additionally informed his patient that his treatment would be terminated if he were to contact the network. The boundary setting worked, and Steve's fear and sense of danger remained safely inside the office walls.

Several variables tend to make people feel unsafe: unpredictability, unfamiliarity, intensity, impingement, silence, and speed (rushing). Space, too, can create a feeling of danger. Hisoka, desiring closeness, once asked DK if he could move his chair nearer to hers. She agreed and he did so, but, as soon as he did, he anxiously began associating with frightening images of cannibalism. DK quickly stepped in by adding, "I forgot to tell you that you can also move your chair back," which he did, with manifest relief. This example illustrates how feeling endangered is often accompanied by an inability to perceive alternatives. DK presented Hisoka with an appreciation that the situation was not fixed and that alternatives existed to decrease the threat.

Of course, safety means different things to different patients in different situations. It is impossible to know ahead of time what a particular patient's requirements for safety will be. Therefore, the therapist needs to remain open and receptive. We mentioned earlier that a supervisee of DK who prided himself in the ease with which he connected with even the most psychotic patients was given a rude awakening after he returned from a week's vacation. He approached a patient with whom he had had a positive connection and playfully asked, "Did you miss me?" The patient instantly punched him in the face and broke his nose. The therapist realized that he had assumed the relationship had remained exactly where it had been before his vacation. What his absence meant to the patient had not yet been explored. The assumption that he had been missed may have been too much for the patient to bear. The precipitous implication of intimacy may also have been experienced as invasive.

Similarly, MS grew a beard one summer, and in his first session back he said to Charles, "You seem to be more cautious than you were before my vacation." Charles replied, "Now you have a beard, and I can't see your mouth like I could before you had the beard. You can hide your expression. Before I could see if I revolted you or not. I know you grew the beard to prevent me from seeing how disgusting I am to you, so I must be careful." The therapist needs to appreciate that a psychotic sense of self and the world is tenuous, permeable, and cannot always be relied on, especially when there has been a pause or change in the therapeutic relationship. Thus, continuity in the relationship cannot be counted on and should be monitored rather than taken for granted. Reestablishment of self and other following separations, and even between sessions, is crucial. MS was made aware of how important continuity is when he noticed another patient, Ivan, smirking after MS made his characteristic closing remark, "I'll see you next time." At the beginning of the following session, Ivan smirked again and said, "I know that's part of the CIA's trick. They send different people each time to wear me down and all of you are instructed to say, "I'll see you next time … as if to conceal the fact that no one shows up twice in a row."

Whereas consistency and continuity are key, therapy contracts might also require greater flexibility when involving patients with psychosis. For instance, if a patient feels that 15 or 30 minutes are enough therapy for one day, they should be able to leave at that point. Or some patients may not show up for therapy when they are feeling dangerous. Rather than interpret their behavior as resistance, the therapist needs to be alert to a patient's way of protecting themselves, the therapist, and the treatment. Self-regulation and the wish not to harm are factors that often go unnoticed.

Amy confessed that she saw (hallucinated) dozens of rats outside DK's office building and that it took her an hour before she perceived (hallucinated) a path, allowing her to run to the entrance. This happened five times a week, for years, and clearly reflected Amy's sense of imminent danger that accompanied her analysis. However, Amy's behavior also demonstrated her strong motivation to overcome even the most extreme fear to engage in therapy. Her ultimate success (she never missed or was late for an appointment) reinforced her commitment to treatment and her inner resources in overcoming her fear and anxiety. This kind of "test" would not be possible in an inpatient setting, where surmounting such a conflict on one's own would not necessarily be encouraged, and such hallucinations would be interpreted as a need for medication. After several years, when Amy developed a sense of safety within herself and in the treatment, the rats disappeared.

It is natural for us to think of ways to make the patient feel safe; however, if the therapist does not feel safe, the patient will not feel safe either. Moreover, it should go without saying that the therapist has the right and responsibility to make themselves feel secure. How does the therapist create an *island of safety* in the therapy room and within the therapeutic relationship? We offer several suggestions.

When the therapist feels that something is increasing a patient's anxiety—making them wild, angry, or stuporous—it is best to back off and comment later. MS once remarked to his patient in such a situation, "I feel we just dodged a bullet." This statement was made playfully, yet it nonetheless denoted the risk and seriousness of what had just happened between therapist and patient. The statement acknowledged that there was a dangerous situation and that "we" were able to remain safe by a tactic of avoidance. Note that there was no explicit delineation at that moment of the precise nature of the danger. Rather, the emphasis remained on safety. By avoiding naming the danger, the therapist allows the patient to elaborate at their own pace or to continue the "dodging." At some later date, the therapist may feel the time is right to raise the issue. "Strike when the iron is cold" is a useful axiom (Pine, 1990).

On a different occasion, with a paranoid patient obsessed with Nazis, MS commented, "There are too many rats in the room." The patient laughed and agreed. Adopting a light tone by calling the Nazis "rats" indicated that the therapist was aware of the patient's dilemma but also that he was not afraid. If the patient appears heated and their behavior seems unpredictable, the therapist might ask the patient what can be done to make the patient feel safe. Or the therapist could do the same for themselves: "Since you just warned me to be careful, I'm going to take your advice. You wouldn't have warned me if you felt there was no danger. So, I am going to open the door. You'll know that it's easier for me to get away if I need to, and that should also make you feel less dangerous."

These examples illustrate the need to develop a dossier of dangerous situations that can be used to guide future behavior. Aggression can be codified, neutralized, and even devitalized by transforming it into language. Thus, another way the therapist can contribute to the safety of the room is by noting predictability and familiarity. To make a patient feel safe, it is important to have a mental map of what the therapist and patient do on a regular basis so that when a deviation occurs, the therapist is alerted to respond to a new situation. If a male patient says, "What's up?" every time he enters the office, note well the time he comes in and doesn't say, "What's up?"

The therapist might say, "I miss you not saying 'What's up?' So, what's up with you today?" The therapist here is emphasizing the predictable flow of a session and the familiarity a certain repetitive behavior has created. The therapist is also suggesting that deviating from that structure may be indicative of something significant and should be explored. Patients who experience themselves as chaotic—and many with psychosis do—will welcome the structure this method provides. To identify a schema, which implies predictability, a therapist might say, "Ninety-nine percent of the times you've stood up and screamed, you warned me beforehand." This kind of organization communicates to the patient that they are not entirely out of control and that there is a pattern to their outbursts.

One aspect of danger relates to the therapist's loss of boundaries in the treatment, a common occurrence in the treatment of psychosis. Sullivan (in Evans, 1996) referred to this as "contagion," and Searles (1959) called the phenomenon "driving the other crazy" the way the patient was once made crazy. There are times—sometimes extended times—when working with a patient makes the therapist feel like they are losing their mind. DK felt like Josh was trying to kill her (not physically) for several months during his psychotic breakdown. His was an intense psychotic transference in which he experienced DK as his hated and demonized mother. During this period, he tried to de-skill her, and for a time she lost touch with her professional capabilities and began to question whether she knew what she was doing. Speaking to another professional helped her to gain perspective.

The introduction of perspective into the treatment often helps both parties handle danger and safety. The therapist might note that the patient has mentioned many situations they deem dangerous. By asking the patient to rank them, the therapist introduces the notion of gradations of danger as well as the therapist's willingness to broach the subject. The message given is that not everything is equally dangerous. And one issue might be easier to speak about than another. "What's something that feels dangerous for you but safe enough for us to talk about?" the therapist might ask, perhaps inviting the patient to begin at the bottom of the list rather than the top. Small victories may lead to increased ambition to take on bigger problems. As therapists, we ask the patient to operate at the highest level of functioning of which they are capable. This ask can serve to reinforce capabilities the patient may not even be conscious of.

## Additional Insights for Outpatient Treatment

Outpatient psychodynamic psychotherapy with individuals experiencing psychosis can be both challenging and enriching. While we strongly endorse the value of outpatient psychotherapy for psychosis, we also recognize the necessity of caution, which must be exercised by both therapist and patient. The exploration of one's mind is inherently a perilous endeavor. One must relinquish control and authority when facing vulnerabilities and fears. The search for meaning can threaten to unravel one's boundaries through the process of investigation. Raw and powerful emotions are experienced as threats to therapists as well as patients. In a film on Bellevue's psychiatric emergency unit (DeLeo, 2001), the doctors' repeated mandate of asking patients in acute distress to "calm down" reveals the anxiety generated by strong affect.

Furthermore, persons with psychosis, many with a traumatic background, are especially aware that human beings have the potential to harm one another. Indeed, Searles (1961) considered schizophrenia as resulting from a person's inability to shut out terror. Karon and Vanderbos (1981a) also state that the only thing a therapist can be certain of when treating psychosis is that the patient is afraid. One need only recall the paranoid schizophrenic who fears others are pursuing them or the catatonic who retreats to a place where no one can harm them. Becoming aware of fear and danger in the treatment relationship has the potential of making the milieu safer and the patient feel less crazy.

We are all vulnerable by ourselves and we are vulnerable to one another. Working with psychosis brings us in touch with human susceptibility, which involves awareness of our radical solitude, danger, helplessness, and mortality (Becker, 1973). Most of us defend against this awareness, which may be one of the reasons why many avoid working with psychosis and also may explain the rush to medicate patients to move them (and us) away from these harsh realities.

There are three critical questions that must be rigorously addressed, for both the patient and therapist, when treating psychosis: What? Where? and When? "What" refers to what type of therapy—pharmacologic, supportive, dynamic, or some combination. "Where" refers to the setting of the treatment: inpatient or outpatient. "When" addresses a particular patient at a particular time. Where and when are closely related; the patient may need the protectiveness of the hospital at a particular moment. The therapist may require that the patient have further developed their capacity for reality testing prior to the two of them embarking on a course of outpatient therapy. The patient, smarting from a recent rehospitalization, may be crushed by the necessity of returning to the hospital and having their outpatient therapy interrupted. The therapist may lack the ability to make the correct judgment about whether the patient needs hospitalization. Clearly, the scenarios are innumerable. Moving between inpatient and outpatient therapy should not be considered in terms of failure or success but, rather, with a recognition that different mental states require different conditions.

The role of regression is a key factor in the "where" and "when" decisions. In the hospital, the patient is informed through word and deed that they have been placed in a situation that encourages or, at the very least, tolerates regression. They are told when to eat and sleep. They live in a confined space with strangers who may be in worse shape than they are. The patient is controlled by hospital rules and regulations that take over decision-making for them in exchange for the guarantee of safety. As described earlier, outpatient treatment works in the opposite direction. The process is collaborative, which means that more is expected of the patient. Resources are limited, indicating that no matter what gets stirred up in a session, the patient leaves and the therapist is unaware of what transpires within them until the two meet each other again.

Then what is the effect of regression on when and where? The therapist's inability to tolerate the uncertainty of the patient's fate between communications (referring not only to sessions, but also to calls, emails, texts, and other patient contacts) is an indication for hospitalization. Paul, a third-year resident, told MS that the interval between sessions with his patient, Jill, filled him with so much dread that he anticipated reading about Jill's murder of her parents every morning in the newspaper. In supervision, it became clear that Paul had avoided discussing his premonition with Jill because he feared it would result in tragedy. Paul hospitalized Jill with the understanding that when both felt there was no danger in examining Jill's relationship with her parents, they would return to outpatient work. Until that time, the safety of the hospital would provide a space where Jill could more freely confront her aggressive impulses.

When is it all right, and even beneficial, to tolerate regression? Josh, DK's patient, experienced three psychotic regressions during a long analysis conducted solely on an outpatient basis. Josh had a strong support system (several close friends and a 30-year relationship with a woman), and he was able to hold onto his jobs despite being quite delusional and paranoid. Although he regressed in sessions with DK, he was able to mobilize just enough ego strength to perform his daily professional duties, though in a minimal way. Because his employers valued his work, they tolerated Josh's eccentric behavior and offered emotional support. He did not miss a session during his psychotic episodes. These islands of sanity (Podvoll, 2003) as well as Josh's earnest desire to stay out of the hospital allowed DK to have enough confidence to continue working with him on an outpatient basis. She either saw him or was in touch with him daily during the acute phases of his psychotic regressions, which lasted approximately six months each time. After Josh emerged from his psychotic episodes, he and DK spent months, sometimes even years, analyzing what brought them on and ways to fortify himself in the face of future regressions. He was very grateful to not have been hospitalized during his psychotic episodes, something he was certain would have turned him into a chronic case. (See Chapter 10 for more on Josh's case.)

## Summary

The greater awareness and preparedness one has regarding the threats inherent in outpatient treatment with individuals experiencing psychosis, the less frightening it will be for both patient and therapist to undertake the therapeutic journey together. We were surprised to find that major psychoanalytic books on the treatment of psychosis (Karon and VandenBos, 1981a; Lucas, 2009; Searles, 1965) hardly include the concepts of danger and safety even though one of the major factors determining whether one hospitalizes a person is whether they are deemed to be a danger to themselves or others. Psychodynamic work with individuals experiencing psychosis is not necessarily more dangerous than work with other types of patients. However, the intensity of the emotional experience for both members of the therapeutic dyad and the traumatic realities they originate from (Fuller, 2012; Jackson, 2001) are often difficult to bear witness to and be drawn into. When a therapist finds a way to navigate these emotional parameters, they can reap the rewards of helping those most wounded by reality to recover their creative life potential.

# Chapter 6

# "Don't Step on Tony!"
## Working with Psychotic Symptoms

Gladys was admitted to the hospital two hours before meeting MS. He had already heard about how upset she had made three experienced and professional nurses. What had aroused the staff was the intensity of Gladys's responses to what they thought were reasonable requests. She shouted at them, calling them murderers, and demanded they get out of her room before they hurt her children. Therefore, MS knocked on her door with some trepidation. After several knocks without any response, he gently cracked open the door and entered her hospital room. Gladys instantly began screaming at MS, accusing him of almost killing "Tony."

Today, many mental health professionals would approach Gladys with certainty that her behavior, with its florid visual hallucinations, and, as it turned out, an organized delusional system, would warrant a diagnosis of schizophrenia. This interrogation would be in the service of a treatment plan most probably necessitating hospitalization or antipsychotic medication to control and eradicate her symptoms. Our approach is very different. We believe in viewing symptoms as adaptive measures and meaning-making systems. When working with a patient and their symptoms, we respect the patient's subjectivity, all the while searching for their nonpsychotic parts to work with.

Many therapists focus on eliminating or managing symptoms rather than exploring them. For example, a patient may develop a psychotic transference and say to the therapist, "I know you love me. I'm going home with you." In response, the therapist may quickly have the patient medicated or show the patient a photograph of their spouse rather than continue in the reflective operational mode by asking, "What does being my partner mean to you?"

This chapter focuses on an approach that works with and is guided by symptoms. We argue that the more conventional approach of immediately

DOI: 10.4324/9781003441519-6

eliminating symptoms does not serve the patient, since the therapist loses a crucial opportunity to understand that person's problems and, perhaps even more important, loses a vital opening into a potential working relationship when symptoms disappear. We seek to understand and reach conclusions collaboratively with the patient, best accomplished by learning about what their symptoms both conceal and reveal.

For example, Carol, a patient of DK, became enamored with her boss. When she confessed her love to him, he did not reciprocate and even told her he was involved with someone else. Carol developed *erotomania* toward her boss and a delusional system to deny the obvious. She wrote him letters and believed he was sending her signs of his love in a variety of indirect ways. She was convinced that every period and comma in the emails she received from friends and colleagues held the secret meaning that her boss was in love with her. She was unable to sleep, and her agitation and hypervigilance grew. In treatment, Carol was medicated just enough to allow her to calm down and sleep so that she could engage in the necessary reflective work of analysis. Little by little, she replaced her claim that "My mind broke" with another idea: "My heart was broken." Her delusional system was her manner of adapting to a reality (her boss did not love her) that was too painful to bear. Much of the therapeutic work centered on mourning her unrequited love.

As in Carol's case, we sometimes have our outpatients medicated; however, the reasons to medicate are not to eliminate psychotic symptoms but, rather, to remove whatever interferes with the patients' sense of safety and development of trust and observation/reflection. If the collaborative effort between patient and therapist cannot contain the intensity of affect, or if there is evidence from outside the treatment setting that the patient is endangering themselves or others, medication may be necessary. Yet even when resorting to medication, the language of the symptom and its communicative function should not be ignored nor eliminated. Furthermore, it is important to note that when medicating a patient, the therapist introduces a third, whether that third is the medication and/or the psychiatrist. This third becomes the object of transference reactions that can represent either positive or negative adjuncts to the treatment. Patients may feel possessed and contaminated by the drug they ingest or they may feel cured and no longer in need of exploratory measures (Tutter, 2006).

It is important to understand that we are primarily, but not exclusively, referring to the significance of symptoms in the initial phase of treatment. It is easy enough to wipe out bizarre symptoms with medication, yet to do so creates patient mistrust in the entire enterprise and a lost opportunity to collaborate in the meaning-making of psychodynamic treatment at its best. At times, medication also removes a patient's social life (i.e., hallucinated others—see Chapter 8). We all have the goal of helping patients expand their understanding of reality, tolerate and regulate difficult affective states, and return to life with better coping mechanisms. We try to convey to patients that they have it within themselves to understand and change themselves. We keep in mind that *psychotic symptoms are a sign that a human being is fighting for their life.*

We now return to the case of Gladys, a patient seen by MS in inpatient treatment for four years, to illustrate how her psychotic symptoms communicated her plight and how working with these symptoms, rather than trying to rapidly eliminate them, led to a fruitful alliance, deep psychodynamic work, and significant progress. What follows is narrated by MS, with comments in italics by DK.

Gladys lived in a single room in a boarding house. She had threatened her neighbor with a baseball bat, claiming that, despite having warned him to be careful of her children, he had twice nearly killed one of them by stepping on the child. After Gladys threatened him for the second time, he complained to the landlady, who ended up calling the police because her tenant refused access to her rented room. When the police arrived, Gladys wouldn't let them in either. She opened the door only after the police threatened to break it down, insisting they stand outside. She said the children were in the room with her, and they were frightened by the appearance of policemen. When the police said they could see only her, she said that was why they were dangerous, and she ordered them to leave. They returned several hours later with a court order for psychiatric commitment to the hospital.

When Gladys was admitted to the hospital, the only information I had was the police report. Gladys provided scant information, except that she lived under severely crowded conditions with small children. When we first met, she refused to discuss her personal history. Her sole purpose in life was to protect her children. I realized that any hope for an alliance would be based on my recognizing her need to be acknowledged as a fierce protectress. Therefore, I told her that she had gotten through to me about her awesome responsibilities. I suggested that the hospital was not a safe place for small children. She must have felt anxious about fulfilling her role as guardian under the present circumstances. She concurred that I had been insensitive to the dangers posed to the children by my opening the door, almost stepping on Tony. She had been shocked that I would ask so many questions when children's lives were at stake. "However, I give you points for finally recognizing that you put my children in danger," she added.

From what the nurses said, I had expected Gladys's shouts to be driven by rage, but what I saw and heard was terror. I didn't see Tony, and I also apologized for scaring Gladys. My instinct at that moment was to reduce Gladys's fear, and then, bewildered by what I had "done," I felt that I was likely to recreate the situation that had panicked her in the first place unless I could obtain more information. Even that early in the treatment, it was important to clarify self–other boundaries: "Though I am sorry for scaring you," I said, "my limited view of your reality does not permit me to be watchful in your reality." To bridge the gap in our respective realities, I first asked if Gladys would be more comfortable if I were to stand directly outside her room. She said nothing nor did she back away. I told her that since I was not able to see Tony, the possibility of my harming Tony remained. I explained that until we could find a way together to reduce this danger, I would not enter her room unless she allowed me to. I needed her help, initially to inform me of Tony's whereabouts, and ultimately to help me to see Tony myself. She said nothing more, and after a few moments, the initial meeting ended.

*MS begins by attuning himself to Gladys's symptoms. He enters her reality while maintaining an objective stance.*

I returned at the same time the following day and, over the next several weeks, the daily 15-minute sessions continued very much like the first one. At first, however, I stood at the door, emphasizing that I did so because I wished to cause no harm to Tony or Gladys. At some point, my back began to hurt from standing, so I informed Gladys that I needed to protect my back by sitting on a chair. In so doing, I suggested to her that I too had something to protect, and I was also making clear that I would do what was necessary to take care of myself.

*MS lays the groundwork for a therapeutic alliance. He and the patient both have something to protect. He collaborates with Gladys to protect them both.*

Before continuing my narration of this first phase of therapy, I will describe Gladys. She was a short, wiry woman whose body never seemed to be at rest. She was hyperalert, as if always ready to spring into action. Her eyes were like a scanning device, and she constantly surveilled the room. She had a sorrowful and weary expression but, over the next several weeks, her terror seemed to lessen. During this time, I learned that Gladys had 17 children, all under eight years of age, living with her in her small hospital room.

I began to feel that the only possibility of an alliance with Gladys would entail my meeting her in her world and not challenge it. I understood, too, that for Gladys to feel safe, it was essential that I not pose a threat to her children. Together we decided that I would not enter the room until we arrived at an understanding of how I would do no harm and even help her in protecting the children. Initially, I suggested that she could inform me of the whereabouts of each child so that I would not harm them, but that placed a great strain on her since she had to do all the work. I wished to share some of the burden with her.

*MS's approach is like that employed in play therapy, where the therapist interacts with their patient in the patient's imagined world without confronting it, interpreting it, or connecting it to the so-called "real" world (Yanof, 2013; Levy, 2008).*

From the beginning of the treatment, even early on, when Gladys viewed me as a potential child murderer, my efforts were aimed at emphasizing that the two of us were in the work together—i.e., both of us needed to feel safe to do the work. I needed to feel relaxed to think, and Gladys needed to feel that her children were not endangered so she could collaborate with me. We both agreed that the salient issue concerned the protection of the children, so we devised a plan for achieving this aim. After a week, I was permitted to enter several feet into the room, when Gladys collected her children around her and left an open space between me and herself and the children.

*How much patience is required to enter the psychotic world and retrieve the person trapped in it! The therapist must be resourceful in containing the painful cost of this patience.*

I asked Gladys if she could introduce me to her children. Since it was Tony I had almost stepped on, I asked if it would be all right to meet him first.

Indeed, she described Tony with such vividness that I began to see him in my mind's eye. Gradually she began to talk not only about his physical appearance but also about his personality.

I asked if Tony ever gave her any trouble.

"Oh, yes," she replied emphatically.

This was the entrée into a theme that Gladys and I focused on throughout the entire treatment: namely, how difficult it was to care for the children and how alone she felt.

*The imagined child, Tony, is a symptom, and in asking about him, MS is looking for clues about the meaning he held for Gladys.*

For six months I paid great attention to how crucial the children's safety was to Gladys and how important being their protector was for her. She became extremely defensive at the slightest hint that she might harbor any resentment toward her children. Her role as protector necessitated the absence of ambivalence.

*She does not resent her symptoms. She still needs them to protect her. Like the hallucinated children in which they hide, her symptoms keep her busy and distracted. They keep her from going to a place where she cannot be helped.*

Within the boundaries of the information Gladys provided about her role as protector of her children, several themes emerged. First, the role of protector was the essence of her identity. Second, the very necessity for her hyperalert protectiveness derived from her view of the world as a dangerous place. Finally, remaining faithful to her caretaking role left little time for anything else in her life. This last point was slowly and delicately developed. As mentioned previously, she was intolerant of any suggestion that her role limited her in any way, and she never complained. Nonetheless, at times I would talk about the burden she carried. I quickly realized that to persuade her to consider the restrictions of her role, I had to first make very clear my appreciation of the importance of her job. Moreover, I had to show that I knew she was doing a very good job as a protector. In fact, in the spirit of helping her do an even better job, I successfully persuaded her to tell me more about each child.

*MS finds the nonpsychotic part of her. She is protective and caring. She resonates with his responsive understanding and tells him more about her children/her symptoms/their meaning.*

Over many months I learned that she had not given birth to any of the children and that they were all orphans who shared a commonality of having been exposed to inordinate cruelty early in life. Though each child's story was unique, they all shared the sense of being the victims of a cruel world and, until Gladys's appearance, they lived with no adult guidance. The vividness of her detailed descriptions of each of her brood permitted us to have lively discussions about the children, their interactions with each other and with her, and their impact on her. I never said the children's safety was the sole goal of the therapeutic work. Rather, the children's safety was a necessary precondition of a larger goal, which was for Gladys to develop a broadened sense of herself in the world. After all, she had been legally committed to the hospital, limiting her life in serious ways. Others, including her family, had found her impossible to deal with.

Gladys's initial descriptions of her children had been glowing. They thrived on love, both in giving and taking. Over time, a more complex picture emerged, which included episodes of ingratitude and competitiveness. At first, Gladys resisted discussing the negative aspects of taking care of 17 children by herself. She stonewalled inquiry, insisting that she had no time to think about herself. Why didn't I understand that? Her resistance was less about acknowledging the burdens associated with her caretaking than about exploring what the children provided her and, by implication, what she lacked, the latter threatening to bring her face-to-face with her impoverished existence.

*The symptoms/children begin to reveal a complex tapestry of meaning underlying her psychosis that involved care, love, resourcefulness, conflict, and more. MS and Gladys are making progress.*

Whenever Gladys spoke of trouble in her Paradise, I felt relief while recognizing that the trouble made me fearful. The good news was her acknowledgment of even modest ambivalence toward her children, suggesting a crack in her defensive armor. My fear was another matter. Initially, I thought mine was entirely about how Gladys would manage her fear. Then, a more troubling thought emerged: I was concerned about my capacity to bear the pain that would follow were she to lose her children, particularly if I contributed to their demise.

*Countertransference signals caution in opening the door to the underlying issues. MS must share her madness while separating himself from it.*

*This indicates the devilish difficulty in knowing when he should back off or delve deeper and how fast he should move.*

I was unsure about which one of us I was protecting. If I was only protecting myself, it could be at the expense of my failing to acknowledge Gladys's capacity to face reality. On the other hand, perhaps I was not reading her communication accurately. Until I resolved this question, my interventions were suspect. As I worked through my fear of becoming overwhelmed, I was better able to concentrate on Gladys. My hesitancy about when to confront and when to support diminished.

*MS is now riding the wave of Gladys's psychosis. He is locked in the curl, balanced, and more confident. He is thus better able to authentically collaborate with her.*

I invited Gladys to become my collaborator both in determining the locus of the fear and in monitoring the pace of the treatment. When our work posed too rapid a threat to the integrity of her delusion and our alliance was insufficient to sustain her moving forward, one or the other of us put the brakes on it.

We were able to capture that process in a metaphor whose origin was Gladys's. She announced during one session that she was afraid that talking to me at that moment was causing her to neglect her children. She would be better able to concentrate if she could first see that her children were okay.

Had anything happened to alert her to this concern, I asked.

Her stomach felt "jumpy," she said, a decades-old signal to her of danger. She likened the jumpiness to a smoke detector in her apartment, which she called a "warning bell."

I said we needed warning bells in this room too and suggested that whenever either of us felt that way, we could reference the metaphor. She might say, "I'm about to ring the bell." Or I might ask: "Do my ears deceive me, or do I hear a bell somewhere?" or "Am I right to ring the bell, or am I being an alarmist?" Creating shared metaphors served many purposes. It was a shorthand reference to what had already been discussed, a special language known only to us. Because the situation provoking the metaphor was likely to recur, albeit in a somewhat different form, its presence became familiar and reliable and represented continuity.

*From their gradual collaboration, which was reaching a tipping point, they now shared a world between sanity and madness, a world where they were communicating in a new way. The alliance is solid. They are connected as if with a rope, he on the outside of her psychosis, she still on the inside but moving toward him.*

Declarations of displeasure with her children increased. She was only one person after all, and there was so much to do, an early indication that a future discussion of her loneliness was possible. As her complaints surfaced, so did tensions within her family. Fights broke out among the children. I reminded her that she had told me she was "only one person." What did she expect of herself? As turmoil among the children increased, she expressed displeasure at their ingratitude.

Taking my cue from her, I again asked about the details of her burden. Did she ever get tired? How did she acquire the knowledge to handle the various problems that arose from caring for so many children? Didn't she need to remain vigilant about the danger the outside world posed to tax her resources?

*The increased conflict between her children/her symptoms signals a growing disgust with her condition, one of Podvoll's (2003) islands of clarity.*

"So how is Gladys today?" Our sessions typically began with that question, whereupon she would provide a detailed description of her experience since the day before. The treatment went predictably in this way, but six months in, Tony suddenly and mysteriously became quite ill. In one of the earliest and least disguised evidence of a treatment alliance, Gladys told me that since I was a physician, perhaps I might be able to diagnose Tony's condition.

I responded that Tony's symptoms did not fit a clear picture.

Remarkably, she informed me that she didn't expect me to have all the answers and that she knew I had limits, but that she was "touched" by my interest, nonetheless.

Tony fell into a coma and died two days later. As always, I went along with Gladys's reality, asking her what we should do with the body.

*Again, MS does not challenge Gladys's reality but works with her from within it.*

Gladys adamantly replied, "Don't worry; he'll just disappear."

I said that might well be the case, but I very much doubted that Tony would disappear from her heart. She became quiet, looked at me suspiciously, and then burst into tears. It was the first time she had shown sorrow in my presence.

*Here is a breakthrough. One of her symptoms disappeared, the main one, and she begins to mourn it.*

Gladys's grief deepened, and soon she refused food. I was torn about how to proceed. On the one hand, I was convinced that mourning was essential for her progress, especially since it seemed that loss was at the center of her difficulties. It was important for her to develop the capacity to tolerate loss. On the other hand, 16 other children still had to be dealt with. So, even though we were gradually chipping away at Gladys's masochism and selfless life in which she nonetheless was at the center, I decided at this point to use her masochism in a constructive way.

"I know this is asking something almost impossible for you to consider in your grief, but think of the other 16 children," I said. "They need you. Only by releasing Tony can you fully give to those who remain."

*This is a clever move that appeals to Gladys's own penchant for responsibility and altruism.*

Over the next year of treatment, 15 children perished. The general outline of Gladys's experience with Tony's illness and death provided the template for these other experiences. Grief was followed by an awareness of her responsibility to the "living." Her grief was intense, and we often sat together in silence. Whenever she refused to eat or, especially during one occasion when she became catatonic, I reminded her of her responsibilities to the living. Though obvious, never once did I directly say that the responsibility to the living was, of course, to herself.

Once I slipped and suggested to Gladys that perhaps she took on such an enormous task because she felt badly about herself.

Outraged, she began screaming and told me I was crazy. "Maybe that's it!" she announced as if reaching a novel insight. "That's why you've never called me crazy for having these children no one else can see. Maybe you're an ass!"

*A rupture. MS goes in for the truth too quickly! This may be a setback, but the alliance is strong enough to withstand a little shakeup, and Gladys feels safe enough to criticize MS and call him a name.*

Thanks to the growing working alliance and the strengthening of the nonpsychotic part of Gladys's personality, she was more comfortable asserting herself. At that moment I realized my interpretation had been premature and dangerous. As with other conditions, when working with psychosis it is vital to leave certain issues on the back burner, sometimes for a very long time. In an attempt at reparation, I reflected, "It's clear that what I just said was quite hurtful to you." Because we had already established a strong working alliance, Gladys and I were able to repair the rupture caused by my premature interpretation.

Each loss of a child was deeply mourned, and I even felt that each loss produced more intense grief than the previous one. When I voiced this observation, Gladys convincingly explained, "Sure, each time I am less scared to feel things. Didn't you know that?"

I assured her that I did not ask questions that I already knew the answers to, but her question allowed me to stress the theme that I emphasized at every opportunity—namely, that she was the principal informant of her life and that what I knew about her I had learned from her.

*MS concedes to the primacy of Gladys's experience, which, again, fosters trust.*

I will skip ahead to the first half of the third year of treatment, a strenuous time that was dominated by the dying and death of Jennifer, Gladys's last child. Her grief was so intense that I began to feel hesitant about the nature of the work. I wondered whether I had gone too far in encouraging her to confront her losses.

"If Jennifer dies, there will be no reason for me to live," she exclaimed while refusing all nourishment.

Despite her request to be allowed to die, I gave the order for Gladys to be fed by tube. The decision to force-feed Gladys helped resolve my countertransference because her starving herself compelled me to confront two issues: first, whether I had the right and responsibility to decide whether she could live without Jennifer and, second, whether the therapy was based on an unjust decision on my part to pursue a strategy of relinquishment in the service of autonomy. As I pondered my function in the treatment, I realized that, whenever I had faltered, Gladys gave me a sign to keep going. My guilt was now getting in the way of what she had taught me. Therefore, in resolving to keep her alive, I was also telling both of us that we could—and would—continue our work.

*Here is a beautiful moment of collaboration between therapist and patient. This work is dangerous, and collaboration protects the therapist as much as it does the patient. This treatment is striking in how much of it involves the protection of vulnerabilities and the integrity of subjectivity.*

Gladys tried to pull out her feeding tube but, curiously, did so only when the nurses were present, thus provoking their anger. I pointed out to her that she had shown no defiant behavior with me, and I wondered with her whether there was a part of her that wished to continue our work and, therefore, not alienate me as she had the nurses. I wondered to myself as well whether the reason she had chosen to provoke the nurses was because she sensed that I had wanted her to punish me and, therefore, she would not get the same response from me as she did from the nursing staff (i.e., I would not get angry the way they did). Perhaps their anger also deflected her focus away from her sorrow.

*She only pulls the tube out when the nurses are there and not MS because she is telling him she wants to live.*

After this discussion, Gladys ceased her selective tube pulling and informed me that the tube was no longer necessary; she was ready to be on her own. I remarked that her poor nutrition was weakening her.

"I know Jennifer's going, and I want to remember everything," she said. "Maybe memories are all that I will have." Since I was unable to see Jennifer, Gladys suggested that she might draw a sketch of Jennifer and that she and I could collaborate to make the sketch as accurate as possible.

The sketch took nearly two weeks to complete. Each session began with Gladys describing how Jennifer looked. I offered suggestions about how to make the drawing a more accurate representation of what she was describing. The drawing was clearly a transitional object (Winnicott, 1975) to help Gladys in her grieving process, as well as an attempt to make something real in the world she increasingly shared with me—an object that we co-created. One day I asked Gladys what she would do with the finished drawing.

"Maybe I'll tear it up; maybe I'll frame it," she answered matter-of-factly.

I said that her choice represented the two ways she could deal with Jennifer's loss: remembering her or trying to rip her out of her mind. Jennifer died the following day.

The next three weeks were very solemn. I joined in Gladys's grief, telling her that I, too, had no words now. For the most part, we simply sat together in silence. But I did ask Gladys which way she was leaning in plans for the drawing. Since she happened to be Jewish like me, I mentioned that our situation reminded me of sitting shiva, the customary way Jews mourn someone who has died.

To my surprise, she remarked that no one had ever sat shiva in her home.

I was astonished: not by the fact of the absence of mourning, but by her sharing, perhaps for the first time in three-and-a-half years of treatment, something about her life before the psychosis had taken it over.

*The death of the last child, the drawing, and this personal information signal a breakthrough on a deeper level.*

I knew I was on precarious ground, lest Gladys slam the door on her past. Yet I wished to take advantage of this opening, so I ventured to say, "You know, for the last three-and-a-half years, we've never talked about anything [that happened to you] outside this room."

She replied curtly that she had been far too busy taking care of her wards.

I asked her whether we might continue to move forward without turning our backs on Jennifer and the others. I tried to reassure her that everything in her life had meaning and that there was a relationship between her life with the children and her past. I asked her to think about whether there might be anything about what happened to her before the children that could help us understand why she had taken on such an enormous task. I also asked if what she had done with these children could help us comprehend how she experienced what had gone on before.

She replied that it was all too confusing for her and that I was rushing matters.

Gladys was correct, and my rush to analyze the connection between her distant and recent past was premature and largely influenced by my newfound awareness that I was going to move within a year and was feeling pressured to tidy things up before leaving. Over the next six months, Gladys taught me that my need to get everything neatly tied in a bow was disrespectful of her considerable strengths, which she had demonstrated repeatedly. After all, 17 very important people had left her already, and she had survived.

*It is only natural for MS to push after another breakthrough, but Gladys helps him keep at the appropriate pace.*

Despite her protests about rushing things, Gladys's story now tumbled out of her in a short space of time. She revealed that she had been an only child. Her father frightened her because he always yelled at her and she felt, from a very young age, that he hated her. She tried to hide from him, especially when her mother wasn't around. (It did not appear that she had been sexually abused.) Gladys idealized her mother, especially because she felt her mother had tried her best to protect her from her father, even though her efforts were ineffectual. Gladys often thought about running away from home, but she never did because she feared some harm would come to her mother.

She was eight years old when her mother died. She was continually frightened after her mother's death and felt even more unprotected than before. As she recounted her story, she laughed and said that she knew it was crazy, but she had felt that perhaps her father would be nicer to her once her mother was no longer in the picture. Sadly, this was not the case.

Three years after her mother's death, another woman moved into the house. Gladys's father never married the woman but demanded that Gladys refer to her as Mother. She refused to do so, and one day the woman told Gladys that everything was her fault, that her parents had married because her mother became pregnant, and if she had "never happened," everyone's life would've been better. By that time, Gladys was a teenager. She finished high school and went to work for the ASPCA, a job she liked very much. She felt a kinship with the animals because they had been given away, which she equated with having been unprotected. With a great deal of sorrow during these sessions, when she narrated her story, she questioned imploringly, "Why didn't anyone want to protect them? They were so helpless!" Gladys described a "birthday" ritual she devised whenever a new animal was adopted and emphasized how the life of the person doing the adopting was completely transformed. These private celebrations were high points in Gladys's life. It was soon thereafter that she developed her delusional system.

The reason she was admitted to the hospital was because her neighbor complained and she had refused to let her landlady into her room, fearing for her wards. The landlady insisted, claiming that she had to see how well Gladys was keeping her room. Gladys then became paranoid and barricaded herself inside, which led to the police getting involved.

Within three sessions Gladys had blurted out her entire history. The remaining time we worked together was spent, as she put it, "connecting the dots." Gladys and I discussed how much she had wanted to protect her wards, and yet all of them died. She instantly associated several memories of the times her mother had successfully protected her as well as the times she had failed. What was even more surprising was that she recalled several richly detailed memories of her father taking care of her. With a great deal of wistfulness and irony, she insightfully came to appreciate the great paradox of her adult life: as important as the children had been to her survival, it was necessary for them to die so that she could live. Yes, the children had to die, but only after she had acquired enough of what she called a "base." And who had provided that base? The children, of course. Up until this point, Gladys and I never discussed whether the children were real. We didn't need to.

My leaving the unit was the last issue that needed to be confronted. Cautiously, we examined the multiple meanings of our imminent separation. Then, a startling event occurred. When Gladys had moments of apprehending the emotional significance of my departure, one or more deceased children would suddenly appear. They never spoke, stayed only a few minutes, and then faded out. The children's appearance soothed her, allowing us to return to experiencing the emotional impact of my leaving. I came to rely on the children's appearance to guide me in knowing when to probe and when to support. After several such sequences, I felt that Gladys was communicating her readiness to examine her delusion.

I pointed out that the children appeared only when we talked about my leaving, especially when she allowed herself to feel her sorrow. That suggested a link between the danger she felt when experiencing my leaving and the children appearing. Were the children saving her, or was she saving herself through the reassuring vision of them?

She felt it unlikely that they had been there all along without her being able to see them. Maybe she was wrong about their having died? But why would they fake their own deaths? Hadn't she given up her life for them? This type of rumination continued.

The answer to her conundrum hinged on her ability to acknowledge how the depth of her loneliness created a crisis demanding relief. Understandably, she had to save herself, even if it meant creating illusory allies. "You provided yourself with the strength to fight another day," I said. To accept her loneliness implicitly meant that she now felt able to declare her loneliness without losing herself. Could the childless Gladys provide her own solace without returning to a psychotic solution? If she were able to reflect on the totality of her mothering experience—to acknowledge it, bear it, and grasp the multiple meanings of her interactions with her children without falling into decompensation—then she would be on solid ground. Happily, the more we examined how Gladys had carried out her caretaking role, the more she appreciated her capacity to be responsible, to manage stress, and to love, even as our work repeatedly reminded her of her loss and her psychosis.

## Guidelines for Working with Symptoms

We would now like to turn to some guidelines for working with symptoms, which can be gleaned from this case history.

1. *Take what you can get.* Symptoms are what the patient offers us, and, therefore, they are the material we have to work with. Often patients with psychotic symptoms are extremely wary, watchful, and guarded. Thus, it is helpful to meet them where they are to establish a therapeutic alliance (Frank and Gunderson, 1990; Selzer et al., 1989).
2. *Respect for symptoms comes as a surprise to patients.* Patients are so accustomed to others, including professionals, not respecting their view of life, that being surprised has the advantage of arousing their curiosity and willingness to work.
3. *Give credit to the patient's strengths.* Rather than treat symptoms as signs of disease, regard them as efforts, however flawed, at adaptation and caretaking. Significantly, Gladys lost her mother when she was eight, and her wards were all under the age of eight. Here was a clear connection highlighting the way she used her imagination to vicariously mother herself after her own mother had died.
4. *Symptoms are adaptations.* Many believe there is a person hidden underneath the psychotic symptoms that needs to come out. We are saying that the person is revealed in their symptoms; symptoms are the window into the person.
5. *Symptoms are a way of attenuating affect.* Gladys was unable to say she was lonely or needed a hug. Yet, she created children whom she could hug and express affection toward at the limits of her tolerance (Knafo, 2020).
6. *Symptoms have tremendous heuristic value.* By paying attention to symptoms, we will eventually understand the context in which the symptoms arose as well as the patient's meaning-making system.
7. *There is continuity in personality.* Once we understand that adaptation arises from somewhere and attempts to get somewhere else, then we can help patients appreciate the continuity in their lives. We challenge

the notion that there is a "break" between a "before" and "after" state and, instead, value the symptom as a *bridge* for restoring a coherent and continuous sense of self (Selzer and Schwartz, 1994).

8. *Establish the authority of the patient.* Even if the patient's symptoms appear like a riddle, one can nonetheless communicate that they are meaningful and credible, albeit puzzling.

9. *Symptoms offer a clue to major issues.* Within the first five minutes of meeting Gladys, her symptoms made it obvious that she was living in a dangerous world in which she was assigned the role of protector.

10. *Symptoms are driven by intelligence and logic.* It is wrong to assume that symptoms are emotions gone berserk. If one takes the time to understand the meaning of symptoms, one can appreciate the enormous logic they contain.

11. *Symptoms communicate.* No matter how tentative, confused, or smoke-screened they are, symptoms are an effort to reveal something. In Gladys's case, the paradox of her life was revealed through her symptoms: she needed the children to live, yet she also needed them to die so that she could go on living.

## Conclusion

Our model of working with psychosis differs from most current practices, even though both models focus on symptoms. The medical model uses the DSM or ICD to ascertain which symptoms are present to diagnose and categorize a mental illness. Our model also looks closely at symptoms, but we use them as guides to understand the patient's dynamics and as invitations to embark on collaborative work. Thus, instead of focusing on symptoms as signs of pathology and dis-ease or dis-ability, we regard symptoms as creative attempts to adapt and survive. Our focus is on patient strengths rather than weaknesses. Viewing symptoms as a pathway toward alliance, collaboration, and meaning-making rather than as obstacles and resistances to be eliminated offers hope to both the therapist and the patient. Similar efforts are being made in communities of those who hear voices (e.g., Hearing Voices Network), where voice hearers learn to understand and live with their voices rather than rush to eliminate them (Romme et al., 2009).

Gladys began treatment with the conviction that she needed to preserve the lives of her 17 orphaned children without understanding how or why she had taken on such a daunting task. She held onto the belief that mourning would result in disintegration and, therefore, devoted her life to a defensive system that precluded mourning. Gladys gradually developed the affect tolerance necessary to withstand her many losses, which she faced together with her therapist. Significantly, with each loss, she was able to feel more and grieve more. Finally, all her children were gone, allowing Gladys to turn to her own interrupted life and "connect the dots." She had become a mother to her imaginary, orphaned children as a way of taking care of the abandoned parts of her childhood self as well as identifying with her lost mother. Now that Gladys's symptoms made sense to her, she was able to let them go.

We hope that this chapter will entice practitioners to see the many Gladyses in the world who will respond well to collaborative work. Even if one's major approach is pharmacology, then we believe that compliance and adherence to medication protocols should not take precedence over collaboration and meaning-making. We are not positioning ourselves against psychopharmacology. Indeed, we believe that medication regimens have a better chance of being adhered to if the treatment relationship is a collaborative one that includes respect for what the patient is bringing to the table (Corradi, 2004; Docherty and Feister, 1985).

# Chapter 7

# Anybody Home? Working with Negative Symptoms

The literature on psychosis and its treatment has focused primarily on positive symptoms, despite the finding that negative symptoms are present in 25%–90% of patients with first-episode psychosis and in 20–40% of patients with chronic psychosis (Lutgens et al., 2017; Makinen et al., 2008). Kraeplin (1919) was the first to note that some hospitalized schizophrenic patients manifested "…a weakening of those emotional activities which permanently form the mainsprings of volition. … The result is dullness, failure of mental activities, loss of mastery over volition, of endeavor, and of ability for independent action. The essence of personality is thereby destroyed" (Kirkpatrik et al., 2001, p. 165). Bleuler (1911/1950) also noted symptoms that display disturbances in association (affect, ambivalence, and autism). The term *negative symptoms* has been used to refer to a lack of energy and engagement in one's surroundings. Anhedonia, apathy, asociality, and avolition are all regarded as negative symptoms, to be distinguished from *positive schizophrenic symptoms*: delusions, hallucinations, and disorganized thought and behavior. Because of the emphasis on the felt absence in negative symptoms, they have also been labeled *deficit symptoms*. More recently, CBT practitioners Beck et al. (2019) and Mote et al. (2018) conceptualized negative-symptom psychosis as a "deficit syndrome," consisting of a "cognitive triad": a person's negative view of self, other, and the future. Mote et al. (2018) work with these negative cognitive schemas through performance-contingent rewards and social skills training. Before describing our approach to working with persons with negative symptoms, we will review the criteria used for diagnosing negative-symptom psychosis.

DOI: 10.4324/9781003441519-7

## DSM Definition of Negative Symptoms

The *DSM-5* (American Psychiatric Association, 2013) distinguishes between mental and physical negative symptoms. Mental symptoms include a seeming lack of interest in the world, not wanting to interact with other people, an inability to feel or express pleasure, an inability to act spontaneously, decreased sense of purpose, not talking much, and difficulty speaking due to disorganized thinking. Negative physical symptoms can include an unexpressive or blank face, monotone speech, lack of gesturing when communicating, lack of eye contact, and physical inactivity.

Like its previous iterations, the *DSM-5*'s description of negative symptoms consists of a list of diminished or entirely absent functions, referring to characteristics that are missing. The *DSM-5* does not mention that these symptoms might be playing an adaptive role, which could indicate what they might add rather than subtract. Indeed, the dramatic and rather catastrophic descriptions of a person exhibiting negative symptoms have discouraged professionals from even trying to approach what seems like an impossible and incurable situation.

In fact, negative symptoms can be secondary to other conditions, functions, or influences, including defensive ones. For example, what appears as asociality may be due to paranoid withdrawal arising from fear. Restricted emotional expression may be the result of drug-induced akinesia. Low drive or apathy, lack of spontaneity, and impaired affective arousal may be the consequences of overmedication with sedative drugs (Hollister, 1974). For these reasons, Carpenter and his colleagues (1985, 1988) divided negative symptoms into primary (deficient) and secondary (reactive) categories to distinguish them, going so far as to support the claim that deficit psychosis may be considered a separate disease. They speculated that negative symptoms can emerge from understimulating environments. Furthermore, Carpenter et al. believed that negative symptoms can be used to defend against psychosis and may not only be a manifestation of it. Indeed, post-psychotic depression can manifest with negative symptoms. Wing and Brown (1970) claimed negative symptoms can also be caused by hospitalization and social isolation.

Not surprisingly, in light of the pessimistic view of negative symptoms, the literature on psychosis deals almost entirely with positive symptoms. Laypersons and many mental health professionals associate the term schizophrenia with positive symptoms only. The pharmacologic literature also lacks a definitive consensus statement about drug management of negative symptoms (Arango et al., 2004; Moller, 2003). The neglect in the literature both reflects and reinforces the consensus that treating individuals who manifest these quieter and more heterogeneous symptoms are more difficult to treat. Surely, it is easier to make vivid, dramatic manifestations of psychosis (e.g., hallucinations, delusions, and disorganization) disappear, or at least attenuate their intensity, than it is to successfully address what is missing (avolition, apathy, etc.).

## Positive vs. Negative Symptoms in Therapy

Working with a patient with positive symptoms is conducive to the therapist playing an active role and being imaginative and curious; the patient wants something, including something from the therapist. The patient may simply wish the therapist would go away and leave them alone. But even that is grist for the mill. "Why do you want me to leave?" the therapist might ask. "Is there anything I can do to encourage you to change your mind?" Both questions invite interaction. Something is going on.

On the other hand, a person who behaves as if no one is in the room presents a different conundrum. "You don't exist" is a very different proposition than "I have to get rid of you." "I don't exist either" adds to the therapist's frustration. In fact, these apparently opposite positions share a common goal in that they are both strategies for trying to remain safe; the difference is the means to achieve that end. The patient exhibiting negative symptoms needs both to hold onto and be unaware of their wish to remain alive. One of DK's patients who had had 17 psychotic episodes, ten of which presented with negative symptoms (one to the point of catatonia) claimed that during these episodes, she was 85% dead. This is not surprising, since withdrawal is never absolute. Short of death, libido can never be fully withdrawn. Even the most isolated patient, by engaging in a withdrawal effort, is revealing a sign of life: their desire to not be overwhelmed.

The distinction between positive and negative symptoms applies to the impact on the therapist as well as the patient. Failing to recognize this fact is a serious omission, resulting in the therapist's being unaware of what might be a significant contribution to the struggles ahead. Patients with negative symptoms appear to offer nothing and seem interested in nothing; there seems to be no one at home. Many have written about the challenges for the therapist who works with such patients. Steiner, in his highly insightful book, *Psychic Retreats* (1993), views the psychotic organization as a retreat to safety from anxiety and the threat of one's own sanity. The therapist, Steiner says, "has to avoid being driven either to give up in despair or overreact and try to overcome opposition and resistance in too forceful a way" (p. 131). In fact, the therapist may be feeling that they need to hold onto their personhood to avoid becoming a void, while the patient may feel that becoming a void is precisely what guarantees holding fast to their personhood. What each clings to differs, but the goal is the same: to prevent feeling overwhelmed and to avoid extinction.

Interestingly, when referring to symptoms of psychosis, therapists tend to describe positive symptoms by attributing them to a person, whereas negative symptoms are described in a disembodied way, as though they were phenomena without an author or owner. Perhaps this is the therapist's effort to soothe their own pain since the lack of recognition doesn't seem to be coming from a person but rather from a constellation of pathologies. The patient's impact on the therapist is daunting and discouraging and can include a lack of awareness that *the patient is a person experiencing something.*

Therapists are taught the importance of asking new patients: "How can I help you?" Implicit in this question is: "What is it you want?" Patients with negative symptoms could find such a well-intentioned question threatening since it attributes desire to someone who regards the denial of desire as necessary for survival. A counterattack, however, muted, could be frustrating and confusing. Withdrawal, by definition, communicates that the patient is beyond need. Once DK pressed her negative-symptoms patient, inquiring whether he experienced a desire for anything at all. His response: to live alone on a deserted island.

## Working with Negative Symptoms

Negative symptoms represent a formidable obstacle for the therapist, but they still offer clues about what the patient is struggling with and point to areas of conflict. Once the therapist recognizes areas of conflict that have led to defensive withdrawal, these resistances can inform and enliven the interaction. "They are showing me something. What can I do with this information to facilitate collaboration?" the therapist may ask themselves. For instance, a patient passes gas in session, and the therapist notes a slight smile on the patient's face, suggesting a form of connection and communication. Though the communication contains a degree of sadism, the patient conveys a message to the therapist about contamination and that there is literally a limited amount of air in the room to breathe.

Though we recognize the challenges of working with persons manifesting negative symptoms, we are more optimistic about treatment than many authors and clinicians claim to be. Our optimism is based on a psychodynamic understanding of the defensive uses of these symptoms and the countertransference in therapists confronting these symptoms, as well as our success in treating patients who present in this way. Negative symptoms reveal as well as conceal and represent the patient's characteristic attempts to shut out the world—to remove themselves from their environments, both external and internal. The patient's goal is to create and sustain a barrier to prevent them from experiencing painful affect, but their negative strategy has an impact on the therapist's willingness to engage with them. The degree to which the therapist attributes their symptoms to a deficit rather than a conflict will influence how he or she approaches the patient. Most essential for the therapist is staying the course while remaining aware of their own wish to withdraw.

Catatonia is the most extreme manifestation of shutting down the self to stay safe at any cost. The patient's underlying fear is of being overwhelmed by their own affect; shutting out the external world is secondary. However, people, events, and experiences external to the patient can trigger affective responses, any of which can overwhelm them. They emphasize the internal location of the disturbance when they announce, "I can't handle this," pointing to the problem as residing within the self. Affect is the enemy. Accepting its challenges raises the possibility of opportunity and hope.

Thus, the therapist's goal is to help the patient feel less threatened by intolerable emotional states such that they no longer feel the need for a barrier. Sometimes this means the therapist must withstand extended periods of rejection until the person feels safe enough to emerge. Gail Hornstein (2000), Frieda Fromm-Reichmann's biographer, claimed that her subject considered no patient, no matter how psychotic or seemingly unreachable, to be beyond hope. For example, Fromm-Reichmann saw a largely mute woman for nearly five years, during which their sessions consisted of the two of them seated near each other, which permitted the patient to feel the therapist's presence without being obligated to talk or make contact. After three years, Fromm-Reichmann expressed the conviction that this patient was curable because she began to appear friendly and seemed happier than before. A young colleague of Fromm-Reichmann told Hornstein how the elder therapist knocked on another patient's door daily for six months before he trusted her enough to let her in. Fromm-Reichmann's empathy, patience, and persistence seemed to always pay off in the end.

Most therapists do not have Fromm-Reichmann's fortitude. They often feel responsible for what is happening and identify their task as one of breathing life into an apparently lifeless patient. At some point, the therapist's focus may shift from a belief that they are providing life-giving breath to feeling as if they are struggling to maintain enough oxygen in the room for both therapist and patient to breathe. The therapist feels they must survive if they are to help the patient, and repeated frustrations can lead to a feeling of hopelessness. Moreover, the therapist's need to see results gets in the way of empathizing with the patient's experience. *It is difficult to appreciate the functions of deadness if one is focused on eliminating it.* Paradoxically, while "playing dead," the patient is struggling to survive by becoming as close to a nonself as they possibly can. Meanwhile, the discouraged clinician continues to conduct therapy in their customary fashion, unconsciously focusing less on the patient's current state and more on the hypothetical state they need to be in. Certainly, the therapist will attempt to locate the need to change in the patient, but they will likely neglect the kinds of mutual accommodations the therapist cultivates when working with patients considered healthier. Therapists who feel unable to help the patient in the way they had hoped may become fearful of losing their professional identity, which means they will not apprehend the utility of the patient's position.

Consequently, there is a hardening of each participant's position. The patient does not appear to acknowledge that either of them exists, and the therapist is often unaware that they are angry with their patient. "Can't you see I'm trying to help you?" the therapist might exclaim to themselves or to the patient. The therapist is unlikely to allow the patient's power over them to become conscious; instead, the clinician insists they are in control to stave off a sense of futility or failure. Therapists might attempt to deal with their felt loss of control by attributing the patient's power to their deficit: "Poor thing, they can't help themselves." On the other hand, the clinician might blame themselves: "I must be doing something wrong."

Neither of these positions is helpful. But how does one deal with a person who seems to want nothing? The answer, as the old Ford ad declared, is to "Ask the man who owns one." It is a surprisingly tall order to grant such a patient credit for knowing how they ought to be treated; however, to do so can make an enormous difference. If the therapist can relinquish their ambition and need to maintain a professional identity and allow themselves to enter the patient's world, the therapist will eventually have a feeling of relief in surrendering to the struggle, followed by a feeling of blankness. It is highly unlikely that the therapist's own withdrawal (*decathexis*) will be as complete as the patient's, but it should be sufficient to allow them access to their patient's existential situation. In turn, the patient will become aware of the therapist's empathic attunement.

Not all forms of withdrawal are helpful, however. For example, a therapist may justify withdrawing from a patient without blaming themselves by taking the view that the patient has a fundamental psychic deficit. The therapist can rationalize that the patient simply lacks the resources to be helped. Nature has failed to provide the patient with the necessary tools to process their affect. The therapist rationalizes that such patients are struggling against the impossible and that to continue pursuing them constitutes a narcissistic venture at the patient's expense. Nonetheless, despite these rationalizations, questions begging for psychodynamic understanding remain: What does the patient think is happening to them? Do they feel they have any control over the process? Is it happening within them, or do they believe they are being invaded? Even if the patient's symptoms are predominantly the result of a deficit, they remain a person, responsive in some fashion to their state. That person cannot be deemed as beyond dynamic understanding, though this may be their wish. True, the patient appears inaccessible. But can that mean they have eliminated all sources of conflict? Does vacuousness tell the entire story?

We teach our supervisees that stalemates caused by fear, insecurity, and/ or boredom can be overcome with curiosity. The problem is that many of the questions the therapist has regarding the patient and their own experience with them must be kept to themselves to not invade the patient's need for retreat. The therapist's need for closeness and responsiveness must be contained. If the therapist were to express these feelings, the patient might rediscover their own desire for closeness, awakening unresolved yearnings and igniting sorrow and rage, the affective intensity of which threatens to annihilate them. Appreciating the value of nihilism, and the resiliency it requires, helps the therapist understand the intermingling of weakness and strength in their patient's defensive retreat. One patient expressed this succinctly to DK: "If my parents died, I'd feel nothing." This man was clearly communicating that if he lacked feelings, he would not need to mourn the loss of significant others. Time after time, he informed DK that he felt nothing when she took her vacations. This stance continued for years until one day when he stated, "I feel nothing," he added after a moment's reflection, "or at least I think I do." Opening himself up to the possibility of having feelings about his therapist's absence marked the beginning of his readiness to allow emotions into the relationship. Eventually, he began to ask DK what others feel in such situations, wishing to learn what a "normal" response to loss looks like.

The blunted person is attempting to avoid facing either who they believe themselves to be or whom they fear they could become. Therefore, the first and most difficult step is to help the patient acknowledge their sense of themselves, after which the patient must be helped to bear and put into perspective their symptoms regardless of their etiology. At times, the first glimmers of access to a sense of self can be provoked unexpectedly and outside of the therapist's conscious efforts. Even a person in an advanced state of dementia who sits immobile for hours on end, seemingly unresponsive to their environment, may be moved by hearing a particular song or seeing an old photo, momentarily "waking up." Being touched by the appearance of a long-buried memory is often followed by the recognition of what is happening to the person in the now (Baird and Thompson, 2018). And the "now" is never only a replay of what was.

## Countertransference Concerns

Eshel (1998) used the metaphor of a "black hole" to describe working with patients whose world appears dead and empty. She posed the question: "How can the analyst be affected, invaded by, taken in, experience and share the patient's pain, terror, unbearable inner objects, psychic illness, and deficit, when facing a '**black hole**' experience—the experience of being gripped, devoured, distorted and annihilated by enormous forces of deadness and death?" (p. 925). Indeed, nowhere is it more necessary to be aware of one's countertransference experiences than when working with patients with negative symptoms. It may seem that the black hole only has room for one, and that is why hope is so important, yet so potentially disruptive to a treatment. If we look beyond the patient's withdrawal and "deadness," we begin to recognize the patient's complexity, which can provide the therapist with a sense of hope. On the other hand, the therapist cannot exploit hope to avoid experiencing the patient as they present. "There's more to him than this. I know it," shifts the therapist's focus to aspects the patient may reveal in the future, as the following illustrates.

Dr. Miller, one of MS's supervisees, appreciated that her patient, Amir's negativity was only part of a more complex picture. However, after that realization, she barely noticed how Amir made her feel. Her focus shifted to finding the 'buried' remainder of Amir. MS pointed out that Amir's negating self was central to his survival as well as the path to discovering the rest of him. Dr. Miller responded with dismay at having once again to focus on his negativity. Fear of one's own desolation is understandable, but the therapist of a patient struggling with negative symptoms can be helped in supervision to recognize that desolation and hope can be experienced together when care is taken not to overwhelm either person in the therapeutic dyad with this complex mix of emotions. The more the patient is "not there," the more the therapist feels attacked or ineffective. The therapist must hold onto their professional identity, lest they fall into the same meaningless void inhabited by the patient. Though most therapists consciously claim: "If only I could reach this person," a more honest assertion might be: "If only I could reach this patient, as long as it doesn't entail finding aspects of myself in them."

A minority of therapists who do not feel threatened by a patient's withdrawal tend to be people who are somewhat schizoid themselves— that is, they experience too much closeness and interpersonal demands as distressing. In fact, they enjoy the analytic situation because its intimacy possesses strict boundaries. They can sit comfortably with a patient's silence because they too need limited verbal and emotional engagement. Patients with negative symptoms may be experienced as a relief for these therapists. Other therapists find that sitting with such a patient stirs up claustrophobic feelings. Ogden (1995) believes that aliveness in analysis takes precedence over everything else. In one paper, he described how treatment with a patient who enacted "entombment" and lifelessness created "countertransference anxiety" in him. Ogden also shared the ways he defended against this anxiety: he obsessively counted the minutes left in session; he fantasized about ending the session early, claiming he felt ill. Most telling is the taking of his pulse as if counting the beating of his heart reassured him that, unlike his patient, he was still alive. Paradoxically, his patient's deadness led Ogden to fight for his life.

We believe, based on our years of supervising therapists, that the majority withdraw against their will from patients displaying negative symptoms as a result of feeling helpless at making meaningful contact with them. Many times, this withdrawal is based not only on a thwarted wish to be helpful but also on a fearful rejection of *identification* with the patient. As long as the therapist's focus remains on the patient's inability to engage, the therapist avoids seeing what they have in common with the patient. Shifting the focus to the patient's impact on the therapist is important. Admitting that frustration and disappointment have left the therapist no choice but withdrawal ironically narrows the gap between them. If one believes, "I am nothing like this person," an empathic connection is impossible. On the other hand, if and when the therapist comes to recognize similarities between themselves and the patient—specifically, the therapist's own wish to withdraw as a way of dealing with despair and helplessness—then that clinician can begin to appreciate what their patient has already learned: oblivion can be the answer, not the problem.

Empathy is necessary for therapy to succeed, but it cannot be programmed. What a therapist can do is examine their own resistance to their evolving empathy. Therapeutic ambition is the most common barrier. Over time, the patient's repeated non-recognition can challenge even the healthiest therapist's narcissism. To be loved, especially by oneself, can require proof of deserving that love. But when the therapist relinquishes ambition, giving the patient and themselves permission to withdraw, the therapist creates a space for a different kind of ambition, which is to build a connection with the patient through a parallel experience that can provide a grounding for more explicit object ties later in the therapy.

## The Therapist's Withdrawal

Bollas (1987) pointed out that therapists who work analytically are always seduced into an interpersonal environment by the patient, causing them at times to live in an unknowable region. Like Freud, who wrote that the analyst "must turn his own unconscious like a receptive organ towards the transmitting unconscious of the patient (1912/1978, p. 115), Bollas insists that therapists cultivate "countertransference readiness" or "freely-roused emotional sensibility" (Bollas, 1987, p. 201), which he claims inevitably transforms the therapist into a second patient. He applies Winnicott's (1971) guidance, borrowing the concept of allowing the patient to *use* the therapist as an object, which leads to his conjecture that to find the patient, one must first find oneself. Bollas wrote: "The afflictions of one person becomes the illness of two persons in the analytic situation" (1987, p. 199).

Bollas's description applies to what takes place in the treatment of patients with negative symptoms. We believe the therapist moves from fear of finding commonality with their patient to discovering pathways of identification with their patient when the clinician begins to feel overwhelmed by the "seeming" impossibility of ever reaching that person. The therapist's initial reaction may be shame for acting like the patient, more so if the withdrawal is experienced as pleasurable. On the other hand, the patient's withdrawal may have been precipitated more acutely by trauma, loss, abuse, a deadened relationship with a primary caregiver, or many frustrations and disappointments experienced over a prolonged period of time. Sitting with this submerged intensity may trigger memories of absences or losses in the therapist's life, negative occurrences that, in ideal circumstances, have been analyzed. Both wounded healers and those with no traumatic past have their reasons for retreating in response to the nonresponsive patient. The deeper the therapist's withdrawal, the greater their appreciation for the patient. The more fully the therapist experiences both of their inner worlds, the more likely the patient is to accept the therapist. This process can occur without words, such as in unconscious communication (Freud, 1915/1978; Bass, 2008). Each, in varying degrees, has depended on withdrawal to survive. The message the therapist now sends assures the patient that they two share the same experience. They both inhabit the same planet, perhaps not in a quantitative sense, but certainly qualitatively. The patient feels known.

One day, John, a 43-year-old postal worker, suddenly stopped sorting mail. His co-worker asked what the matter was. John did not respond. After several hours had passed, his colleagues called 911, and John was sent to the ER. After a brief hospitalization, John was discharged. During his hospitalization, he only marginally cooperated with the staff's requests, reacting but never initiating. Post-discharge, his family prevailed on him to seek help—requests he initially ignored—but when his father told him that getting help was a condition for remaining at home, John reluctantly agreed. In treatment, he repeated his behavior in the hospital, answering what he called "fact questions," such as age and background, but refusing to respond to inquiries about how he was feeling or what mattered to him or to comment on his inner life. After several months of his nonresponsiveness, his therapist began to show irritation. The patient retreated even further. Once, the therapist detected a smile, which she interpreted as his pleasure in dominating her, and she became even more irritated. Frustrated, she sought supervision from MS. Her first sessions were marked by an inability to discuss her patient, and she spoke only about her frustration. One day she apologized for "too much complaining." MS told her that accepting her complaining was the first step for her, and that only then could she begin to comprehend that her patient may also be complaining but in his own way.

MS accepted her complaints as an understandable and necessary part of the therapeutic process. She became curious about her patient, reviving her initial interest in why he was the way he was. Her questions were no longer aimed at helping him gain insight but rather served as ways to collect information about "Who is this person?" She found herself interested in aspects of him unrelated to his symptomatology. Gradually, the patient responded, albeit in a limited fashion. Fourteen months later he told her he had dared to recognize her because "you stopped trying to give me something. Before, I thought you were after me to change." He added, "I'm a person, even if I don't act like one."

## Holding and Containing

One way to conceptualize normality is to think of it in terms of one's capacity to know and deal with reality, a world perceptually and conceptually shared by a human collective, grounded first and foremost in their best understanding of their physical experience of the surrounding. We say that a person who is "normal" has the ability to distinguish between their inner world and the external world, between self and other. An acceptance of reality also includes being able to accept the differences between expectations, needs, and what is possible. By contrast, a person with psychosis often creates their own reality. A person experiencing psychosis with positive symptoms may experience reality as whom they have become—for example, "I am Jesus Christ" or "I am Moses." The treatment goal for such a patient is to help them come to terms with who they are rather than whom they believe themselves to be. On the other hand, patients with negative symptoms experience the reality of what they are not—they are in a state of omission. The goal for these patients is to help them move from negation to assertion, from "I am not" to "I exist."

Over time, as they become more secure, patients with negative symptoms open an entryway into their psyche, cautiously giving access to particular outsiders. That remnant of the patient who knows they are still alive and wants something—the "split in the ego"—provides the pathway to a therapeutic alliance. Finding that pathway can be quite difficult and takes time, though it is always present. One of DK's patients barely spoke and exhibited indifference to her and everyone else, but one day he brought in a self-portrait. The eyes in the drawing revealed a deep longing, something he was unable to convey verbally or in the office they shared. DK received her patient's message: "There is more to me than I have been showing you." Once the glimmer of aliveness makes itself known, the therapist can attempt to collaborate with that part of the patient. The therapist moves slowly and cautiously toward that faint light since the patient continues to fear that the therapist wants something from them. The therapist's reaching out to the patient will initially increase their appearance of remoteness. With exquisite sensitivity, the patient monitors the therapist's response to limit arousal both within themselves and in the therapist.

Even after the patient emerges from their shell, the original conflict is not fully resolved. As the patient struggles to reconnect, they again risk becoming overwhelmed; the degree of danger is inversely related to the strength of the alliance, the therapist's steadfastness, and how much of the process the patient has been able to internalize. The end goal is to eliminate the patient's reliance on withdrawal as their survival method and replace it with affect tolerance. Affect tolerance can be achieved when the patient experiences the therapist's *containment*. Bion (1959) first wrote about containment in relation to *projective identification*, emphasizing the importance of the mother's ability to deal with the infant's primary aggression and envy by remaining balanced and comfortable. He also noted that in clinical situations, projective identification makes it possible for the analyst to contain the patient's powerful emotions (p. 106). We are referring to containment and projective identification when we say the therapist embodies withdrawal in response to their patients with negative symptoms. Because the patient's withdrawal is a communication that can be held by the therapist, the process gives the therapist important information regarding their patient's state of mind. Steiner (1993) suggests that the therapist can, very gradually and carefully, give back these projections to the patient. Steiner accomplishes this task by avoiding "patient-centered" interpretations that aim at understanding, replacing them with occasional and well-timed "analyst-centered" interventions whose purpose is *being understood*. A therapist might say, "I'm beginning to understand you because you have been so deft at shutting me out. Your impact on me has been helpful to me by showing me things about myself." Such a statement implies that a shared experience exists between patient and therapist and that the patient, by excluding the therapist, is, in fact, relating to the therapist. To shut someone out implies a powerful interaction. Continued containment leads to integration and eventual growth in one's interest in understanding and not just being understood.

As the therapeutic collaboration becomes more active, the patient helps the therapist to help them by showing evidence of withdrawal when the therapist gets ahead of what the patient feels they can tolerate. The therapist helps the process in two ways: the clinician notices when the patient fears being overwhelmed and monitors themselves accordingly, and, through holding and containment, the clinician increases the patient's capacity to tolerate their own affect.

In Winnicott's (1960) notion of *holding*, the mother/therapist creates a milieu, a "holding environment," in which the infant/patient feels secure because their needs are met with care and concern, which eventually leads to autonomy and the development of a true self. Bion's (1959) notion of containment refers to an active intrapsychic and interpersonal process that involves the mother's/therapist's reaction to the child's/patient's projective identification. This is a two-person, largely unconscious phenomenon, during which the recipient/therapist feels at one with their patient, allowing the therapist to not only identify with but also to become the patient. Ogden (1979) describes projective identification as creating a third object that is both therapist and patient and also neither of them: a co-created object that transcends both of them. Once this third object is created, a new dialectic becomes possible within the treatment. The patient feels unburdened; the therapist can empathize with their patient; and both can accept what has been avoided. Clearly, both holding and containment are necessary for the treatment of patients with negative symptoms. Winnicott and Bion understood that the therapeutic relationship takes place in a realm created by both partners—in a space somewhere between conscious and unconscious, self and other, and reality and fantasy— no matter how overtly involved or uninvolved the dyad may appear from the outside.

The last step in treatment occurs when the patient makes the therapeutic process their own through internalization. Then the patient is able to acknowledge, tolerate, and put into perspective their affective life. Experiencing intensity no longer comes at the risk of becoming overwhelmed.

In a scenario in which the patient refuses to acknowledge their therapist's presence, the patient implicitly declares that they are better off alone. If the therapist does not protest, interpret, or leave, over time, the patient recognizes that neither they nor their therapist has been destroyed through this rejection. Both have endured. The therapist has withstood the patient's withdrawal and lack of collaboration and has done so without retaliation (Winnicott, 1954/1975). However, the patient continues to feel they lack the capacity to manage affective experiences on their own and indicates as much to the therapist. The therapist wisely resists the temptation to reassure the patient that they may be underestimating their capacity to tolerate affect. Signaling their appreciation that the patient continues to feel precarious, the therapist might say instead, "Dealing with the danger of being in over your head at this point takes precedence over the reward you might get from jumping in too soon."

## Revival and Mourning

The patient benefits from gaining a complete picture of what their withdrawal has provided for them. All too often, therapists focus on the limits and destructiveness of retreat to the exclusion of its gratifying aspects: security, mastery, and control. Patients with negative symptoms use numbing and withdrawal to avoid mental pain and feel some modicum of control. The best chance the patient has to relinquish psychic retreat as a defense is by appreciating the complex meanings it has held for them. Acknowledging what they have lost (both positives and negatives) while moving away from defensive withdrawal strengthens their reliance on containment. There are two aspects of withdrawal the patient must mourn if they are to reconnect with themselves and the world. The first aspect is the pleasure and safety they associate with withdrawal; the second aspect is the opportunities they have lost as a result of their withdrawal.

The patient loses a sense of safety, the power of negation, the feeling of being in control of the situation, not having to tolerate and regulate emotions, and a belief in themselves as invulnerable to consequences. Yet paradoxically, the patient cannot experience intrinsic pleasure until they are less withdrawn. When severely withdrawn, the patient's entire focus is on feeling nothing. Wanting nothing eliminates frustration, disappointment, and envy, but entails a loss of affect. Similarly, lack of ambition avoids the possibility of failing or pleasing oneself, a perverse, or more accurately, an inverse form of grandiosity. Traditional grandiosity holds, "I'm capable and deserving of everything," while the patient with negative symptoms declares "There's nothing I need nor want." The former refers to the freedom to be and to have anything; the latter refers to the freedom from the tyranny of need. As the patient tentatively ventures away from the state of withdrawal, they belatedly become aware of the thrill of their omnipotent defense, the need for no one, and the conviction that others are replaceable.

A quote from Samuel Beckett aptly describes the arc of the movement away from withdrawal and toward investment in life: "In the silence you don't know, you must go on, I can't go on, I'll go on (1973, p. 279). At points along the road to reinvestment in the world, the patient is likely to regress to disengagement, though not as severely as before. Regression involves the consequences of having lost the indirect rewards of omnipotence, namely feeling nothing and the intrinsic pleasure of being beyond pleasure and pain. The recovering patient experiences powerlessness, the loss of the armoring they believed they had acquired in the face of vulnerability. Negation made them feel above the fray. Now the loss of the omnipotent fantasy challenges the patient to survive in spite of being vulnerable.

The temptation to regress may also be an expression of the patient's wish to flee from sorrow, a response to their realistic appraisal of what withdrawal has cost them. Recovering patients believe that, in their search for safety, they have squandered their lives and will never be able to make up for lost time. The therapist's task is to reacquaint the patient with the self they had no choice but to withdraw from and to facilitate the patient's capacity to empathize with themselves. Now that they are able to see that all they did to survive, which felt like death, was, in fact, a waystation to survival, giving them breathing space between where they were and where they are now. While working with the patient to develop a perspective on what has happened, the therapist must simultaneously confirm both the reality of the patient's loss, including an appreciation for the context in which it arose, as well as their need to mourn the loss. Because the patient fears their sorrow will overwhelm them, mourning for what could have been will arouse the temptation to reinstate withdrawal. Here the therapist can intervene with containment. To do so effectively, the therapist must first trust that their intervention will be temporary and that the patient will again take over on their own.

The cycle of doubt, questioning, tentative acceptance, and eventual wonderment about what has transpired must be returned to again and again. Asking "How did this happen to me?" requires the patient to first acknowledge that *something has happened*. Repetition and working through (Freud, 1912/1978) is central to the therapeutic process. Though the cycle may need revisiting again and again, the intervals will become longer between setbacks, and both therapist and patient will be quicker to recognize when there's trouble ahead. They've already been through a lot together, and the patient survived without withdrawing, "going dead," or shutting down.

## Summary

This chapter has examined the challenges of working with patients experiencing psychosis who exhibit negative symptoms. These patients present as unreachable due to a protective wall they've constructed to prevent them from being affected by the world and to allow them to avoid painful affects they fear are overwhelming and dangerous. The goal is safety and survival, even if it comes at the cost of living in a deadened state. We have explicated a process by which the therapist first struggles to feel effective and distances themselves from the numbness in the patient. Alternatively, by offering holding and containment and staying the course, the therapist can reach an empathic understanding, but only after relinquishing their wish to heal. This relinquishment requires a corresponding withdrawal from the therapeutic self, which in some way mirrors the patient's withdrawal. The patient, feeling understood and safe from intrusion, ultimately dares to relinquish retreat in favor of investment, a reinvestment in themselves and their world. Both patient and therapist have survived deadness and disconnection. The chapter that follows presents a detailed case of a patient who presented with extreme negative symptoms.

# Chapter 8

# Alone in a Crowded Mind

## When Psychosis Masks Loneliness

The charcoal drawing of the whitened face of Marcel Marceau, the great French mime, greeted clients at my office entrance. One analysand, Amy, very fond of Marceau, avoided eye contact with me (DK), though she never failed to nod hello to the expressively sad face of the mime, who held out his white-gloved hand in supplication. They were two of a kind, she told me; they understood each other implicitly. Following the exchange with Marcel Marceau, she sat down and began speaking. Before leaving, she would again bid the mime goodbye.

One day, appearing troubled, Amy paused before the drawing, and flatly announced, "Marcel Marceau is dead!"

"Oh," I said surprised, feeling sad. I knew Marcel Marceau was old, but I hadn't yet read the newspaper or heard of his demise.

Toward the middle of the session, I noticed something unusual taking place. Amy repeatedly shifted her head from side to side—as if she were watching an imaginary tennis match. I asked her what was going on.

"You don't see him?" she asked incredulously.

"No," I replied. "Can you tell me what you see?"

"There's a homeless man in your office," she said, still in disbelief that I was unable to perceive him. "He's mute," she added. I quietly noted the connection between her hallucination and the silent art of the allegedly deceased mime, Marcel Marceau.

"Can you describe him to me?" I asked.

"He's ragged, thin, hungry," she offered.

I asked her why she had been moving her head from side to side.

She told me that the mute was scurrying back and forth, running to hide in the corner and then, ever-so-slowly, approaching me. She demonstrated how the mute stretched his hand out to me, nearly touching

DOI: 10.4324/9781003441519-8

my leg— the gesture uncannily identical to the one in the drawing of Marceau.

After I finished work and had time to check the news, I discovered that Marcel Marceau was alive and well. Amy had evidently killed him off and created a mute homeless man to take his place. For the next three months, Amy and I shared our sessions with the mute. I could not see the homeless man and, therefore, relied on Amy to be my eyes. Each of us needed the other to perform the therapeutic dance. She rendered him visible to me, and I, through my understanding of his function, converted his muteness into words. "He seems lonely," I said. "He seeks connection." I was blind; she was mute. She allowed me to see, and I allowed her to symbolize. We both engaged with her hallucination, I as a co-participant.

Amy, a middle-aged woman, lived alone. Her sessions with me comprised the primary human interaction in her day. She told me she saw (hallucinated) rats on the way to see me five days per week, demonstrating her courage to overcome psychotic obstacles and engage in challenging psychological work. She had difficulty knowing her emotions and telling me what she felt. Her creation of the homeless mute served multiple functions. He helped us both understand her loneliness and fear and expressed her hunger for human contact and nourishment better than her words ever could. The mute also assured her of company; she could feel less alone. He additionally stood in for the mute unconscious and was a hallucinated figure of the other. The homeless mute man was the ghost of Marcel Marceau, something dead in her yet whose spirit might be brought back to life. Finally, the mute tested my capacity to care for her and keep alive a desperate, neglected, and emotionally famished human being.

Loneliness, a universal human experience, wrought by a significant gap between one's actual social relations and desired social relations, is, for many, the most painful mental state imaginable (Cacioppo and Patrick, 2008), one that is subjectively felt as a kind of fraught emptiness often accompanied by fear, anxiety, or even panic. Loneliness is different from solitude, the condition of being alone; loneliness is the felt pain of one's isolation from others and/or the subjective, emotional, and cognitive evaluation of one's social position. One can feel lonely, unseen, and unknown when surrounded by people or fulfilled and complete when physically alone (Knafo, 2012). While solitude can inspire creativity (Knafo, 2012a, 2012b, 2013), the impact of loneliness is largely negative and can result in a compromised immune system, reduced quality of life, anger, depression, early death, and even madness and violence (Cacioppo and Patrick, 2008).

Patients diagnosed with psychosis are up to six times more likely to report having felt lonely in their lives than people without psychosis (Kimhy et al., 2006; Meltzer et al., 2013), with the majority (80%) reporting that they had felt lonely in the past 12 months (Badcock et al., 2015): a staggering 74.75% of people with delusional disorders and 93.8% of those with depressive psychosis suffer from loneliness. Rates are significantly higher than those in the general population—around 35% (Badcock et al., 2015). These statistics surface many questions. Do some people experience psychosis because they are lonely, or does their psychosis isolate them and lead to loneliness? Clearly, psychosis and loneliness are entwined. The disposition and personal history of those suffering from psychosis predisposes them to not feel understood, known, or seen. At the same time, they are already isolated, and such isolation can bring about and deepen psychosis.

This chapter discusses the relationship between loneliness and psychosis and how the former affects the latter and can even trigger psychosis in some individuals. We examine some strategies individuals with psychosis use to cope with loneliness; in particular, we look closely at paranoid delusions and hallucinations as defensive coping mechanisms against loneliness and how loneliness plays a role in the psychosis of people with negative symptoms. We also argue that hospitalization and the use of medication can further isolate a person, increasing feelings of loneliness and stigma. We discuss how therapists who are treating psychosis experience a particular kind of loneliness in the countertransference. Finally, we present DK's detailed case study demonstrating her work with a very isolated patient.

The world of the person with psychosis is singular, solipsistic, and difficult to share (except in therapy, and even then, it is mostly shared indirectly). The psychotic world is a lonely world, yet, we have observed that psychosis is often a communication from the depth of a person's radical aloneness, unconsciously fashioned to hold clues to the person's recovery. Despite the prevailing view that psychosis is an asocial retreat from reality and relationships, we maintain that, in most cases, there exists in the patient a hidden desire for relatedness. The psychotic state itself, as manifested in its symptoms, contains a deep cry for connection and understanding. Too much aloneness can already be a form of madness because people need others to reinforce and uphold what the collective calls reality. *Human reality is inherently relational* because human beings are social animals. The innate relatedness of the mind demands others as an anchor for one's individual reality. Each person learns reality at their caretaker's knee and through their nonverbal and verbal communication. We all come to know ourselves and the world through each other. The psychotic break is a rupture of the link between oneself and others that sustains a vision of reality the collective calls "normal." Extreme loneliness creates a state of isolation and disconnection, often triggering psychosis, and psychosis further guarantees isolation in a negative feedback loop.

## Psychoanalytic Literature on Loneliness and Psychosis

There is a dearth of psychoanalytic literature on loneliness and even less on its relationship to psychosis. In "The Neuro-Psychoses of Defence" (1894/1962), Freud described the case of a woman suffering from unrequited love. Unable to tolerate her lover's rejection and her feelings of abandonment and loneliness, she entered a hallucinatory state in which her lover arrives and speaks to her in a "dream state," in which she lives happily for two months. Though Freud used this case to illuminate the concept of repudiation or foreclosure (*Verwerfung*), it can also be read as a psychotic defense against loneliness. Later, in his analysis of Schreber's memoir (1911/1958), Freud explained how the patient's psychotic symptoms were his way of trying to reconnect with the relational world. Freud understood early on that Schreber's delusion of a deadly world catastrophe, a common experience in psychosis, expressed profound loneliness. One is always alone in one's catastrophes. But what is truly catastrophic in psychosis is the nature of that loneliness—*loneliness for reality itself,* particularly for the safety of reality in its coherence, meaning, and connection.

Erich Fromm wrote in 1941 that: "To feel completely alone and isolated leads to mental disintegration just as physical starvation leads to death" (p. 19). Harry Stack Sullivan (1953), with his emphasis on interpersonal relations, believed that loneliness is the most painful of human experiences, more painful even than anxiety. He pointed out the different forms of contact humans require at various stages in their development: infants need physical contact, tenderness, and protective care; children need adult participation in activities; preadolescents need acceptance from peers; and adolescents need intimate exchange, friendship, and love. Failure to receive these forms of human exchange can lead to loneliness and derail the development of personality. For this reason, Sullivan encouraged active engagement between patients and aides at Sheppard-Pratt Hospital where he worked, which was the origin of milieu therapy (Blechner, 1995).

Frieda Fromm- Reichmann (1959) was one of the first to explicitly note a connection between loneliness and psychosis. In her final paper, published posthumously, she wrote: "I offer the suggestion that the experiences in adults usually described as a loss of reality or a sense of world catastrophe can also be understood as expressions of profound loneliness" (p. 5). She believed that lack of attention and acceptance from significant adults during infancy and childhood result in later loneliness and yearning for interpersonal closeness that can take the form of psychosis. Based on our experiences with patients diagnosed with psychosis, we believe such an environmental deficit weakens reality formation and increases the probability of a psychosis arising, following a catastrophe experienced by a person later in life. As reality itself is installed via embodiment—the lived repetition of actions, thoughts, words, relations, and meaning from infancy onward—the installation will be more firmly grounded in some people than in others, depending on constitutional and environmental factors. A supportive environment establishes a strong sense of reality—one's own and the world's. Whenever the self slips away, the world slips away with it.

Melanie Klein (1963) believed loneliness to be the basis of paranoid and depressive anxieties, derivatives of the infant's psychotic anxieties. She believed that everyone possesses these anxieties, but they are more pronounced in depressives and schizophrenics. According to Klein, schizophrenics feel little or no sense of belonging to another person or group and have split-off parts of the self that are projected into others. This fragmentation ensures that "One is not in full possession of one's self ... one does not fully belong to oneself or, therefore, to anybody else. The lost parts, too, are felt to be lonely" (p. 302). Unable to internalize the good mother or secure a stable foundation for social connection, the schizophrenic, according to Klein, "is left alone...with his misery" (p. 303). With psychic fragmentation, it becomes difficult to distinguish between good and bad objects and between internal and external reality. Paranoid distrust emerges, resulting in social withdrawal and more profound loneliness. The predisposition to psychosis, however slight, may bring about behavior that increases isolation and may crack the psychic fault line, leading to full-blown psychosis, which gives rise to even further isolation in a vicious cycle. This is no surprise since we now know that people who have never experienced psychosis often develop "reactive prison psychosis" during prolonged solitary confinement (Grassian, 2006). Such people display "florid psychotic delirium, characterized by severe confusional, paranoid, and hallucinatory features," and "intense agitation and paranoia (p. 328)."

Even though Winnicott (1965) viewed the "capacity to be alone" as a developmental milestone, he defined psychosis as an "environmental deficiency disease" (pp. 135-136). Harold Searles (1965) thought that people with psychosis repress both dependency needs and feelings of loneliness. Undoing the repression of the former, he found, revealed the chilling presence of the latter, along with the knowledge of the shortness of life and the perennial feeling of separateness from other people. Searles said:

> Probably there is no greater threat to the schizophrenic than the repressed knowledge of his aloneness, the realization that he, who yearns so strongly for oneness with another person, not only has the same inevitable aloneness as every human being, but in addition is even more completely cut off from his fellow human beings by reason of his isolation within his schizophrenic illness. (p. 123)

## Loneliness and the Onset of Psychosis

DK treated a middle-aged man, Cornelius, who had been married for 25 years before his wife abandoned him. Because the couple worked together, his means of support and social network quickly evaporated after the breakup. As he scrambled to survive his losses, he confessed that his "harrowing, bone-aching loneliness" was driving him insane. He said he had to continually check to make sure his wallet and keys were where he had left them because he was possessed by the absurd idea that they might disappear. Several times during his sleepless nights he approached the window to make sure his car was out in front because he was certain someone would steal it. Every stranger seemed threatening to him, and he heard strange noises every night, unsure whether they were coming from within himself or the world around him.

Eventually, on the verge of suicide and about to hang himself from a hook he'd fastened to the ceiling, a spider building a web nearby "spoke" to him, convincing him not to go through with it. Cornelius had had no previous psychiatric history nor did his parents or grandparents. Since Cornelius was a writer, DK encouraged him to journal as one way of coping with his suffering.

Here is one of his telling entries:

> When I roll up in front of the shanty where I now live, the driveway is empty and the streets eerily quiet. No one waits for me to return. No one calls to ask when I will be coming home. I will climb a set of foreign stairs and enter a strange apartment. It will be empty. There will be no dinner, no wife, no daughter, no one making small talk about the day. There will be no friends with whom I can raise a glass or share a laugh. Roxanne will *not* sit next to me on the couch. She will *not* hold me in her arms anymore. She will *never* again look at me and smile just because I am the one she is looking at. We will offer each other *no* further comfort.

> When the sun finally sets on this day that takes so long to end, I will still be alone, facing an even longer darkness. The black night will become a desert and my desire to sleep a narrow tunnel, dimly illuminated by the flashing phosphorescence of unbearable thoughts. Choking on my solitude, I will crawl my way toward another bleak and lonely dawn. I will lie awake in my bed most of the night, astonished at how much pain it is possible to feel. When, craving oblivion, I will finally doze for a few minutes, yet even sleep will be torturous, periodically jerking me awake in terror, and I will reach for her, and she will *not* be there. Each time I awake with a gasp, I find that, yes, it's true, *her absence is real.* I will face this unbelievable reality and whimper in the darkness like a mortally injured wolf. What will keep me company during this time is the very thing that will make my solitude especially unbearable: the shame and humiliation of a loss I do not comprehend.

Not surprisingly, initial psychotic episodes usually occur in late adolescence through early adulthood, when young people first experience the separation and loss of loved ones, finding themselves alone and on their own for the first time. During this time, a young person's "reality" is undergoing major revisions. A 2018 study conducted in the Netherlands (el Bouhaddani et al.) found that social exclusion during adolescence is closely related to psychotic experiences. Identities are not yet fully formed, and external pressures to perform in school, at work, or in new social groups can feel like too much to bear. The loss of people and function leave the person feeling alone and lonely—susceptible to regression, dissociation, and fragmentation. When one is constitutionally vulnerable and/or has a traumatic history, the possibility of a psychotic break becomes more likely. Cacioppo and Patrick (2008), known for their research on loneliness, found that "people misuse their powers of cognition in their attempts to self-regulate the pain of feeling like an outsider" (p. 77). In other words, people distort reality and delude themselves to assuage the angst of isolation. This misuse can take extreme forms in the cases of those most vulnerable and wounded.

## Conventional Treatment of Psychosis and Loneliness

That psychosis results in further loneliness is patently obvious. People diagnosed with psychosis are hospitalized and medicated, placed in seclusion rooms, and separated from their loved ones and families, all of which puts them in further exile from themselves. Many have complained that antipsychotic medication makes them feel like zombies, dead inside. Furthermore, the stigma of psychosis and hospitalization is internalized (Switaj et al., 2014), and the patient feels shame and further withdraws. Although hospitalization may be needed at times, such treatment erodes individuality and autonomy and, because patients are frequently treated like children, encourages regression (Knafo and Selzer, 2017). As they become part of "the system." Chronic patients often develop additional symptoms to allay loneliness. The more one undergoes inpatient hospitalizations, the more loneliness one suffers (Chrostek et al., 2016). On the flip side of this coin, some patients stop taking their medication or find another reason to be re-hospitalized because the hospital is the only place where they find people who talk to them and take an interest in them. The hospital offers some semblance of safety and coherence and serves as a manageable reality for the psychotically exiled.

Pesach Lichtenberg, developer of Soteria House (SH) in Israel, an alternative to acute institutional care, told DK that SH employs "companions" to accompany the residents during their time of crisis to relieve the loneliness problem (personal communication, October 20, 2022). A new social movement has emerged in the early 2000s in a Japanese fishing town, Urakawa, in southern Hokkaido, *Tojisha-kenkyu* addresses the absence of the collective in the experience of serious mental illness. (Ayaya and Kitanaka, 2023). Self-reflection is encouraged, and, importantly, shared with the community, thus advocating a place in society. Like the 12-step approach to addictions, the creation of a safe environment and community support are central.

## Psychotic Symptoms as a Way of Coping with Loneliness

Bereft of social relationships, one can become maddened by loneliness and use psychotic symptoms to both express self–world exile and attempt to cope with it. Amy created a mute homeless man to convey her sense of loneliness to DK and also to provide herself with some companionship. Searles (1965) described a woman who hallucinated bugs and turned them into people to have some company. In Chapter 6, we presented the case of a woman who hallucinated 17 children as a desperate tactic to care for her abandoned child self while providing herself with a family.

The number of people experiencing psychosis who complain about loneliness contradicts the hypothesis that individuals with psychosis are alone because they retreat from reality, preferring their inner world. Like Mentzos (1993), who argued that psychotic symptoms possess object-seeking functions—in particular, in their attempt to balance the conflict between object needs and self-safety—we, too, consider psychotic symptoms as ways of coping with loneliness in their attempts to establish ties to the object world. This understanding informs our interventions and treatment in general. Paranoia, for example, seems to be a natural consequence of extended isolation. Cacioppo and Patrick (2008) claimed that because we are social beings who require support and resources from each other, aloneness can feel threatening: "Feelings of isolation and perceptions of threat reinforce each other to promote a higher and more persistent level of wariness" (p. 31). That sense of threat and wariness can evolve into full-blown paranoia. *If no one is with me, everyone must be against me.*

DK treated Richard, a paranoid man who had developed an intricate delusional system. He was convinced that he was being targeted as a serial killer. Signs everywhere pointed to this accusation: television, radio, and even strangers in the grocery store. While growing up, Richard's mother had been a highly anxious parent, never permitting young Richard to leave home alone; someone was always watching him. This anxiety literally followed him into adulthood and fed the obsession that others maintained a constant interest in his whereabouts and activities. His mind recreated a world that mimicked his childhood, in that he was never alone. Lee (2006) wrote that a delusion is a narrative, an "encrypted blueprint of an earlier relational trauma" (p. 44). This description fits precisely: Richard's hovering and obsessed mother was duplicated in a crowd of imaginary snoopers who were convinced he was a serial killer.

Sullivan (1956) believed that paranoia emerged from a need for intimacy coupled with the conviction that one is incapable and undeserving of that intimacy. He wrote in a paranoid's voice: "I want to be close to this person for a feeling of warmth which I need because I'm lonely; but if I move toward him, he will regard me as inferior and unworthy and will deny me this warmth because he won't warm to so inferior a person" (p. 160). Likewise, Josh (see Chapter 10) explained to me how, for him, paranoia and psychotic delusions functioned in partnership. Whereas his delusions cut him off from the world, paranoia kept him (distortedly) attached to it. The paranoia kept people at an optimal distance: "If I let people get too close, I fear they will find out I am really a nobody and will abandon me, which is my worst nightmare. But if I keep them too much at a distance, I lose them and am still abandoned" (Knafo, 2016). Josh nicely illustrates the compromise between remaining somewhat anchored in the world but not so much as to become overwhelmed by it. In some cases, severe OCD can also be understood as a form of paranoia. Patients who fear being contaminated or contaminating others maintain constant negative internal dialogue with the figures of other people—a sad antidote to loneliness.

Auchincloss and Weiss (1992) considered paranoid delusions to be desperate fantasies magically connecting their bearer to others, thereby undoing object inconstancy and perceived indifference to the object world. Simply put, we feel connected to others if we imagine they possess some of the same thoughts we do, or, at the very least, that they are thinking of us. One patient said, "If people don't get inside each other's heads, how do they relate to one another?" (Auchincloss and Weiss, 1992, p. 1014). The person exhibiting paranoia is split between total indifference and complete relatedness— needing connectedness and therefore projecting delusions onto others. Projection functions not merely to externalize unwanted wishes but to keep the other close, even merged (Schafer, 1968), albeit as part of one's delusional system. Fairbairn's (1952) suggestion that a bad object is better than no object is relevant here. To this, we add that a bad reality is better than nearly none at all. In the delusions of psychotic minds, we find furious psychic power at work in the creation of a reality that is masked by the shared reality of common folk. As brain damage sheds light on features of the neurotypical brain through comparison, so too does psychosis shed light on "being normal." As Cornelius put it, "Sanity is not about being some way. It's not about being normal. It is about holding your own in the struggle not to go mad."

Understanding the object needs of paranoia can guide the therapist's intervention by focusing that understanding on the paranoid person's adaptive solutions to their conflict. The therapist can point out to such patients that they are not only trying to get rid of something; they are trying to *get* something—object connection—through indirect means. Untethered to reality, these magical fantasies, if left alone, ultimately backfire, leaving the paranoid person vulnerable to invasion and exploitation or, worse, delusions that the world is coming to an end, which really means that the person's object world is ending. One patient told DK, "It's lonely because others cannot even imagine the pain of feeling I caused the end of the world!"

Psychotic symptoms as substitutes for object relations are further evident in visual and auditory hallucinations. Not all persons who experience psychosis hear voices, but those who do usually hear more than one. And not all such voices are negatively experienced, nor do their bearers necessarily wish to rid themselves of such strange company. Narimanidze's (2015) qualitative study on the relational aspect of hearing voices revealed that many of her participants preferred to keep their voices. This finding may seem surprising since much of the literature on auditory hallucinations connects them to overwhelming, negative, or frightening content (Birchwood et al., 2000). Even violence and suicide attempts are often considered responses to auditory hallucinations (Falloon and Talbot, 1981). Yet there are people who hear voices that do not disrupt their lives nor lead to acts of violence (Romme and Escher, 1989). Eigen (1986) aptly noted:

> In hallucinations, the object-world comes back in flagrantly distorted ways, but it does return …[The] hallucinatory object-world can tell the story of past wounds and wishes. In them may be read the remnants of a broken history, and at the same time, they represent partial, at times

total, fulfillment of the subject's deepest longings. Wounded wishes find a home in hallucinations. (p. 47)

Eighty percent of participants in a study of 100 individuals diagnosed with serious mental illness reported that being alone had exacerbated their voices (Nayani and David, 1996), and a significant number of Narimadnize's (2015) subjects dated the onset of their voices to a particularly desolate time in their lives. They described going through phases of isolation and loneliness or feeling the need to escape harsh realities, just prior to the onset of auditory hallucinations. Some voices became attached to imaginary companions. One participant said: "I started having imaginary friends because…until nine years old, I wasn't very sociable…I realized from a young age that I had an ability to create something to drown out whatever dysfunction was going on around me" (Narimadnize, 2015, p. 65). Another participant located the beginning of his voices at age seven: "I'm usually the one by myself most of the time...I hear these voices in my head. When I was a kid, I thought it was normal" (p. 65). Another participant said his voices were due to "being alone too much, pushing myself away from other people, not being in contact with friends, family" (p. 65). Still, another questioned if his voices responded to a lack: "I don't really have that many adults to talk to…I work with children…but I don't know if that's why I have conversations in my head" (p. 66).

All participants reported an intimate relationship with their voices. "I feel like they know what I've been through," (Narimanidze, 2015, p. 45) said one without a trace of irony. Some engaged with their voices to cheer themselves up, seeking them out as companions during long stretches of being alone, for example, while at work or on the road. Another heard a voice that sounded like his deceased mother, including "conversations we used to have just before her death…I feel like it probably gives her some closure that I'm still her son and that I still listen to her, [am] there for her, still supportive" (p. 64). From keeping one company to providing refuge from a hostile, fragmented reality, voices can, for some, provide a kind of self-care that they are unable to obtain otherwise. If antipsychotic medication costs the psychotic person their "social life," no wonder so many stop taking their meds. As one participant poignantly noted, "If the voices would stop, I would always kinda be alone…like something was missing…sometimes when I haven't heard my grandmother in weeks or whatever, I feel a little funny…like I haven't had anybody to talk to…I tend to be like…What's going on? Maybe the medication is working too well (Narimanidze, 2015, p. 92)."

Clearly, hearing voices is not always a positive or comforting experience. Yet, as opposed to the medical approach, which treats the condition with drugs, the Hearing Voices Movement is a peer-led organization that helps voice hearers live comfortably with their voices rather than eliminate them (Hearing Voices Network, 2019). Indeed, research conducted by Romme and Escher (1989, 1993) and Craig et al. (2018) indicates that engaging with one's voices can ameliorate the distress experienced by voice-hearers. Interestingly, some with psychosis are now being successfully treated by interacting with avatars created from their own hallucinations (Craig et al., 2018).

Most of Narimadnize's (2015) participants kept their voices private due to fear of being ostracized or deemed incompetent (and thus forbidden to care for children or perform at work). This secrecy can have the effect of exacerbating the isolation that may have precipitated the onset of the voices in the first place. Even in hearing friendly voices, the person with psychosis is still on the inside looking out, suffering a special kind of isolation, what one of DK's patients called the "loneliness of being crazy."

In this chapter, we have been discussing the connection between positive symptoms of psychosis and loneliness. When someone experiences the negative symptoms of psychosis—symptoms that produce blunted affect, anhedonia, social withdrawal, poverty of speech and thought, and low attention and motivation—loneliness and its effects can be even more acutely felt. What follows is DK's description of her treatment of an exceptionally reclusive young Japanese American man who could not endure being around others. The case reflects the existential and psychological difficulty embodied in flight from a historical rupture that was not processed or symbolized. The case narration shows how the levels of concealment embodied in a defensive solitude provides hints and clues to the patient's liberation.

## Hikikomori: Loneliness and Negative Symptoms

Hisoka, a reclusive Japanese American male, first sought therapy with me 19 years ago after his therapist left the clinic he was attending. At the time, he was 19 and never ventured out of his home except for therapy sessions. Even when home, he hardly left his room. He was a true *hikikomori*, the Japanese term that literally means "pulling away or being confined." Although the term *hikikomori* came into the literature to describe a culture-bound syndrome, there is now wider recognition that this syndrome exists in the United States and elsewhere (Conti, 2019). Often *hikikomori* begin by refusing to go to school, which leads to complete withdrawal from social life and extreme degrees of isolation and confinement. (The term *hikikomori* refers to both the sociological phenomenon as well as to people belonging to this societal group.)

When he first came to see me, I noticed that Hisoka was extremely thin and had a stiff, affectless demeanor. Though obviously shy, his enormous eyes met mine and stayed there. We both felt uncomfortable. Hisoka sat opposite me without saying a word, waiting for me to initiate a topic. He looked at me without blinking, resembling an aloof Buddha, leaving me clueless about what he might be thinking or feeling. He responded to my questions with one or two-word answers.

After sitting silently for 20 minutes, he said, "I'm nowhere" to explain what brought him to see me. "I have no goals, no future, no motivation," he added ten minutes later. He felt "empty and helpless," was tired a lot, and slept 10-12 hours a day and stayed up at night. His social withdrawal began in high school and increased to the point to which he felt depressed and suicidal. He had been hospitalized twice for suicidal risk after which his isolation became complete. He needed to be homeschooled to obtain his high school diploma.

Trying to find out more about him, I asked him about his relationship with his family, to which he responded with one word: "detached." His mother had been quick to tell me that she believed Hisoka's problems stemmed from the fact that he had been adopted at nearly two years of age.

Hisoka disagreed, adding that he thought adoption was "no big deal" and had had no influence on him; he was a strong believer in nurture over nature. He fought with his Italian American adoptive parents when he was in fourth grade because they wanted him to attend Catholic services and Sunday school. He won this battle but also felt he'd lost something—he felt himself floating at sea with no meaning or destination.

I proposed that perhaps he and I could make that our therapeutic goal, to make meaning of his life and give it direction. He nodded in agreement.

Treatment proceeded in this manner: Hisoka and I stared at each other, week after week, month after month, with him occasionally offering one-word answers to my questions. Exasperated with this routine, one day I finally asked him if he remembered his dreams.

Surprisingly, he said he dreamt daily. I was thrilled with the opening. He recounted the dream he had the previous night in which he was lost and not able to find his way home. His sister was in the dream, but he clarified that she was not really his sister. After he recounted the dream, he adamantly insisted that he did not believe dreams had meaning. I did not argue with him but offered that the dream he brought me was not so far-fetched given what he had told me about himself. Here he was looking for a home (perhaps therapy?) because he was with a family that wasn't really his family (referring to his adoption). He smirked in what appeared to be agreement.

Very slowly, Hisoka began sharing his inner world with me. He loved anime and horror films and novels. He knew about serial killers, stating that he liked "gore with relevance." I thought he liked being scared because it helped him to feel. I also thought he was entirely cut off from his anger. He spoke about art and books, theories, research, and ideas. He could engage in high-level intellectual and philosophical discussions, and he argued his points beautifully. We discussed religion, animal rights, libertarianism, gender differences, cinema, and more. He skillfully employed intellectual defenses, and I gradually pointed out that he stayed away from personal and emotional topics. He agreed but added that he really didn't know how to speak about noncognitive matters.

Once I mentioned that it seemed much easier for him to speak about animals than humans, to which he replied, "Dogs don't ask me personal questions."

The sessions with Hisoka gradually became less tense, and he began to initiate conversation now and then. He shared his love of music and even sang his favorite "bittersweet" songs for me in session. As I became a person to him, he confessed that he Googled me and even found some of my family members. He discovered that I was French Moroccan.

I asked him what he thought of that, and he replied with a straight face, "I don't like Moroccans."

I was shocked until I realized he was joking. I began to understand the extent of Hisoka's social awkwardness and how little he understood about how he affected people. I realized we'd need to practice a lot of interacting in session and that I would have to bring more of myself into the sessions with him to accomplish the goal of improving his social skills. I told him he had hurt my feelings and explained why. He was puzzled, but gradually, as more of these situations took place, he began taking me into consideration, recognizing that I had a separate subjectivity.

Once he saw me with my son and asked me, "Who's that kid?" immediately answering his own question with, "It's not your kid. Perhaps it's a neighbor's child. Perhaps you molested him. Perhaps he's not a child at all but an adult with a disease."

These fantasies clearly represented Hisoka's fear and aggression triggered by seeing a potential rival. I was becoming increasingly important to him. Eventually, he reluctantly accepted the fact that I had a child, though he projected a lot of himself onto him ("Maybe you switched babies at birth"), and he sometimes asked me about my son. After a while, he wished to give me a cat so that my son could have a pet. Hisoka confessed that he believed no one had ever "got him." He seemed surprised when I said that I would like to. In one session, Hisoka told me he didn't want to share, and he didn't want to begin. But then he began talking about animals. He liked dogs, he said because they are interactive. We discussed whether we were cat or dog people.

Since he seemed disappointed that we were both cat people, I said, "Perhaps you wish I were more like a dog."

Though he nodded silently, I thought he found relief in the thought that I could understand his feline ways.

Hisoka sometimes missed sessions and never called to cancel. Afterward, we always explored what might be going on for him. At times, it seemed he felt too close to me and needed to create distance. At other times, he was depressed and even suicidal and couldn't bring himself to move. He always felt bad, as he knew I was waiting for him.

"When you are ready," I said, "I'd like you to try to come in when you are feeling down so I can see what it's like." It took nearly two years of treatment for Hisoka to share his dark moods with me in person, although by then they had become less frequent. I tried to help Hisoka see his dilemma: he wanted closeness yet feared getting hurt. He admitted that the fear was stronger than his desire.

We spoke of taking small steps toward changing his life. His greatest goal was to go back to school and finish his college degree. He had tried twice but dropped out soon afterward. I knew he'd need to be able to join the rest of the world by sleeping at night and staying awake during the day. After he had this schedule down, I had him take the family dog for a walk several times per week to develop discipline and the ability to adhere to a schedule. Besides these changes, there was not much alteration in his external life from session to session, so he thought he had nothing to say. I taught him to free associate at these times, and he did so quite successfully. He also brought dreams, though he said he still believed they were meaningless. He shared a "vampire dream" to which he associated, "You have to feed on people to survive." Yet he still denied his own dependency. Despite the fact that Hisoka was clearly getting closer to me, he did not seem to know it.

When I returned from a three-week summer vacation and asked him how it was for him to not see me, he said, "Nothing. Sorry." After a while, he said, "I either felt nothing or I am not aware that I felt anything."

I pointed out that there could be a world of difference between those two.

Soon afterward, he said he thought I wouldn't care if he stopped coming to therapy because I had many other patients. He admitted that he felt I was more important to him than he was to me because he had only one psychologist while I had many patients. He stated that he didn't want to have to think of others' feelings. For the first time, we spoke of how he could use me and our relationship to become more comfortable relating to others. He began asking me about relationships.

"What does it mean to be attached to someone?" he wondered out loud. "Is attachment to one person the same as to another?" Hisoka began weighing the pros and cons of attachment versus solitude.

I empathized with how difficult it was for him to move out of his isolated space. As someone who was exceedingly shy as a child, I understood Hisoka's defensive retreat and knew I had to avoid saying or doing anything that he might experience as impinging. I needed to make the world safe enough for Hisoka to emerge from his hiding place.

Eventually, Hisoka signed up for an online college course: Dog Psychology, but he fell behind and dropped out of the course. I learned about this attempt afterward. I didn't let him give up, and we decided he'd try again, but we'd make his class part of our sessions to explore his difficulties when they arose. His next course was Introduction to Psychology, and he aced it. The following semester, he took two courses and excelled in both. Hisoka's confidence grew, and he began to discern a future for the first time in years. Yet at times, he sank into a depression because he thought he was progressing too slowly, and he didn't feel his accomplishments were sufficient.

One day Hisoka shared a story he wrote about a prisoner who was tortured and placed in solitary confinement. We never found out what crime he had committed nor whether he had been wrongfully imprisoned. When we spoke about his story, we discussed the things that help one survive under such conditions. We spoke of the writings of concentration camp survivors, Victor Frankl and Elie Weisel. We discussed *The Diving Bell and the Butterfly* (1998), a heroic and poignant account by French journalist Jean-Dominique Bauby, describing his cataclysmic life after suffering a massive stroke that left him with a rare and horrific condition called Locked-In Syndrome. In essence, we spoke about enriching Hisoka's inner life to help him withstand suffering.

We had an unusual session in which Hisoka expressed his feelings for me and his desire to know more about my feelings for him. He asked me if I liked him.

When I said I did, he asked me to distinguish between caring and liking. He clearly had trouble believing I liked him. I said I liked him because he's a character and I like characters. I said I liked his purity of thought and that I liked him more as he opened up more.

He said he liked me too because I value honesty and keep my word.

I said I liked working with him even though I found it challenging.

Hisoka began to think more psychologically, admitting that one could be influenced by unconscious forces. Once he said, "When a dog has a bad experience with a garden hose, it remembers the emotion but not the actual event. And it reacts every time it's exposed to a garden hose." Indeed, he asked if I would feel bad if I had to get rid of a dog I adopted. We traced this question to his feelings about having been adopted—gotten rid of. It took us two years before he was able to explore the topic of his adoption, mirroring the two years he lived before he was adopted by a couple in the US. I raised the concept of reconstruction, and that piqued his curiosity.

Could we piece together his early life even though he remembered nothing?

He was skeptical but willing to give it a try.

We each did our homework. I researched adoptions from his native country, and he brought in early photos and adoption documents given to him by his parents. We closely examined the photos and observed a plump, well-cared-for infant. We read the documents that told us he had been with his birth mother for approximately a year and a half. We pronounced his original name out loud. We surmised that the father had left the mother and she didn't want to, or could not, be a single mother and thus put him up for adoption.

"Maybe she was arrested and went to jail?" he proposed.

I said, "You turn her into a criminal because you feel she behaved criminally toward you."

He then lived with a foster mother to whom he became attached until arriving in the US. We spoke about his good fortune to have had a long early attachment with his Japanese mother who clearly wanted him, and he had a loving Italian American mother who raised him. We also spoke about the misfortune of having had two maternal attachments and one paternal attachment brutally severed. We spoke of how difficult it might be for him to open himself up to becoming attached after that. Although he criticized our reconstruction for not being an exact science, he seemed to accept what we came up with as a "reasonable narrative" of his early life.

In truth, what more could we expect? The losses he suffered occurred so early in his life that they could not be processed as something that had happened to him or symbolized as such. Nonetheless, they were radical losses that shaped him at the most primary level, disrupting the process of secure attachment and the sense of being loved and wanted. His losses imbued him with a pall of lifelessness and meaninglessness that had left him adrift in a dead world devoid of hope. When he first came to me, he could not even realize the barest sense of his place in a longstanding and loving family. He lived in exile from his very own life. Reconstruction was the best we could do.

One day Hisoka asked me if there is a critical time for things to take place and, if they don't, could they occur with effectiveness later. We related his question to the attachment rupture of his early childhood. Is it possible for such a catastrophe to be repaired? Soon he compared his situation to Helen Keller's life, mentioning that she was taught to communicate despite having lived as an isolate due to being blind and deaf.

I asked whether he was questioning whether I could teach him the language of emotions, as Ann Sullivan had taught Helen Keller the language of expression, and I brought him Helen Keller's autobiography in the next session.

He read it overnight but was disappointed because he "wanted more about the miracle of transformation." Nonetheless, after this discussion, Hisoka asked me if he could move his chair closer to mine. He did and then associated to cannibalism, revealing how terrifying his dependency needs were. "What would you do for someone you love?" he both questioned and answered, "Hold your breath till you faint? Not blink? Not eat them up!" Later, he asked me, "How do you separate yourself from your patients? I couldn't do that." He began to say that his need for people, though still slight, was increasing: "After a week of solitude, I get bored." His entry into social life began with online video games that demanded more personal interaction and communication.

When discussing the merits of graphology one day, Hisoka and I compared handwriting. He only printed, stating, "If I were to write in script, it would change everything because the letters would depend on what comes before and after." I connected what he said to his relating style of keeping large spaces between him and others as well as to the break between his early past and what followed. His trauma destroyed a sense of continuity and connection. I repeatedly showed him how he minimized the effect others had on him as well as how he used defensiveness to minimize his dependency needs.

After a difficult session in which I had become overly impatient with his oppositionalism, Hisoka arrived for the next session and told me the previous encounter had depressed him.

I was taken aback because that was the first time he had let me know I could hurt him. I told him that, although I was sorry that he felt sad, I was pleased that he could express his feelings rather than miss a session as he'd done in the past when he felt depressed.

Subsequently, Hisoka brought more and more dreams to session. In one session, he recounted five, with repeating themes of violence, betrayal, trust, death, special knowledge, powers, and conflict. His dreams became richer, opening up a path to his unconscious life and expressing sadness and mourning while revealing a new ability to face his losses.

He wrote an essay for school with the theme of how people needed a purpose or cause more than happiness. Whereas he felt he had no meaning at the beginning of therapy, he now named a few causes he believed in: education, vegetarianism, and personal growth.

I asked him to think about where people fit into this schema.

He came in the next session telling me he didn't think a 35-year-long happy marriage was an accomplishment. He said the only time he felt strongly was when his pet lizard died.

I, in turn, felt powerful fear during this session, as I saw how clueless Hisoka still remained regarding the importance of relationships. I shared with him my fear for his future. I asked how he imagined his future would be after his parents passed away, and he simply said that he had no idea.

"That's what scares me," I said. In the next session, he brought in a dream about a family tree and questioned where he belonged.

After feeling rather hopeless for Hisoka, I was surprised one day when he started talking about identity. "How does one describe another?" he asked. "How does one describe the self?" He began by trying to describe me and stated some facts he knew: psychologist, in her 50s, liberal, socialist, likes art, isn't athletic, reads more than watches TV, likes movies, feels she doesn't have enough time to do what she wants, has allergies.

I told him that was very good and asked if he could describe me from a relational perspective.

He said I am sometimes frustrated with him, and I don't like to be abrasive; I like listening more than talking and don't say much about my personal life unless I think it's relevant. I am habitual (the way I end the session) and have a punctual urinary-relief schedule.

I said he moved from my group identities to my behaviors. Could he now move to more personal feelings he had about me that helped him know me?

He looked puzzled and said simply, "You're a cat." After describing me, Hisoka turned to himself: agnostic, vegetarian, Asian, adopted, male; has an Italian family. He is quiet; likes music, anime, and books; is not athletic; likes animals; and is not so great with kids. He moved deeper by adding that he is not so emotional and is restrained and unstable.

When I asked him to describe himself relationally, he said he was quiet, especially in large groups, and not always polite. Then he said he, too, was a cat.

In a phone conversation, Hisoka's mother told me that he was changing at home. He was coming out of his room more and socializing more with the family. He was taking care of his hygiene more.

I ran into his psychiatrist that same week, and he too told me he was amazed at the work I had done with Hisoka, comparing it to carving a "David" out of a block of marble. I was thrilled that our work was beginning to manifest in outside changes. Indeed, he was looking different. Something in his face had transformed. He looked more relaxed and open, less depressed. He looked young and more animated.

After ten years of work, Hisoka came a long way. He obtained his undergraduate degree; he got a job and worked part-time, then full-time. He was promoted to manager. ("Can a cat be a manager?" he asked me.) He even moved out of his parents' home to live on his own. He paid for his new home from his own savings. He smiled and laughed, began to hang out more with his brother, played basketball, and frequently ate dinner with his family. Most important, Hisoka started to confront the uncomfortable truth that he desperately needed people.

One day, Hisoka sent me a photo of himself with a dog. He no longer wished to live alone, so he adopted a dog. Hisoka, an adopted child, now adopted a dog. He then brought the dog to a session so that I could meet him. Several years later, he signed onto an internet dating site. He asked me to take his profile picture, which I did. Not surprisingly, the only women he seemed to communicate with lived overseas, offering little prospect of meeting them in person. He needed the distance which, at the very least, helped him practice how to dialogue with a potential romantic partner/ friend.

Hisoka and I recently ended our treatment. Coincidentally, we planned to broach the topic of termination on the same day, illustrating that we were both on the same wavelength. We both felt that, despite still having work to do, especially around dating, Hisoka was ready to continue on his own. We are both assured that he can do so. Terminations are never complete. They do not need to resolve all problems. Freud (1913/1978) cautioned analysts to be wary of their ambitions, which may exceed those of the patients. Most important is the sense in both parties that the patient can take it from here.

During the COVID pandemic, Hisoka did something he had aggressively maintained held no interest for him: he connected with his biological parents (who had separated after his birth). At first, they corresponded by mail, and then he traveled to Japan to meet each of them in person, along with extended family. He has begun to learn Japanese.

Hisoka, the young man who for years refused to leave his room, now makes plans to travel the world. I offered him a travel journal as we parted. He offered me a gift he had ordered from Morocco, my birthplace, which he had once made fun of.

Hisoka's case demonstrates the importance of anchoring when derailed attachments harm a person's ability to embody a stable reality. Hisoka felt so alone when he was very young but did not even know he was alone. His aloneness turned in on itself, and he substituted anime for reality and a single room for the world. His parents carried him while he lived in the deadened womb of his room, facilitating his parasitic position. He felt miserable about that; he felt like a loser. The relationship with me eventually allowed him to anchor himself to the world, or, to put it more directly, to attain an embodiment that enabled functioning within it.

When I asked Hisoka if I could write about him, he was surprised. I explained that I was writing about solitude, and he quickly nodded, saying simply, "That would be me." Despite the fact that Hisoka is an extraordinarily private person, he agreed to have me present our work because he felt it was important to me, and he believed in the significance of my subject.

## Case Conceptualization

Hisoka could never process the breach that had occurred with his first two mothers. In a sense, those losses occurred before he came into existence as a knowing and fully conscious self and preceded the capacity to associate to and symbolize them. These losses formed the very soil in which he grew and in which he could not put down roots of attachment. The soil was initially so barren that even the rich layers of care and love placed on top by his third mother could not root Hisoka in healthy attachments to his adoptive family. Hisoka was in desperate flight from intimacy, as if, after losing two mothers, something inside him pledged, *this will never happen to me again.* And then he forgot his loss and additionally forgot that he forgot it. He fled from others, taking false refuge in a self that had no purpose; without connection to the other, the whole meaning of the term "purpose" faltered, but he did not know that he was in flight. He only knew that his existence was like a tiny flashing light afloat in a dark and bottomless ocean. The best he could do was to identify with small pets and animals.

Hisoka initially cocooned himself inside his small bedroom, surrounded by his computer games, videos, and porn, fully dependent on his family while feeling completely detached and in need of no one. He took a perverse pleasure in being able to spend months alone, taking his meals by himself, staying awake all night while others slept, and sleeping all day while others were awake and productive. Yet, he was haunted by the feeling that he had fallen too far behind, that his life had no meaning. As he became more and more alone, he found himself alone with nothing. He found himself in fact *a nothing*, hardly a self. He was in a double bind: erasing others, he had erased himself; reveling in isolation, he himself began to disappear, and his disappearance prevented saving action of any kind. If his mother had not taken him for help, he might likely be dead.

When I think of Hisoka as having come to me in a state of flight, I find myself asking from what or to whom was he fleeing. Inevitably the same idea recurs to me: *he was in flight away from the mark of death and toward the mother*. By the mark of death, I mean how each individual's history has shaped a terror that symbolizes extinction. By being in flight towards the mother I mean how each individual requires a maternal (parental) rectification of what has not been addressed, processed, and integrated. Hisoka was young enough to be my child. From our very first session, I saw breaks in his icy distance, a moment when his eyes became hungry and searching while they looked into mine seeking himself there, revealing his desire to be born in a blinking instant. With time, those instants became far more frequent. He sat closer to me, made more eye contact, hung out with his brother, came to dinner with his family, continued his online schooling, got a job and then another, confronted the uncomfortable truth that he desperately needed his family and considered the possibility of extending his love beyond pets and animals into the human dimension. He fled the terrible rupture of his infancy toward the *very thing he fled*: the face of the mother, that existential place where he could be brought to his senses, where his life could be restructured and rendered with purpose. Not surprisingly, he wrote an essay that defended the idea that it was far more important to have a purpose than to be happy.

It is often said that a good mother knows her child's needs. Recently I realized that in my many years of clinical work, I have disclosed more about myself to Hisoka than to any of the hundreds of people that came before him. I sensed that he needed to know his therapist as a person so that he could feel "close" and adopt me as a partner in his hidden world. He could not trust me if I did not show myself, so I never evaded his direct questions. With him, it was a matter of following clues and looking for inroads into his mind. Our initial breakthrough came when he told me he recalled his dreams, which provided me with pointers about what to explore with him. Animals, too, played a major role in connecting us and opening a path for displaced discussion. Reconstruction also played a major role in creating the first layers of narrative needed to establish a symbolic context into which he could incorporate his losses and his flight from them. When Hisoka and I parted company, we each went our own way, carrying the other inside.

## Loneliness in the Countertransference

Since persons with psychosis often have difficulty with social relations, therapists sometimes become their sole human connection, the session the only time during the week in which they deeply interact with another human being and themselves. This is a privileged place to be for a therapist as well as an enormous responsibility that can at times feel like a burden. Therapists confront solitude as they listen to endless stories that leave them questioning the meaning of their patients' lives, their lives, and life in general. The analyst is Sullivan's (1940/2006) "participant–observer," the juxtaposition that comprises a paradox: engagement and disengagement; relatedness and solitude. Analysts simultaneously participate in the transference and countertransference while attempting to stand apart as an observer of the patient's and their own psychodynamics and defenses. In some cases, analysts sit behind the couch, out of view, a solitary figure set in a singular personal space, attentive to the patient yet open to private reveries, engaging the patient on conscious and unconscious levels.

Warren Poland (2000) rightly observed that silently witnessing the patient's self-inquiry is a major part of the analytic process, and Charles Hanly (1990) stated that genuine analytic work involves respect for the solitude of each person as they relate to themselves. The therapist often feels alone and adrift in a sea of confessions. Though the analytic relationship is deep and intimate, cracking open the patient's most private and personal inner landscape, it does not include the analyst as an individual who discloses fully because most of the focus is on the patient and because this allows the transference to develop. Additionally, the analyst is cautioned not to speak of these intense encounters due to confidentiality concerns. Psychodynamic psychoanalysis is lonely work. At the day's end, the analyst may carry in their heart and to their home worlds of sorrow and loss, the angst of human existence along with its innumerable forms of pain.

Working with patients who exhibit psychosis is known to induce loneliness in the therapist, and those with negative symptoms can generate even greater loneliness in their therapists. Therapists (especially beginning therapists) often feel frightened or lost when working with psychosis. They do not understand the patient's communication, or they feel unable to reach the patient. They may identify with the patient's hopelessness and despair or feel hopeless with regard to being able to help them. They may feel an absence of empathy for the patient's condition, or the patient might be angry over the therapist's aloofness. Collaboration may be lacking. All of these experiences can result in the therapist feeling disoriented, alone, unsure of their professional effectiveness, and, worse, unsure of their personal identity. Most of all, we therapists are often made to feel the utter loneliness and alienation that our patients who experience psychosis feel.

Perhaps most important, the encounter with psychosis reminds therapists what people's sanity costs in terms of lies and denials. These patients remind us that our character development does not simply accommodate the vector of our constitution and personal history—it defends against the nature of reality itself (the utter indifference of nature; the immensity of the cosmos and our smallness within it; the fact that our existence is an accident and yet matters so much to us; the heartbreaking fragility of all whom we love or hope to love; the impossibility of having with others what we dream about; and the finality and annihilation of death). The person with psychosis in treatment stands with the therapist on the borderland between a humanly ordered world and the chaos from which humans draw order. The therapist must accompany the patient into that terrifying territory, one that the vast majority of "sane" people mightily repress and avoid. One is reminded of madness. One is reminded that one can go mad. And one is reminded that one's sanity itself is also a kind of madness. If reality itself is too threatening to bear, then psychosis can be understood as a process by which the imagination runs rampant, overpowering reason and the repression necessary for its proper functioning, creating delusions and hallucinations that mirror the tragedy of being human while creating a "world" that idiosyncratically expresses that tragedy while attempting to preserve life.

Each of us must do something when the gap between our social reality and desire for company becomes too wide, lest it become a devouring abyss. What we wind up doing with the gap is a vectorial result of our constitution, our personal history, especially its unconscious derivatives, and our conscious intent. The responses to existential and personal loneliness fall across a wide spectrum, though they have one thing in common: the need to have the other, whether a person or thing. That other may be a new friend or love, a fully absorbing life project, religious or spiritual engagement, or an addiction in the form of alcohol, drugs, gambling, or sex. As we have seen, sometimes the other is madness itself—in the form of hallucinations and delusions or extreme seclusion. As analysts, we work with the last two components of the directional life trajectory, hoping to provide a therapeutic relationship that encourages the patient to realize life and form self-enhancing relationships. We would like to close with another entry made by DK's writer/patient Cornelius:

> When the burden of your existence has so little left to contain it, your very reality as a person is destroyed. Without the rigor of an identity and the social scenes in which it is defined and belongs, you spill into a shapeless slick mess, like an oil spill, or jump from surface to surface like a fire out of control. You become a terrified animal who knows too much but not enough. Exiled from the homeland of your very self, no place inside or outside is safe, and there is nothing in you to separate the two. Everything is gone except a throbbing mass of sentience invaded by a strange and ugly world. Yet there still beats within you the tiniest of all hearts, a pulsing fist raging with white heat. Inside that clenched fist is a black piece of paper holding a request written in blood in a language bubbling up between the living and the dead. This is an ancient and universal language made up of the sounds of the night, of terrible loneliness, of mortal conflict, and of death cries, the lingua franca of original desperation. Translated that request says:
> *I am here. Please see me.*

## Summary Guidelines for Working with Loneliness in People with Psychosis

1.  Loneliness can manifest in unusual and sometimes hidden ways. For example, paranoia is a way of never having to be alone. Similarly, hallucinations can keep a person company. Psychotic symptoms simultaneously express self–world exile and attempts to cope with it. Understanding this paradox can guide the therapist's interventions to address the patient's desire for contact, not only the desire to retreat.

2. One should be careful when speaking of a patient's desire for a relationship because they often are not aware of it themselves.

3. Relatedness can feel dangerous to some and, therefore, the desire for contact and the need for safety should be considered together when making an interpretation.

4. When a patient can acknowledge that they are lonely, they are making progress. For someone experiencing psychosis, a confession of loneliness is intimately associated with a sense of vulnerability and, therefore, of being exploited. As compensation, the patient may rely on a distorted myth of self-sufficiency.

5. Loneliness is, in essence, the awakening of desire. Therefore, to reach the patient's recognition that they want something, the therapist must first respect the danger the patient feels were they to become aware of their own desire.

6. It is important to keep in mind that persons who are diagnosed with psychosis are far more likely to suffer from loneliness than the general population.

7. Hospitalization and medication can exacerbate loneliness in those with psychosis. Many feel the medication makes them feel detached from themselves and their thoughts. Therefore, one should try therapies of all kinds (individual, group, family, occupational) to help patients stay connected with others and feel less lonely. In cases where medication is necessary, the therapist should consider prescribing the lowest effective dosage as well as antianxiety meds over antipsychotic meds.

8. It is key to be aware of one's own loneliness when treating patients who do not respond to the therapist as a subject. Supervision, talking with peers, and having a life outside of one's work all help the therapist to maintain the patience required for working with these states.

9. All patients, whatever their diagnosis, should be met with sincerity, openness, and approachability. However, these qualities in a therapist are even more important when they work with psychosis.

10. There is no such thing as anonymity, especially with patients who are keenly tuned into the therapist's unconscious. The real relationship that goes beyond transference and countertransference helps initiate the patient into an interpersonal and relational world. Acknowledging the nature of this relationship does not mean oversharing. It means being

real and showing the patient what relating feels like—given to them in small, incremental doses—at a rate that is tolerable to the patient.

11. Because psychosis isolates patients from others, it is important to show empathy for their state, even if one does not fully understand it. The therapist can say, "You feel it is inconceivable that anyone can fully appreciate your plight. Is that so?" Such statements can go a long way in helping the patient feel less alone.

12. It is vital to be aware not only of the patient's withdrawal from connectedness (including from the self) but also of their wish to connect. Ideally, the therapist–patient interaction tilts the scale in favor of the patient's wish to connect. Understandably, the patient often becomes horrified by recognizing that they have given up relationships to feel safe. The patient then finds themselves at a crucial waystation between isolation and connectedness. In this fragile position, the patient will, over time, confront the dilemma that they have a choice and, therefore, that they are *in conflict with themselves*. They realize that they want two things that appear in opposition to one another: closeness and safety. What they will choose is equivalent to the outcome of the therapy. During this time, the therapist must remain nonjudgmental regarding this delicate balance. Only by refusing to take sides can the therapist encourage the patient to make an autonomous choice.

# Chapter 9

# Coming Undone

## Acute Decompensation and Creating a Narrative

### Pre-psychotic Panic

It takes years for some patients to develop psychosis, but that *gradual* process can be retroactively tracked over time. The process involves increasingly awkward and detached relations with family members and the outside world. These patients can become either overly withdrawn or exceedingly aggressive, both of which tend to remove them from social relations. Such behavior changes usually begin to take place during their high school years, though they can begin even earlier. Some can continue to function on this pre- or borderline-psychotic level indefinitely (e.g., white psychosis); others have what is commonly referred to as a *break*, when they leave home, go to college, or experience other types of life demands that exceed their capabilities.

A second group of patients experiences an abrupt disturbance, an *acute* attack, wherein they suddenly become disorganized and feel confused and frightened by the changes they begin to perceive in themselves and their thought processes. When this happens, one usually can find an identifiable stressor, such as a significant loss, trauma, or marijuana or other drug use (Bebbington et al., 1993; Berenson, 2019; Rabkin, 1980; Räkköläinen, 1977). For a brief period (usually a few weeks), the patient feels as if they are living between worlds: the prior way of seeing things and the new, "psychotic" way of understanding. This in-between state creates conflict that can be highlighted by the therapist to strengthen the nonpsychotic part of the personality. Though the nonpsychotic elements have been weakened in the battle against the encroaching psychotic part, the therapist can appeal to its reasoning powers and adherence to reality. Working together to reduce conflict and confusion is a way of establishing a therapeutic alliance. When this work is not accomplished, the psychotic part of the personality seeks a

DOI: 10.4324/9781003441519-9

quick solution to flee from the uncomfortable state of fear and confusion. What results is "psychotic insight" that aims at explaining everything (e.g., "They're after me" or "I'm God") and finding corroboration for such insights (Arieti, 1974b).

If the therapist intervenes quickly with persons experiencing the sudden onset of psychosis for the first time, they can help arrest the progression into full psychosis. When the patient is still in conflict about what is happening to them ("I don't understand what is happening to me"; "I don't feel reality is real; I am not real"; "I'm confused"), the therapist can optimally step in and validate the questioning, contain the panic, help the patient tolerate strong affect and uncertainty, and reassure them that this process does have an explanation. The therapist can reassure the patient that they will help them reach a true understanding of this experience. Unlike the situation in which people gradually develop psychosis, acute psychotic episodes can be only that—episodes. When the therapist views the break as episodic—i.e., temporary—they can also help their patient accept the fact that such dysregulating periods are ephemeral and given to change. The patient internalizes the therapist's faith in change, as well as the therapist's ability to contain and tolerate affect, which makes it easier for the patient to trust the process rather than flee.

Instead of viewing the beginnings of breakdown as the first phase of a chronic condition that can be treated—not cured—by hospitalization and/ or a lifetime drug regimen, one can approach such a crisis as a necessary opportunity for change. We agree with Bollas who, in *Catch Them Before They Fall: The Psychoanalysis of Breakdown* (2013), calls for immediate treatment of persons experiencing breakdown to prevent them from becoming "broken selves" (p. 5), diminished in their capacity to function for the remainder of their lives, indifferent to their lives, and detached from their object world. He proposes a radical treatment: creating a temporary holding environment to prevent the breakdown from taking hold, by meeting daily with the patient during their episode until they emerge from it, or meeting with the patient for all-day sessions. We have also employed, with positive results, extended sessions and increased frequency of sessions with persons in an acute pre-psychotic state.

Some clinicians believe that those demonstrating psychotic symptoms need to first be calmed by medication and/or hospitalization before being treated therapeutically. Conversely, Bollas writes, "When the person is at their most vulnerable—and especially in breakdown—they are usually particularly amenable to help, and to the development of insight into the self" (2013, p. 7). The timing is ripe to explore what exactly took place in the days leading up to the breakdown, and time is of the essence. The therapist becomes the container, the holding environment, for the patient's bizarre thoughts and experiences, all the while helping them to understand what has happened to their inner and outer world and why.

Open Dialogue, an increasingly popular approach to first-episode psychosis, also has the therapeutic team stepping in very quickly at the first signs of decompensation, meeting frequently and intensively with the patient to prevent devolution to chronic symptom patterns (Seikkula and Alakare, 2013). Initially implemented in Finland, Open Dialogue does not resort to hospitalization but uses the support of the patients' family members and significant others as well as a consistent treatment team. This approach has shown a recovery rate (measured by fewer hospital stays, decline in psychotic symptoms and medication usage, return to work or studies) of over 80% (Seikkula et al., 2006). The Parachute Project (soft landing from a psychotic episode) similarly advocates early intervention (within 24 hours), along with psychotherapy and crisis orientation, family meetings, and continuous accessibility to services for up to five years. Both Open Dialogue and the Parachute Project use no medication or administer the lowest effective antipsychotic dose possible, along with psychotherapy. Hospital stays are avoided whenever possible because the belief is that personal attention, low stimulus, and noninstitutional settings show the best results (Cullberg, 2006).

## Psychotic Insight Following Decompensation

If therapists do not have the opportunity to see the patient during their prepsychotic state, then they will usually encounter them post-decompensation. Following the acute crisis, these patients frequently describe fantasies of world destruction and report that an "internal catastrophe" (Levy et al., 1975, p. 1) has taken place, leading them to conclude that they are no longer themselves and that their premorbid selves no longer exist. A patient's sense of catastrophe occurs when their internal vulnerability encounters what they perceive as overwhelming external stress, resulting in the terror that annihilation is about to occur. The current self is not up to the challenge. Therefore, what is about to be lost must be replaced by a self that is no longer fearful of extinction. Finding a way to survive is all that matters.

Following the break, making sense of the world becomes less important than creating a structure to help the patient hold on. Many such patients believe that maintaining the experience of continuity within themselves has broken down and they react by "reinterpreting the outer world to create a new coherence" (Cullberg, 2006, p. 43). This self and world re-creation takes priority as the patient becomes convinced that they alone are the origin of repairing the threatened dislocation within themselves. To this end, they utilize imagination and projection, as exemplified in persecutory as well as omnipotent fantasies, to provide themselves with a new solipsistic basis for continuity. Since the world, as it has previously existed, is no longer relevant, it cannot represent an ordeal for these patients. That statement itself is misleading in implying a sharp distinction between past and present and inside and outside, yet one of the patient's core problems is their failure to maintain a self–other boundary. Boundary dissolution is a primary symptom necessitating the blowing up of one's former world. As a result, the extent to which patients with psychosis acknowledge the existence of the world determines the degree to which they will fear being invaded by it (Arieti, 1974b).

Consistent with the patient's belief that they have "lost" themselves, some mental health professionals have developed a theory of ego deficiency in psychosis, which posits a "dissolution" of self and object representations and a "fragmentation" or "disintegration" of the ego and personality. We believe that any such theory of internal disintegration or lack unfortunately, and of necessity, commits the therapist to a process of "reconstruction" or structure building, sets a limit on treatment goals, and fails to consider patients as equal partners in their recovery. We believe that the patient has not lost themselves but, rather, disconnected from a part of themselves, even reinventing themselves to do so. By collaboratively understanding their unconscious motives and the meaning of their symptoms, the therapist creates a bridge to the part of the self that has been ousted from their consciousness.

Yet, it is true that the acute psychotic episode plays havoc with the patient's previous sense of themselves. They no longer feel themselves to be who they once were and are uncertain about whom they will become. They may ask themselves what is occurring and why it is occurring to them. Have they done something, or is something being done to them? Tragically, their ability to address these urgent questions is limited by their cognitive challenges, intense anxiety, bewilderment, and panic. The patient's fear of losing their sense of continuity and coherence is not about what is happening now, but, rather, about making concrete what the patient anticipates will occur. The "internal catastrophe" has elicited a sense of being unable to exist in the world, resulting in a degree of terror that will overwhelm them.

## The Illusion of Discontinuity

The sense of discontinuity in psychosis can take many forms. Identity can be invaded by an alien force—e.g., the patient may be transformed by being given special powers or may be a target of a conspiracy. In extreme cases, for example, as seen in Capgras Syndrome, (which can also be caused by neurological damage), a patient recognizes one or more persons closest to them as imposters. DK saw an African American patient who believed her real parents were imposters and was convinced that her true parents were the actors Cary Grant and Doris Day, which indicated a defensive severance from the patient's past. The therapist's apprehension that a patient with psychosis had originally felt a life-or-death need to separate from their former self makes it easier for that patient to accept what they did and why. Containing the patient's affect while providing a context for their flight from themselves facilitates their ability to experience their former self. Because they now have a partner in their therapist, what had been sealed off can begin to see the light of day.

Every person experiencing psychosis, whether they acknowledge it or not, has developed a way of thinking about what has happened to them. They may believe that they held too lofty a goal and are now paying for their hubris, that envious people brought them down, that they have a brain disease, that the cause of their ailment is unknown and unknowable, or even that nothing significant has occurred other than that the world is misperceiving them. Clarifying the patient's particular theory of what happened to them is central to the creation of a narrative. Without this acknowledgment, adaptation makes no sense; with it, the effort at adaptation acquires coherence and dignity. Fixing that point in time allows both participants to explore the patient's life before the catastrophe to determine what has and has not changed. "Catastrophe" is itself a metaphor that allows patients to manage certain painful events. A man diagnosed with "chronic schizophrenia" held a conviction that he was dead (See Chapter 2). This belief served to concretize a series of painful and confusing experiences, provide him with an explanation about what had befallen him, support his passivity, and offer him a rationale for avoiding interaction with others.

Although we write about psychosis as an expression of discontinuity of self, in fact, advances in neuroscience have uncovered that continuity of self is a useful illusion that allows people to survive and feel like they possess a continuous consciousness (LeDoux, 2002). The stability and continuity of the self is a judgment call about self-representation within a presumed bandwidth. In psychosis, a person is operating outside of the survival bandwidth of what is considered "normal."

## Developing the Narrative

A life narrative (Schafer, 1992) involves the reconstruction of the patient's experience of their life to date, the examination of what they feel has happened, is happening, and will likely occur in the future. The narrative is a rich compilation of the patient's roles, interests, ego functions, relationship to time, attitudes about causality, assumptions about their place in the world, self-appraisal, and relational history. A tale of one person's perception of their past from the vantage point of the present moment, the narrative assesses the past and predicts the future but is less about those actual times than it is about the present. In all probability, the narrator has experienced life differently in the past and will hold a different perspective on these same events in the future. In other words, narratives are never finished. They are constantly being revised and rewritten in light of new information and insights.

Developing a narrative is a component of any psychodynamic therapy. However, there are several factors unique to those experiencing psychosis that render the construction of a narrative both essential and challenging. For most people, personality can be understood as reflecting a series of integrated self-appraisals. The sense that one's personality has changed reflects an altered self-appraisal such as, "I no longer can work," or "I'm not as good at meeting people as I used to be." In psychosis, patients experience themselves as either disconnected from who they once were or transformed into someone new and different. Thus, they are prone to interpret changes as due to an intrinsic alteration or fragmentation of their personality rather than to the fact that they have unconsciously changed the way they think about themselves.

Along with a denial of the past, those experiencing psychosis, and, on occasion, their family and friends, act as if there exists a moratorium on the patient's life. It is on hold until the old, often idealized, version of the premorbid personality reappears. The patient and their family join in a conspiracy to deny that the patient's current existence has meaning. One father lamented to MS that "We are waiting for the old Eddie to come back." The narrative recreates a story about object relations with significant people from the past, including the patient's former self. Thus, there can be no hiatus until Eddie returns; there is simply the Eddie of now and whatever connection to his past that is discernible, as well as speculation of his future based on his current self. The creation of a narrative imposes a structure on the patient, the therapist, and the family, providing a focus and serving as a nexus for collaboration.

A narrative involves a process that goes through several iterations, each providing a valid picture of how patients choose to see themselves. Persons with psychosis may insist that they are entirely their own creation, indebted to no one and nothing. Considering that anything or anyone has mattered to them may be too painful to acknowledge (e.g., as in the case with Hisoka, in Chapter 8, this volume). Thus, they may wish to remain unaware, which they achieve through withdrawal and disconnection. The therapist's efforts at creating connections between events in the patient's life can be read as proof that the therapist does not believe the patient: "If you put away your stupid theories and just listen to me, you would be searching for the source of the radiation that changed me," or "You are asking me to describe my home life so we can figure out what I ran away from when, in fact, I was kidnapped." Psychotic insights reveal that the current danger is so overwhelming that nothing that has gone on before is worth mentioning.

Bollas (2015) calls the patient's early narratives "mythic," consistent with the patient's view of themselves as discontinuous and transformed. He believes the mythic narrative must be addressed prior to developing a conventionally understood linear story. Information about the patient's actual historical past will emerge later, making clear what the patient has been trying to overcome, and highlighting the mythic narrative's adaptive function in their survival (as in the case with Gladys in Chapter 6). Linking past conflicts with current efforts at survival aids the patient's owning their mythic narrative as well as its necessity. The patient may remain fearful of their fragility and vulnerability to further psychic confusion and terror, yet they can develop respect for what they did to survive. Separation from one's former self can never be complete, as illustrated by the intimate relationship between the new sense of self and the previous personality. For example, a man who has always been a suspicious person, following the catastrophe, comes to view himself as having been transformed by an envious persecutor. A woman with a formerly depressive sense of self becomes a foul-smelling, worthless individual, deserving of eternal damnation. The patient's ability to see themselves clearly has been obscured by their need to separate from their old self. Their difficulty stems from the failure to appreciate that the revised picture retains properties belonging to their original self as well as manifestations of their adaptive efforts. Developing the narrative requires the patient to struggle with change and, therefore, with loss.

Just as they cannot entirely distance themselves from their pasts, so too are individuals experiencing psychosis never able to completely accept their new psychotic self, though at any given moment it may appear that they do. There is always a nonpsychotic part of the self that observes and questions what the psychotic part does and believes. The closer one is to the onset of the episode, the more these doubts will surface.

Developing the narrative relies on the patient feeling heard. The patient feels validated when the therapist attends to what they are saying, even when the patient contradicts themselves in the very next statement or action. Thus, the path to developing the narrative begins with the therapist's validation of the patient's current sense of themselves. Validation refers to acknowledging the patient's subjective state, whether it confirms external reality or not. The therapist whose patient believes they have been invaded by evil might say, "You have been taken over by a malevolent force, leaving you not in control of yourself." Following on the heels of validation, the therapist next addresses the fact that the patient has changed, though the nature of that change requires more clarification. Along the way, the patient is likely to have experienced conflict with others over the legitimacy of their position. They may wonder how they have managed, what assumptions they have made about the nature of doubters, and where they think their therapist fits into the chorus of skeptics.

Just because the therapist is able to empathize with both the patient's psychic pain and their need for psychotic defenses does not mean the therapist has to accept the patient's solution as the only way of dealing with the situation. The therapist's task is to help the patient to see there are alternative solutions that, in the long run, will require less constriction and offer greater access to a wider world. Two obstacles stand in the way. First, such patients believe that hiding from themselves and the world has been lifesaving rather than life-robbing. Second, these patients believe they must avoid the real world since nothing but menace or ensnarement awaits them upon reentry. These resistances notwithstanding, as the implications of the psychotic self are explored, the patient will find their psychotic self to be less credible.

Developing the narrative is a delicate undertaking that may stall at any point, necessitating the patient's return to an earlier, more primitive, psychotic position. The patient may find their story unbearable, reverting back to being Lord of the Universe. There is nothing the matter with them; it is the therapist who has a problem, the therapist who envies the patient's power. In developing the narrative, the patient risks becoming overwhelmed by the disparity between their current and premorbid selves. If they can mourn the loss of aspects of their former self, they can continue to investigate what has happened to them. However, for a person with psychosis, mourning is especially challenging because it is a direct acknowledgment of loss. Loss, or the threat of loss, is often what triggered the psychotic process in the first place. Mourning threatens the patient's tenuous attempts to replace what they fear they have lost or wish to get rid of with psychotic defenses aimed at making them invulnerable. Nonetheless, as the therapist makes clear that they are able and willing to help the patient contain their affect, the patient becomes more able to share their loss. Their newly found willingness to mourn can then proceed along more traditional psychoanalytic lines, resulting in integration.

Not all patients are able to negotiate the mourning process. Those unable to do so will "seal over" (Levy et al., 1975), a technical term referring to the unconscious denial of catastrophe. *Sealing* refers to a lack of awareness and failure to place one's psychotic experience within a personal context. The clinical manifestations can range from, "I'm fine now and always have been" to "I know something happened to me, but I'm better off not thinking about it and just getting on with my life." Daring to ask, "What happened to me?" can feel too dangerous. A sealed-over person must remain vigilant lest evidence of the prior assault on the self reemerges. Their ability to function depends on keeping a tight lid on the memory of the catastrophe. By contrast, a patient who is able to mourn and go on to construct a complex narrative integrates their psychotic experience into a story that includes past, present, and future. As a result, they are far more flexible and achieve a better therapeutic outcome.

## Trauma Narratives and Dissociation

Psychotic breaks refer not only to the patient's attacks on linking (Bion, 1959); they refer to their traumatic experiences. When we speak of catastrophe, we are almost always speaking about trauma. And when we speak of trauma, we speak of rupture. One of the major reasons people experiencing psychosis have difficulty creating a narrative is because so many of them have been traumatized, and their trauma has resulted in what Boulanger (2007) calls "catastrophic dissociation." Trauma expert Dori Laub has said, "It is the nature of trauma to evade our knowing it" (Laub and Lee, 2003, p. 449). Dissociation naturally poses difficulties when a person is attempting to develop a cohesive narrative.

Up until recently, mental health professionals have considered psychosis as biologically generated, while dissociation has long been considered psychologically linked to trauma (Moskowitz, 2011). Yet, recent research demonstrates the degree to which early trauma is highly correlated with the development of psychosis and just how much psychotic symptoms are, in fact, ways of dealing with trauma (Bentall and Fernyhough, 2008; Davoine and Gaudilliere, 2004; Kirshner, 2015; Krabbendam et al., 2004; Moscovitz et al., 2019; Read and Ross, 2003; Shevlin et al., 2008).

Boulanger (2007) distinguishes between lifeless narratives and living narratives in trauma survivors. The former is due to dissociation, lack of agency or the sense of an "I"; memories are fragmented, chronology is jumbled, and there are gaps that reflect the patient's reluctance or fear of being retraumatized. Lifeless narratives may be recognized as repeated in the same way with muted and little affect, almost like a boring story. There is a poverty of description which masks rather than reveals. Facial expression and body language are flat and unaffected, expressing the inner deadness tied to the event. Such dead narratives are a mark of how far the patient is from insight and relief. A living narrative, on the other hand, is dialogical and in touch with affect; it is meant to be heard by another who can engage and respond empathically to what the patient has endured. With a living narrative, the therapist breaks through their patient's "traumatic loneliness" and becomes a "transitional witness" to the patient's suffering until they can witness and recount their own experience (Boulanger, 2007,

p. 137). Only then can the patient develop the agency, affectivity, physical cohesiveness, and continuity that brings life to their narrative.

## Rationale for Using the Narrative

Not everyone who experiences trauma develops psychosis. But for those who do, the construction of a narrative takes on peculiar characteristics. The illusion of the obliteration of self challenges the continuity of one's life story, and clarifying what has happened allows for an appreciation of continuity. Since the narrative tests the patient's sense of fragmentation and need for dissociation, many resist its construction. Some examples the authors have encountered include the following: One man who experienced trauma and developed a psychotic explanation for the catastrophic dissociation in his life insisted that the only thing that mattered was his sudden, miraculous transformation into the Savior. What may have gone on previously was labeled irrelevant or false. A female patient repudiated her origins, asserting that her "so-called parents" were impostors. To buttress her claims, she declared that people knew her true identity but withheld recognition out of envy. One patient described his past as "stolen from me," which he rationalized as occurring so that "I could appreciate what Holocaust survivors went through." Still another claimed to have been a crown prince who had been sent to an orphanage by an unscrupulous uncle at birth because he wished his own son to become king.

What these assertions share is the patients' insistence that their (alleged) past bears no relation to the present. It is less that they are disconnected from their past than that the alleged past was propaganda. Only they know the truth, or, if others do, they've chosen to conceal it for their own reasons. This is an imaginative, highly adaptive way to deny the painful truth of the past. Patients who resist constructing a narrative generally do so either because of the fear of returning to the pain of who they truly were or the fear that they would yearn for what they had been. Since returning to that self seems impossible, it feels essential for them to remain cut off from whom they imagined themselves to have been.

## Journaling

Individuals experiencing psychosis frequently display fluid boundaries, cognitive impairments, and difficulty containing affect, all predisposing them to have difficulty tolerating ambiguity. For these reasons, they favor premature closure. During an episode of psychosis, the individual may insist on pseudo-resolutions whenever the developing narrative threatens to become confusing or complex or to cause affects to emerge. For example, they may present parts of themselves that contradict other parts yet insist on the absolute truth of whatever aspect they are currently presenting. The patient is saying, "Disregard whatever I said a moment ago. This is the one and only me."

While developing the narrative reveals the patient's cognitive difficulties in managing information, it also provides opportunities for investigation and remediation. Issues arise about how to assign credibility to newly surfacing data, how to establish priorities, how to deal with gaps in information, and how to handle contradictory information. "How else might we understand what you just described?" the therapist might ask. "Is this more important than what you said a minute ago?" Or the therapist might say, "I don't get the link here." These are examples of interventions that will expose areas needing further exploration and remediation. The therapist is identifying the patient's limitations, all the while offering ways for the patient to approach these problems and expanding their sense of what they can become capable of achieving.

Concreteness anchors, so journaling is a useful technique. The narrative can be written down in a book (Furlan and Benedetti, 1985) or amplified by photographs, letters, or other references to the past. Maintaining the narrative in a written form also facilitates its use as a transitional object (Winnicott, 1953). Patients can take the journal with them when they leave the session and work on it on their own. If they find working alone too difficult, the therapist might encourage the patient to wonder about the analyst's reaction: "What might I have said at that point?" or "Did it occur to you that I'd think it's remarkable that, in the face of God's warning you to stop creating the journal, you persevered?" A patient can write to their therapists in the journal, continuing their dialogue and joint venture while physically apart.

Nathan had chronicled his manic episode while in the hospital because at the time he believed he was Jesus and wished to share his insights with others. In treatment, DK and Nathan reread together what he had written. They then spoke of what life was like before his manic episode, making connections between the two time periods. Nathan continued journaling during the treatment, often while in session. The journals became Nathan's narrative, which he continues writing to this day.

## The Therapist's Role in Encouraging the Development of a Narrative

Most individuals experiencing psychosis have scant experience with people wanting to hear their story. For that reason alone, as well as the many others we've mentioned, the therapist is mindful that the process of narrative development takes precedence over creating the final product. Many patients with severe trauma histories may be reluctant to share their stories, not only because they wish to avoid being retraumatized, but also because they do not wish to traumatize their therapists. One woman with a history of parental abuse said she thought DK was too young to hear such stories and that she did not wish to destroy her innocence. Such patients need to be reassured that their therapist will survive exposure to extreme tales of trauma. The takeaway message is: if the therapist can survive, so can the patient.

The journal itself can serve as a metaphor, representing a progressively shared activity. Initially, the therapist is the keeper of the record, both literally and metaphorically. While working with a suicidal patient, DK had him bring his suicide notes to session, tracking the daily changes in their expression. During an erotomanic episode another patient had with her boss, DK kept her love letters written to her boss in her office until the patient was no longer in danger of sending them and ruining her employment. These written accounts became part of the patients' narratives, and they were held safely within the treatment confines. Therapists may write down what they are learning, concretizing the significance of the endeavor. Keeping journals and other written materials safe between sessions symbolizes the therapist's role as a protector not only of the narrative but of the treatment process as well. Producing the journal at each meeting demonstrates object constancy of the journal, the therapist, and the treatment relationship.

The therapist addresses their patient's attacks on linking (Bion, 1988), creating connections between past, present, future, and themes that appear throughout the patient's life. The therapist does this by making links between new information and what the patient has previously recounted: "What you said just now reminds me of what you said two weeks ago when you talked about ___." The therapist makes explicit how what they have learned forms

the basis for their next assumption: "Since you already described yourself as
___, it's not surprising that you did ___." Gradually, the therapist expands
their inquiry, moving from the literal to the imagined. "If instead of ___
having happened, what if ___ had happened? What do you think the result
would have been?" The therapist can also use the subjunctive to help the
patient consider information too threatening to approach directly. "If you
had become angry at your father, what might the consequences have been?"

## Summary

Not infrequently, the patient, family, and therapist collude to support the
illusion that patients are no longer who they had been. This powerful myth
serves multiple defensive functions, and patients can use it to justify their
apathy or their optimism. Patients view their past as irrelevant, thereby
protecting themselves against regret and unprocessed trauma. For the
therapist, believing the illusion of discontinuity has considerable significance.
If their patients are disconnected from their pasts, the therapist may see
them as having lost whatever resources they previously had and view them
as needing the therapist to take over. In that scenario, the therapist does not
feel they are dominating their patients but rather providing what they need.
Another path to the same end occurs when a therapist, unconsciously afraid
of being dominated by their patient, provides himself or herself with a
rationale for exercising control over the patient. Alternatively, the therapist
might adopt a stance of therapeutic nihilism: "Since there's nothing there to
work with, I can't do anything."

We have argued that maintaining the illusion of discontinuity is costly
for all involved. Acceptance of discontinuity is tantamount to the patient
becoming mired in a state of chronic isolation created by the outside world
and their own past. They must constantly work at maintaining their psychotic
fantasy lest their inner associations or events in external reality reveal that the
sense of being disconnected is an illusion. Unless the therapist can help the
patient examine their fantasy, growth cannot occur. The patient's recovery
depends on their ability to recognize that, though they have changed, they
have not lost themselves completely. An underlying, sustaining kernel of
selfhood is always there. When a patient says, "I've lost myself" or "I've
been invaded," they are acknowledging that some part of them is capable of
evaluation and remains alive and well, watching and remembering. An "I"
is formulating a judgment about the self.

In many cases, the life the patient has lived involves extreme trauma. Once a narrative exists—verbal and/or written—it becomes clear to both therapist and patient how and why the patient became who they are and developed the coping strategies they did to survive and make meaning of their experiences. At that point, the illusion of discontinuity is no longer necessary.

Chapter 10

# Going Blind to See

## A Case Study of Trauma, Regression, and Psychosis

At times we have found regression to be a necessary part of a healing process that leads to new possibilities for growth and development. Like Winnicott (1975), we consider regression as a psychic interruption or breech that carries an underlying purpose of returning the patient to a traumatic episode or constellation of episodes in which their reactionary, armored self first developed. The defenses formed against such trauma prevent psychological growth and limit the self's possibilities. The regressive return offers the opportunity for self-repair by working through the original trauma in a safe, holding environment. Today's public psychiatry offers only the elimination of regressive symptoms with either medication or hospital admission. Without psychotherapy, however, many individuals experiencing psychosis become frozen in a lifetime of chronic illness.

Winnicott's treatment of Margaret Little, an analyst herself, who experienced psychotic anxieties, is detailed in her book (Little, 1990) and in Winnicott's paper on regression (1975). In this chapter, we present DK's treatment of a man who experienced three regressive psychotic episodes. DK chose to work with this patient analytically so they could both understand what vital communications lay embedded in his delusions, and what secret order hid within the chaos he expressed in code. The following first-person account is written by DK. DK's account is followed by the patient's view of his analysis and recovery.

### Josh's Entry into Therapy

Josh began his therapy in a state of profound crisis, his voice shaking with emotion when he greeted me with the words: "You found me at the worst time of my life."

DOI: 10.4324/9781003441519-10

That he should deny his agency in asserting that *I'd found him* already conveyed his sense of helplessness to me. Having been forced to leave the home he'd rented for 30 years because the landlord he regarded as a father was selling it, Josh felt an overwhelming sense of betrayal, rejection, and abandonment.

I was quickly able to link Josh's present state of crisis with an event from his early life. His relationship with his parents, especially his mother, had been highly disturbed, though he did not initially offer much detail. He had an older sister from whom he was also estranged. While still a teen, he wished to drop out of college, but his parents threatened withdrawal of financial support. Josh thought his parents were being unreasonable and uncaring. He left school temporarily, and his parents stopped paying his way. Consequently, he stopped speaking to them and remained estranged from his family for nearly four decades. The withdrawal of financial support was merely the straw that broke the proverbial camel's back. Josh harbored hatred and resentment his entire life because he had always felt unloved, unwanted, unworthy, and cruelly treated by a bloodless and icy mother and a weak and traumatized father. He saw life through the lens of victimization with dependency, abandonment, and betrayal figuring prominently in his narrative. Josh's intense hatred and externalizations made it clear that powerful paranoid dynamics were at play.

A few months after beginning treatment, Josh lost Gena, his girlfriend of 20 years. Gena had been a powerful maternal figure for him, even supporting him financially over the previous year. She had discussed Josh's plight with her analyst, and they decided it was best for her to leave him, give him a sum of money and a deadline to find work and begin supporting himself. Thus, Gena left open the possibility that they might resume their relationship if Josh's work status changed. He retorted that he was unable to do so and felt intense anger at being forced to "grow up before his time" (he was 56). Though the parallel to the earlier parental situation leaped out in crystal clarity, it remained largely unacknowledged by Josh. He was losing his paternal landlord and his maternal girlfriend all at once.

Josh's anxiety and depression increased, and he began contemplating suicide. His false parental substitutes—a house of cards—had collapsed, and he felt terrified and cast out. He confessed he'd always felt like an imposter, afraid to be discovered as the person he believed himself to be: a helpless man–child with no secure sense of self and no grounding in the world.

He linked his ghostly self with "schizophrenia," saying, "I never felt part of the world...The world didn't matter to me. Only my inner world mattered. It was a scary fantasy world. I made up the rules. It was frightening. I didn't feel I had a self. It was like a house of horrors in there. I was trapped. That's why I have no idea who my sister, mother, or father are." He said he felt good to finally be able to say this to someone. Analysis was clearly offering him a second chance at life, a chance to come alive as an authentic being.

Josh regularly spoke of his emotional states in terms of "body armor" and "body blocks." The most common complaint was the "block behind my eyes," the first indication of the blindness theme. He described the block as if it were a physical obstruction. I understood Josh's focus on the body as part of his regression, like the preverbal infant who communicates through the body. Encouraging him to translate his physical conditions into affective communication, I found that for the most part, he could not express his emotions and, when he did, could not differentiate them from each other. The only emotions he knew with certainty were fear and fury.

Josh demonized his mother, deceased for many years, refusing to speak about her at first because he felt that if he did, he would be giving her "airtime." Still, she peeked in on our early sessions. He recalled her as a cold, unaffectionate, and critical woman who held Josh responsible for her misery. From his early childhood, Josh was convinced that she wished he had never been born, an example of Brett Kahr's (2007) theory proposing an infanticidal attachment relationship that predisposes one to develop schizophrenia. Trying desperately to please his mother, to garner some love and tenderness, Josh always failed because she "constantly changed the rules of the game." Thus, he grew more confused, helpless, and angry. Josh's rage and fury were palpable. His face darkened dangerously whenever he spoke of his mother. Although I functioned as an idealized mother figure in the transference, I expected that one day I'd be cast as the demon mother. I hoped that by then Josh would grow to entertain multiple viewpoints.

Josh pitied his father, whom he deemed weak and pathetic, expressing sadness and anger that Dad could not save him from Mom's wrath or offer meaning to his experiences. Josh recalled his dread and confusion when he heard his father's nightly screams as he awoke from World War II trauma nightmares that replayed his experiences as a soldier.

Josh had an older sister with whom he had also severed ties; by his own account, he had sexually abused her while she slept when they were adolescents. He initially felt entirely justified in his acts because it was one way he found to take revenge on his mother ("If I can't have her, I'll take the closest person to her"). It took years before Josh could talk about the abuse and experience a measure of guilt for his actions.

Josh reported a dream early on in which he could walk despite the fact that (in the dream) he was sitting in a wheelchair. This dream cautioned me to be alert to his feigning dependency or making himself out to be more disturbed than he was. I'd soon come to learn that his dependency needs were accompanied by rageful, angry demands that his mother, Gena, or I take care of him. Existing beneath his intense rage and panic was an unbearable longing for love and validation that had never been fulfilled, partly because he had felt too vulnerable to express his needs.

During the first crisis, Josh wrote daily suicide notes, most of them addressed to Gena, enacting a revenge fantasy to make her feel guilty for refusing to continue to support him, just as his parents had. At times, he spoke to me in his suicide notes, assuring me that nothing was my fault. I believe his expressing anger in this way kept him alive because it prevented him from internalizing his aggression. Yet, while I was away for a few days he crashed into a truck and totalled his car. A few days later, he bought a gun. Now I was scared. I firmly insisted that if he wished to work with me, he had to return the gun immediately and consult a psychiatrist for medication. Although I consider medication a last resort, I am open to the needs and desires of those with whom I work, and I am fortunate to have psychiatric colleagues with whom I can work and talk about dynamic and medical issues. This was one of those times when I did not wish to feel alone in the treatment of someone with serious violent urges.

Josh cried and agreed to do as asked. We made a pact: He would not kill himself, and I would not give up on him. We continued to stay in daily contact, and he took his meds for a brief time, hating the side effects. Much later, Josh told me that my faith in his ability to reconstitute without medication or hospitalization helped him trust me. I did not insist on his continuing on the medication after I witnessed the terrible side effects he suffered. Most important, my faith in him helped him believe more in himself and his ability to survive.

Gradually Josh began building inner strength. I nurtured him as a mother would a young child while not allowing him to exaggerate his weaknesses. Within six months, he sent out his resume and got a job. He was a pulmonary function technologist and respiratory therapist. He took on a second and then a third job, increased his sessions, and we finally began an analysis. As his confidence grew, he reconnected with Gena. As he became stabilized in treatment, Josh began to express some negative feelings toward me, evoking a negative maternal transference, which opened the door for his becoming aware of his paranoid dynamics.

One day he became enraged because I had pronounced Van Gogh with the "ch" sound, as the Dutch pronounce the artist's name, after he'd pronounced it as "Van Go." He was convinced I had intended to humiliate him. But the breakthrough came when something he said about his "head block" reminded me of an artwork by Man Ray. When he looked up the work he also read about the life of the artist and became convinced that I intentionally wanted him to see the similarities between him and Man Ray, particularly the Jewish link. He began to think I had sent him a secret message that he was "nothing more than a poor little Jewish kid who didn't know who he was." He worked himself into a fury, unleashing his anger at me, his mother, and even Man Ray. He hated his Jewishness and associated it with everything he despised about his upbringing: feeling weak like his father, set apart from others, and left behind. In the throes of paranoia, he fumed at me for being sneaky and indirect. Why didn't I simply say that I wanted him to address his Jewishness?

He was shocked to discover that I knew nothing about Man Ray's personal history. For the very first time, Josh accepted that he had been paranoid and confessed he had Googled me and that my accomplishments made me more inaccessible to him. His rage grew.

I remarked that Josh felt castrated by me, and he agreed. "Man Ray set me off," he shouted.

I responded, "Man, the name, and you're not feeling enough of one."

"Bingo!" he replied.

Clearly, Josh's mother had failed to nurture him, and his unmet needs were converted into rage. He easily experienced me, his mother substitute, as a persecutory object who wanted to harm him and destroy his self-esteem. In this case, he perceived me as trying to fill him up with Jewishness, the hated part of himself and the part he associated with his hated parents. He projected his calculating destructiveness onto me, and I became the secret manipulator, his sadism now residing in me. I was the bad mother/object, a paranoid persecutory object who wasn't to be trusted. The simultaneous awareness of me as a loving object and the encroachment of me as a persecutory object was terrifying to Josh.

Realizing that he was reliving the sadomasochistic mother–son dynamic gave him greater insight into his paranoia. He clearly saw that it was ever-present, a basic mode of functioning, and realized that he used his paranoia to regulate his emotions, especially his anger.

"By claiming I am being attacked, it provides me with a 'hair-trigger' excuse to give vent to a lifetime of repressed anger," he noted. Ironically, Josh's paranoia made him feel safe "because it gives me an excuse to regress to my 'safe place.'" Josh's "safe place" was one in which he hated the world, became withdrawn, and felt justified in his desire to die "because no one will ever love me." A cascade of insights followed. He said that when paranoid, he regressed to an early state in which the world revolved around his own needs and wishes. He also saw how paranoia and schizophrenia worked together. Whereas schizophrenia cut him off from the world, paranoia kept him attached to it, albeit in a distorted manner. The paranoia helped keep people at an optimal distance. "If I let people get too close," he said, "I fear they will find out I am really a nobody and will abandon me, which is my worst nightmare. But if I keep them too much at a distance, I lose them and am still abandoned."

Josh's abundant insights about his paranoia and schizophrenia were very impressive to me. Yet, I wondered whether they were too intellectual. How much was Josh able to feel them and not just think about them? I knew that they needed to be lived and felt, repeated and enacted, and worked through in our relationship and in his relationships outside of therapy. I knew too that we were on our way.

As our progress continued, the work gradually began to center on Oedipal issues. He continued Googling me and expanded his snooping to all my family members to uncover more about me and "get" what he felt he had been denied. I interpreted his actions as parallel to his having taken sex from his sister while she slept and stealing cash from his father's coat pockets—these previous acts of revenge and transgression also illustrated his conviction that no one would give to him willingly, and so he had to take what he wanted without asking permission or getting consent.

Becoming aware of his enactments made Josh sad, and he experienced two new emotions: guilt and concern for others.

He shared a wish to bring his mother back to life so that he could strangle her. I wondered if his ability to feel safe in the analytic relationship allowed him to verbally murder his mother, which, in effect, helped him to grieve the lost opportunity of a murder never committed. The gap between his wish to bring his mother back to life and his wish to kill her is where much of our work began to focus. By bringing his mother back to life in the therapeutic space, and by using me as a surrogate mother, he could have a corrective experience and begin to repair his past enough to further liberate himself from its unhealthy restraint. Perhaps then, I hoped, his second wish would fade.

"My rage covers up my longing for my mother," he said insightfully, as he recounted two dreams that placed him in his mother's bedroom. I appeared in these dreams in a condensed form as both myself and his mother. In one, I was dying, and he watched me get old before his eyes. He drew on my face and bald head in a desperate attempt to re-enliven me. Josh realized that he wished to bring his mother back to life, through me, so that she could see him as a grown man; so he could finally get her love and take it in for the first time; so he could offer her his love as he never had before; and so he could finally make reparation for what he had done so that he could begin again.

While associating to the dream, Josh recalled visiting his mother on her deathbed, at her request. As in the dream, he found her incredibly aged. "She wanted me to tell her I loved her before she died, but I wanted to punish her, to hurt her. I would not tell her I loved her," he said. In his dream, Josh returned to this scene with a wish to change it. Now he wanted to say to his mother, "Look what I've become. I'm a man now. Now will you love me?"

I remarked on how, in his dream, Josh had reversed the situation in which he took advantage of his sister while she slept and his mother as she was dying. Now he revived women from their sleep/death state, saving them from death and from him.

He replied, "Yes if they are awake, I can't take advantage of them. That is how I am feeling now. I couldn't be direct then. I didn't have the power in me. Now that I feel empowered, I can give. I wish I had felt that as a kid."

## Psychotic Regression

All was going quite well with Josh in our six-year analysis. He was working steadily and had reunited with Gena, but as we motored along, I began to perceive danger signs that we were heading toward rough waters. I had mixed feelings about Josh's inevitable regression. Part of me wished to do something to prevent it, and another part knew that the regression might be his only chance for achieving deep and lasting change. Josh went over the rapids in a psychotic episode that lasted six months. I now saw that he had correctly assessed a fragile psychotic core at the heart of his being. Ironically, the better he got and the more he understood, the stronger his ego became. Thus, he could more easily regress to a psychotic state because he had developed sufficient ego strength and felt safe enough with me and in his relationship with Gena to give in to a regressive pull and not have it cause permanent damage.

Josh's regressive psychosis had three triggering events: the presidential election; Gena's new interest in sex; and Josh's own breakthrough prior to the episode. During the 2008 presidential election, Josh's paranoia began to resurface, and he spent hours in analysis raging at the liberals and Democratic candidate, Barack Obama. He confessed that he was afraid "the Blacks" would take over the country and that he would lose control. He feared something terrible would happen. When questioned about specifics, he could only say that Obama would be assassinated. Only later did we realize he was predicting his own psychotic breakdown.

The second event concerned Gena, who, during the previous 10-15 years, had never had sex with Josh. On a conscious level, Josh feared that adding sex to his relationship with Gena would result in his losing the good mother she represented. Whenever he mentioned the subject, or when I broached it, he became extremely anxious and defensive and refused to go further. Having worked through some of her issues of sexual abuse in her own analysis and having found a lubricant for her vaginal dryness, Gena had announced that she was ready to have sex with Josh, emphasizing that she would wait patiently until he felt ready. But all he heard was that her newly moist vagina awaited him. He quickly regressed to a state of dependency, began to experience physical symptoms, and believed he was suffering from a fatal illness. He'd always complained of sight problems, his vision blurring when things went poorly, but now he feared he was going blind and began to focus exclusively on his body, losing the ability to think symbolically. Yet, I immediately suspected that whatever blindness he suffered was an acknowledgment of his refusal to go further in analysis. He spent hours on the internet identifying with lists of symptoms and diseases, visiting doctors, and taking medical tests.

Eventually, Josh arrived at a psychotic insight: *he was going blind!* He believed he was literally losing his sight; the block behind his eyes, an early complaint, had come to full fruition. He claimed the world was dim and dark, unclear, and frightening. I understood Josh's "blindness" as a concrete metaphor for what he was experiencing. As a man who could readily reflect and associate, he had now become obsessed with his blindness and was no longer able to link it to a broader network of associations. Melanie Klein (1975) wrote about hypochondriasis as a felt near presence of the persecutory object about to enter the damaged body. Was Josh's blindness related to his mother's felt presence overtaking his weakened sense of self? Was it the ultimate castration signifying his refusal to see, as in the original Oedipus story when Oedipus blinds himself after realizing he had slept with his mother? Or was it related to his terror that his inability to perform sexually would diminish him in Gena's eyes? Interestingly, De Masi (2009) has written that in psychosis the unconscious is blinded and prevented from coming into contact with the perceptual part of the self. Now, because of his blindness, Josh could regress to being completely dependent on Gena. He would not have to reconcile her maternal function with her sexual needs. He blinded himself to the intense conflict between a desperate need to be taken care of and the terror associated with the intimacy of sex. Closeness meant castration; distance meant abandonment. There had been no in-between for him. In his mind, there was no way out, no resolution, and no bottom.

His destruction of sight reflected the need to rid himself of perception and thought, the very organs that could recognize inner and outer reality (Bion, 1959). Josh's "sickness" became the manifestation of his breakdown. Paranoia found a home in his body in the form of extreme hypochondria. The horror of the outside world became the horror of his inside world, boiling beneath his skin. Without sight, he became terrified and ridden with annihilation anxiety (Hurvich, 1989), the symptom he had intended to manage in the first place. Interestingly, within a short time, he complained of going deaf. By trying to avoid the terror-charged conflict of intimacy vs. dependency, he created a far greater fear. He felt threatened by the system he had defensively created, and this process destroyed the very means that would have helped him work through his core conflict (De Masi, 2009).

I had always felt that Josh's life had been permeated by childhood trauma, mostly around the powerful negative emotions he felt for his mother. When he spoke of her, I was reminded of Aulagnier's (2001) theory regarding the origin of psychosis as the consequence of primary violence perpetuated by the mother's mind on the child's mind, which prevents the autonomous development of his inner world. Josh's mother could not, or would not, contain his anxiety, aggression, and envy. Nor could she respond to his powerful longing for her. Thus, his unbearable anxiety was directed back at himself, plummeting him into nameless terror. Josh recalled his mother abandoning him as a small boy on a crowded street in New York City to teach him a lesson not to stray. He compared the panic and helplessness he was feeling now to the panic he had felt then. Josh learned to hate early in life and to construct an omnipotent and fragile self-system and destructive superego. His warped superego wanted to punish and kill himself and others. He knew he carried within him a primal malfunction, which he called schizophrenia.

Because of his extreme reaction to Gena's invitation to sex, I now began to wonder if Josh had been sexually abused by his mother. If he hadn't been physically abused, he certainly had been crushed by the power she wielded over him. Surprisingly, he compulsively attempted to have sex with Gena during his psychosis and "nearly died from abject terror." The room was dark, and he could hardly see, but he told me the "presence of my mother haunted me throughout." Naturally, he was unable to perform. "I thought of my mother. I had a baby dick. Too small. Not big enough. Not erect enough. It was futile." He associated his childhood home in Brooklyn with "darkness, no direct sunshine; the blinds usually were drawn. It felt sinister, secretive." He began to think he had set up sex with Gena to replicate a scene from his childhood. When Gena touched his penis, it felt like a baby penis.

During this time, I saw my function as containing Josh's rage, fear, and anxiety and naming his emotional states, and helping him own them without being destroyed by them. Meanwhile, he sought out one doctor after another: five ophthalmologists, two neurologists, several otolaryngologists, and two neuro-ophthalmologists. He had CAT scans and MRIs. He had acupuncture and Feldenkrais, a type of movement therapy used to promote flexibility. We considered medication under the care of two psychiatrists, and he did try antidepressants, anti-anxiety, sleep medications, and even antipsychotic medication, though he stopped them all when he experienced severe side effects.

Josh had trouble falling asleep, and when he did, he awoke in a sweat and a panic and was unable to get back to sleep. Once he dreamed that he buried his father alive in a pit that resembled the pit he had hidden in during World War II. Josh seemed to be repeating his father's trauma by awakening every night at the same time his father had. By making this connection, I helped Josh "see" the intergenerational traumatic identification he had internalized.

Josh began to look exhausted and frightening—dark rings under his bloodshot eyes, his face a continual presentation of grimaces as he shouted and stormed during treatment, wrangling attention and support from everyone he knew until they reached the limits of patience. We both considered hospitalization, but he begged me not to have him hospitalized, convinced that his life would be over once he'd become a psychiatric patient.

I encouraged him to hang on and assured him that the intensity of the episode would eventually subside. I knew that part of him heard me even though he was unable to do any analytical work. I am certain I was trying to convince myself as well. I assured myself that, since Josh never missed a session, his attachment to me and the work would win out over time.

Josh exhibited what Pao (1979) called "organismic panic." He had seen and felt too much and so created a delusional world of blindness in an attempt to not feel overwhelmed by what he could not face. Again, Josh became hyper-anxious, sleepless, and suicidal. I held on to Winnicott's (1975) notion that the individual, being unable to defend the self against failure, freezes the situation in the unconscious with the hope of unfreezing and repairing it at a later time in a safe environment. I remained alert for what Podvoll (2003) called "islands of clarity," areas in which ego functioning and ego integrity still exist, and also reminded myself of Podvoll's call for compassionate action. Amazingly, Josh continued his treatment four times a week and still worked two of his three jobs. He also kept all his friends. These were three beautiful islands of clarity.

His dependence on Gena increased, and I saw them together several times, as I needed to ascertain what support he had on the outside. Fortunately, Gena was on board. I suggested that she not encourage his dependency and speak to the highest functioning part of him. Gena's loyalty, patience, and love played a central role in Josh's eventual recovery. Of course, Josh began to split between Gena and me. She was the "good mommy," and I became the "bad mommy." Part of what Josh needed to experience in his regressive psychosis was the overpowering rage he felt toward his mother, and I became her embodiment. Gena reminded Josh of the positive role I had played in his life, and this helped to counter his paranoia. He felt guilty about the intense rage he directed toward me, and I felt overextended and unappreciated during the hours of his sustained abuse.

The third trigger for Josh's psychosis was his own breakthrough. He'd always felt a profound disconnect between his mind and his body, often complaining about tightness in the back of his head. A few weeks before the onset of his psychosis, he claimed to have had a "breakthrough in consciousness." He stated that for the first time, his body and mind were in sync, and he was thrilled to feel a unity he'd hoped and waited for all his life. Unfortunately, this breakthrough came at a time when his girl-friend was offering him sex. He now saw clearly what lay before him: his fear of performing as a man, his limitations, and most of all his mortality. Though Josh was now 63, he was physically fit and athletic. He claimed he felt as if he were 20 and that there was nothing he couldn't do physically. All at once, he needed to face his limitations, which included his stage of life.

"Suddenly, I thought, Oh my God! I am a living thing. That means I can die!" he told me. "I am afraid of life. I am flesh and bones!" He realized that he had lived in a haze, disavowing his mortal, animal body, ignoring time as flesh. Though he had a partner, career, and many friends, he carried within him a sense of alienation and disconnection that flared up when he became ill; during these times, he was overtaken by existential anxiety. In his psychosis, he could not forget his animal fate, the fact that he would die—the terrifying inevitability and finality (see Becker, 1973, for more on the denial of death). He said, "I have to go through everything again, but with my eyes open, not from a remote contact-less state."

One day, after an emergency forced me to cancel an appointment, a blood vessel burst in Josh's eye. He panicked, convinced that, indeed, he was going blind. He then had trouble connecting to me, "I don't know you,'" he said later. "You've become a blank. When I feel people don't care, I crawl up in a ball and want to blow my brains out." Still, he continued treatment.

He was terrified of being alone. He'd cry, "I want my mommy," and "I'm watching myself disintegrate." At times, he felt as if what was happening to him was a punishment. His dreams were filled with menacing people, death threats, bombs, killing, and castration. He was unable to associate to their contents. He felt he had to defecate all the time, and, because of this symptom, he developed a fear of going out. Incapable of containing the feelings exploding inside of him, he wanted "to shit on the world!" His thoughts and emotions had become concrete objects to be expelled rather than expressed.

He quickly returned to a highly dependent position, as if he needed to relive his infancy and childhood and all that had gone wrong. He felt helpless even though he continued to function (minimally) and work (hardly). He was in a constant state of panic. But when he saw me, he "let it all out": his fears, rage, terror, extreme dependency, feelings of being emasculated, and despair. I became the bad mother of his childhood on whom he would take out his rage. At times, he expressed murderous desires as well. But I was also the good mother who was consistently there for him, who cared for him without fail and believed in him, and who did not abandon him even when he expressed his fury.

Meanwhile, that fury increased. He suspected that I did not think it likely he was physically ill, and each time a test result returned negative, he'd be disappointed; then catch himself and say he was relieved. He felt as if I were unwilling to acknowledge that his persecutory objects were multiplying in his body and that he was desperately under siege, his body, a castle about to crumble. On my side, I believed that the annihilating work of the persecutory objects had created Josh's "blindness." He saved his harshest criticism for the doctors I recommended.

"You're not supposed to smile at someone who hates you," he said to me one day when I smiled at seeing him enter the office. He attacked every connection that sustained him (Bion, 1959): his connection with me, with the progress he had made over six years, his friends, and even the link with Gena. Every session began as if no work had preceded it. The links between days, sessions, events, and even thoughts dissolved in the storm as he disassembled before my eyes. I continued to speak to what was most integrated and functional in him all the while remaining a reliable presence that could withstand his rage, dependency, and anxiety while attempting to contain his regression and psychosis.

Rage, spite, and vengefulness characterized Josh's relationship with his mother. He became a failure in school to spite her. Nothing could top the reward of revenge. His mother could not be dead enough. In one fantasy, he imagined strangling her, throwing her out a window, stabbing her with a knife, spitting on her, defecating on her, and stomping on her head. After he recounted the fantasy with no affect, he suddenly panicked: "Oh my God! I killed the one person I'm most dependent upon. What have I done?"

I knew that Josh was speaking not only of his relationship with his mother but also of his connection with me. Indeed, he removed the "Dr." from my name when he wrote his checks, stating with a smile, "I demoted you." I had failed him as the perfect mother, he said.

When I asked him what a perfect mother would look like, he replied, "Someone who would keep me a baby."

"Then that's the mother you had," I said.

He answered, "I need you to help me see this red thread in a way that doesn't destroy me."

Indeed, this red thread was the tightrope we walked, Josh and I, as we attempted to enable him to see just what he could tolerate without deteriorating or going totally blind.

In a moment of insight, he said, "I spent my whole life hating my mother any way I could, even when I was not connected to her, even in her death. And you represent that."

It was difficult for me to watch this very large, 63-year-old man reduced to a weeping blob, crying for his mommy. I had to remind myself of the work we had accomplished together for six years. At times, I wondered about my own sense of reality. Had he ever been better? Was he physically sick? Had I missed important aspects of his character? Was he driving me crazy as he had been driven crazy by his family (Searles, 1959)? And was this a failed treatment rather than the success story I had thought it was?

Yet Josh sometimes arrived at his sessions announcing, "I want to work." In one such session, he tried to convey his primal terror: "I feel so helpless as if I was literally just born and someone is telling me to run a company." Once, after running to the hospital with a false emergency, he was calmed by being seated in a wheelchair. He felt the wheelchair was luring him, and he had to fight its temptation. I reminded him of the dream he had reported early in treatment in which he sat in a wheelchair even though he was able to walk. The seduction of the psychotic solution—his "blindness"—was in constant conflict with what I could offer him.

I taught Josh breathing exercises to calm himself down. I pointed out the secondary gains he was receiving from his psychotic behavior. He loved the attention from his friends who called him daily. I solicited the scientist in him, inviting him to be curious about the symbolic meanings of his blindness. Little by little, we began to see "psychosis-free intervals" (De Masi, 2009), during which he started to engage in analytic work aimed at understanding and "seeing" the meaning of his psychotic construction. Often when we had a good session, characterized by an appearance of Josh's curiosity and willingness to engage with me in trying to understand and gain control of his predicament, his vision would "miraculously," though temporarily, improve.

At times, he'd say, "The real Josh made an appearance today," or "Today I feel almost normal," illustrating the new fluctuations in his condition.

I tried to help Josh monitor his affect states to develop a sense of control over them, knowing when to resort to anti-anxiety medication and when not to. Josh's occasional insights, his motivation to live and to work, his desire to transcend his past, his connection with me, Gena, and his friends, and his ability to work: all of these still existed, even in minimal forms, and I spoke to them, enlisted them as my co-analysts, and they eventually nudged us over the hump.

I was less afraid of Josh's regression than I was of his despair. I can still recall seeing Josh, a large man now literally melting away (he had lost 50 pounds!), with a desolate and despondent faraway look in his eyes. He could barely sit still, his entire body shaking, and concentrating was too much to ask. Naturally, I feared he'd take his life, and we spoke of that possibility constantly. I knew many professionals would have had him hospitalized. I was fortunate to have worked with two psychiatrists who also encouraged Josh to try to get better without hospitalization. Yet, despite his appearance, Josh continued coming to treatment, believing it was his only hope. Gradually he began to consider the possibility that his blindness was psychogenic in nature. He started to take risks and venture out into the world.

The turning point took place after my August vacation, during which I maintained contact with him by email and phone sessions. Providing continuity was, I believed, essential while I was away because it helped

Josh feel and "see" my dedication to and concern for him. In short, while he was demonizing me, I remained fully committed to our relationship, even extending the treatment parameters. Surely, he would internalize that truth over time.

At first, Josh didn't even realize he was improving. For example, one Monday he told me he had been blind all weekend. Later in the session, he mentioned that he had played tennis twice and had gone shopping. When I pointed out that he couldn't have been too blind to engage in those activities, he lashed out at me but later agreed with my obvious inference. He reported a dream in which he gave oxygen to a father figure, which I interpreted as Josh's attempt to revive his father from death, and, by association, himself from a deathlike state. Indeed, Josh began to show signs of life as he slowly attenuated his antagonist behavior. His neurotic defenses reappeared, replacing the psychotic structure; he was gradually recovering his vitality and feeling much better.

Indeed, Josh again began to speak psychologically. "My mother was blinding me," he said. "She gave me no affection, love, or security. And I am blinding myself for the sake of pleasing her, even though I say I don't want to be attached to her." For Josh, the blindness was "what she wants" and also "how I get back at her."

I ventured to sum up: "We have been reliving your childhood, your neediness and lack of love from your mother, your hatred of her, and, of course, the stalemate you found yourself in with her—the terror of the world and feelings of unpreparedness. You are saying to me and to her, 'Don't you see? I cannot manage in this life without the necessary foundation!'"

Within his break, Josh had rendered us both blind to recapture the disconnect between mother and son. "She made me impotent, sexually and emotionally. She made me a slave. I couldn't break away," he said.

Josh had a dream in which he reconnected to his sexuality: he was attracted to several voluptuous women, women shaped like Gena, something that would have put him off in the past. We began to do the work of separating Josh's childhood from his adulthood yet retaining the continuity that existed between them.

"My childhood was one big emergency. I couldn't get out of it. I could only hide," he observed. Whereas he had previously demoted me by taking away my professional title, now he gave me a raise. "I'm sleeping better," he admitted. "I'm feeling better. I feel I am coming out of this. I've been hiding out. I can give now. I feel what you did for me." He had a dream in which his arm was cut, and the flap of skin opened. "I am getting rid of my emotional cancer," he interpreted.

One day he brought me a bag of light bulbs for my office and a dream in which he sought a better view. "I just couldn't accept that reality was real," he said. "And now that I am through avoiding, let's talk about sex and death."

Josh admitted that needing sex from a woman, especially one he loved, gave her power over him, subjugating him since his need might be greater than hers. She stood above him, her body a desirable object to which he must join himself, forced by dint of his desire to perform. This could be a beautiful dance for him except that he felt he'd lose himself within it, disappear, be absorbed and enslaved, and die in darkness again. He loved her and wanted her; he was terrified by his desire and the possibility of being dominated through his desire; he feared the loss of whatever ego resources he had built; he hated her for being at the nexus of his conundrum. At last, he saw clearly.

## Regression and Psychosis

Winnicott (1975) claimed that it takes courage to regress, and Nass (1984) maintained that the capacity to experience and tolerate early modes of functioning requires a strong ego rather than a regressed one. Kris (1952) argued that a strong ego is, in fact, partly defined by the flexibility of its various functions, including the capacity to tolerate and come back from regression. Josh was able to survive psychotic regression because he found receptive containment in me for his toxic impulses and because he had enough ego strength to get him through it.

Regression is especially important for individuals who have experienced trauma. Josh returned to the site of his environmental failures (hateful, punitive mother and traumatized father). Meanwhile, the holding environment I consistently offered helped him get in touch with his primitive rage and fear so that he was able to regress and examine his trauma within the safety and stability of our relationship. Although he fought me and the treatment, he never left. He used me and the therapeutic setting to act out his trauma without the threat of censure and retaliation. In the simplest terms, Josh went from a person who developed in reaction to and defense against his trauma to a person who *saw* and knew what had happened to him. To truly understand what has happened does not mean the patient arrives at some invariant objective truth. Rather, the patient deeply and insightfully decides on the meaning of their experience in a way that saves them.

Josh regained his ego capacities and symbolic functioning. "I am still Josh," he said after emerging from his psychosis, "but now I'm Josh hooked up." We worked for more than a year to make meaning of the psychotic regression he experienced, and Josh remarked that he couldn't imagine having recovered without it. He said, "It sounds crazy, but I've never felt stronger. I had to split to protect my life. I had to face what happened to me. The trauma had to be released. I faced my terror and death. I am calming down now. I am emerging."

Josh made a full recovery from his psychosis, not only maintaining his sanity but continuing to grow—until Hurricane Sandy hit New York in 2012. Once again, Josh, now 67, was forced to leave his home. For a third time, he felt rejected, abandoned, and homeless (though he lived temporarily with Gena). He regressed for a third time into a psychosis that was more virulent than the previous two episodes. Once more, he believed he was suffering from a life-threatening illness. Most concerning, however, was the powerful negative therapeutic reaction that emerged. The rage against his maternal figure I had glimpsed at the beginning of treatment now took possession of him, and Josh seemed determined to destroy me, himself, and the treatment. He was like a suicide bomber who didn't care who or what he destroyed. He wished to take revenge on his mother (and surrogate mother) for not having given him what he needed. This regression was the most trying because his unrelenting rage was directed unswervingly at me. He needed me to be his masochistic partner and suffering mother.

The pleasure Josh took in describing to me his death-dealing fantasies was disconcerting. In the countertransference, I felt that he was de-skilling me and, in fact, killing me. I also felt it was important to him (and of course to me) that I survive his death threats. Struggling to regain my bearings, I asserted my boundaries and communicated firm limits. I declared to him that I would not allow him to destroy me though I could not prevent him from destroying himself. He reacted with enormous rage; however, he then emerged rapidly from the psychosis. One year later, he told me that his strategy for killing me had not worked, and he had to try something else. That something else was analysis—for him to finally realize how much pleasure he derived from sadistically bringing me down and merging with me (as the demon mother) in my weakened and dead state. "I wanted to kill the thing I love the most," he said, knowing now that I represented his icy mother: "You freeze me, and I'll burn you!"

My having survived Josh's destructive yearnings helped him to see us as two separate beings. Josh began to use me (Winnicott, 1971) as well as express care, remorse, and guilt toward me and others. Owning his rage and its deadly consequences, and mourning what he had never received from his mother became central preoccupations in the analysis. In fact, several years after his last psychotic episode, Josh became clinically depressed. We both awaited the reappearance of his psychotic symptoms, but they never showed up. Instead, he experienced true mourning along with an expressed wish to live. Josh was mourning the ending of his professional career (he retired), the ending of his youth, and, of course, the people he had lost along the way. Most of all, he mourned the wished-for relationship with his mother. Only now was he finally mourning his losses—including not having a family and not having sex with his partner for so many years. Josh remained in this state of mourning for many months, and I sat with him and shared his sadness and grief. Although this phase of treatment was difficult for us both, it had a very different feel than his psychotic episodes. This time, he was present, in touch with his emotions, confronting reality and its losses head-on.

I still work with Josh, who continues to make progress. When his landlords were selling the house he lived in, Josh and Gena decided to purchase it. For the first time in their 40-year relationship, the pair decided to make a home together. After his retirement, he has been occupying himself with tennis, gardening, making music, and, most of all, building and sharing a life with Gena. More recently, after decades of being alienated from his past life, he has begun to reconnect with some of his family members.

## Concluding Remarks

Josh experienced three psychotic regressions and one major depression during two decades of analysis. He had a strong support system (several close friends and a decades-long relationship with Gena), and he was able to hold onto his jobs despite being at times quite delusional and paranoid. Although he regressed in sessions with me, he was able to mobilize just enough ego strength to perform his daily professional duties, at least minimally. Because his employers valued his work, they tolerated Josh's eccentric behavior and offered emotional support.

He did not miss one session during his psychotic episodes. Due to his islands of clarity (Podvoll, 2003) and Josh's earnest desire to stay out of the hospital, he worked with me on nearly a daily basis during his psychotic regressions, each of which lasted approximately six months. After Josh emerged from his psychotic episodes, he and I spent months, and sometimes years, analyzing what had brought on his episodes and discussing ways he could fortify himself against future regressions.

Josh's case illustrates several key elements in the treatment of psychosis. Most important, it shows that psychosis can be treated with analysis and demonstrates that regression is sometimes a necessary and even a healing component of the treatment. In addition, making meaning of the psychotic symptoms is an integral part of treatment. When dealing with psychosis, Bollas attempts to understand the patient's reasoning and then communicate that meaning to them, emphasizing how it is reasonable for them to behave and think the way they do, given their specific historical and psychological circumstances (Personal communication with DK, December 11, 2011).

Josh's "blindness" was profoundly symbolic (i.e., he had indeed been blind to many aspects of his experience), and it also represented his desire and need to regress to a state of dependence. His blindness was also his wish to deny his own body, especially his sex organs. Treating psychosis is often like entering someone else's nightmare or trying to defuse a bomb. No wonder many shy away from such work. On the other hand, daring to visit the limits of experience, where almost anything is possible, necessarily taps into the therapist's creativity because creation always takes place on the threshold of the unknown. Having faith in the resilience and natural healing potential of people, no matter how bizarrely they present, offers them containment and acceptance, which can turn into increased possibilities for growth.

Josh's eyesight was restored, accompanied by improvements in his insight. *He went blind to see!* He has become increasingly open to better understanding and managing his psychological life. He now calls himself a "realist" because he sees himself more objectively than ever before.

For me, the work with Josh has deepened my belief in the importance of the relationship in the therapeutic process. The relationship is the transparent vehicle in which all the content of therapy resides, as well as the literal crucible in which transformation takes place. When I shared this chapter with him, Josh cried and said, "You told my story."

I responded, "I told *our* story."

## Josh's Narrative of Psychosis and Recovery

*Well before I met Dr. Knafo, while I was seeing another therapist, I had a distinct memory of being in my mother's womb. This was not a dream, or a fantasy, but an actual memory. It was dark, cold, and terrifying, and all I wanted to do was get out. Although I didn't, and couldn't, escape my surroundings, I distinctly remember leaving my body, looking back, and seeing only my physical shell, minus my spirit. In hindsight, I believe that splitting from my body was probably the only way I could break free of my emotional and physical pain. Since then, I have spent my entire life trying to reintegrate.*

Although I could easily write a book about how analysis with Dr. Knafo saved my life, I believe this short commentary about my experience with psychotic regression will clearly illustrate this point. The main questions raised in her account include, "Are psychotic regressions sometimes necessary for the healing process; can therapy with psychotic patients be done on an outpatient basis; and can therapy, in cases such as these, be done with a minimum (if not the absence) of drugs?" For me, the answers are, "Yes, yes, and yes."

My first regressive psychosis was triggered by my landlord and his wife (clearly, surrogate parents) informing me they were selling their house and moving to Florida. I was with them for nearly 30 years. The news threw me into a state of panic, and I regressed to a very infantile, dependent state. I felt abandoned, rejected, betrayed, helpless, and unbelievably paranoid—I wished I would just die and contemplated suicide almost constantly. Although I was convinced no one could help me, I desperately reached out to anyone who would listen to my tale of woe. These feelings were literally non-stop, 24 hours a day, lasted six months, and made me feel like I was swimming in some sort of hell. I couldn't sleep, hardly ate, lost a ton of weight, looked like a cadaver, and ended up roaming the streets of my neighborhood at all hours of the night, frantically trying to exhaust myself so I could collapse and get some rest—but to no avail. Sometimes when going out, I could hardly stand and felt I would defecate on the spot. I was terrified of lying down, and when I was "lucky" enough to drift off for a short nap, I was plagued by nightmares and woke up in a panic, drenched in sweat. While awake, I was shaking all the time, punching walls, banging my head into trees, and had the attention span of a gnat. Other than that…I was fine :-).

It was shortly after the onset of the regression that I began therapy with Dr. Knafo. Despite my condition, what I call my "schizo intuition" was still intact, and the instant I met her I felt she knew what she was doing. I sensed she "got who I was," and she seemed confident in her ability to help me—this was combined with a sweet compassionate nature, which was an absolute requirement. Over the years, I've come to believe that for any therapy to succeed, there has to be some "magic" between the therapist and the patient, and I've felt blessed to have her as my doctor.

My chief complaint (aside from the litany of symptoms from the regression) was that, for my whole life, I felt as if I was living in some sort of purgatory, disconnected from both my body and the real world. I told Dr. Knafo I felt as if I had no ego, and even though she insisted technically I did (but a weak one), I still didn't believe her. I also told her that my gauge for being "cured" would be if, and when, I'd ever feel linked up.

We agreed from the outset that we wanted to do therapy, if possible, without the use of drugs, believing they were mostly a band-aid that dulled the senses and hindered the progress of therapy. My expression was, "It's like pouring perfume on vomit and thinking the smell would go away." We did use some drugs, however, for a very short time, but therapy has been conducted almost exclusively without them.

We got through the first regression after much hard work, and I remained fairly stable for nearly six years, making steady progress. One of the most powerful tools to get me through the regression was *free association*. At first, what came gurgling up from my subconscious didn't seem to make any sense. However, for some reason, it expanded me, as if I were being embraced. Having had few, if any, hugs from my mother, any feeling of warmth was more than welcome. In time, the associations began to knit together and took on structure and meaning.

And then…a few years later, I woke up in the middle of the night with runaway anxiety that was so intense, I felt like I wanted to rip my skin off! The analogy I made was that of an overflowing bathtub: the water was my anxiety, but when I tried to turn off the faucet, it wouldn't budge. I remember feeling that this had to be some sort of "cosmic joke." I couldn't believe this was happening again! I thought I'd paid my dues the first time around.

The onset of this second regression came just before Dr. Knafo was leaving for her yearly vacation, following an incident where I burst a blood vessel in my eye. Like the first regression, I had all the same symptoms, but this time I was convinced I was going blind, which ramped up my condition, and, as Dr. Knafo pointed out: "There were things I didn't want to see." Seriously concerned about me, she made me promise to e-mail her every day while she was on vacation. If not, she said she would consider committing me. I think I wrote her only half the time, needing Mommy's approval on the one hand, yet wanting to torture and worry her on the other (there was a defiant little imp in me that knew exactly what he was doing, but I couldn't admit it to myself). But Dr. Knafo took it, probably knowing full well that acting it out would help. Combined with my girlfriend's incredible love and support, the "three of us" made it through regression number two.

Approximately a year after the second regression, I reaped my first huge reward from therapy. I had an image come to mind in one of my sessions of a tree seedling growing through a crack in the concrete. It was one of the most profound experiences of my life. I was the seedling, and I knew it was the beginning of my finally having an ego (small though it was). Throughout my life, whenever I thought of myself, the image was never of being positioned inside my body. Rather, I was this etheric, ghost-like entity hovering above my right shoulder, but not connected to myself. That time, however, and for the first time in my life, the feeling and image were no longer there. I could sense that my mind and body were finally linking up and felt the beginning of my lifelong dream of reintegration. Since then, that seedling has grown into a mature tree, and I have a strong, steady foundation based on a sense of self.

Anyone who has lived long enough has suffered life's ironies. And so, two years later, having been ejected from my home after Hurricane Sandy, and told by my new landlords (my second pair of surrogate parents) that I had to move out for four months (for repairs), regression number three reared its ugly head. This time, combined with my landlady, it was yet another mother that rejected me—Mother Nature. But it was different. I still regressed to a somewhat dependent, infantile state, but not nearly as bad as the last two regressions. Instead of *wanting* to die, this time I wanted to live, but was certain I was dying. I developed physical symptoms that were so severe that I was absolutely convinced I had either multiple sclerosis (MS) or ALS. Extensive testing, however, proved me wrong. And Dr. Knafo wasn't buying it either, insisting she thought it was all psychosomatic. But I had an agenda, and I was not to be stopped. Now that I had adequate ego strength, if I was going to die, I was taking her (Mommy) down with me.

The emotional battle that followed between us was epic. All we needed was Cecil B. DeMille to direct! Neither of us knew who would survive, or if either of us would survive. However, Dr. Knafo made her position quite clear: "If you want to die, go ahead, but you're not taking me with you!" Regardless, I tried. I was absolutely relentless and couldn't help myself. I recruited, and convinced, all my friends that she was incompetent and wasn't the least bit concerned that I was seriously ill. This culminated with a psychiatrist friend of mine lambasting her on the phone and accusing her of malpractice.

Regression three lasted nearly a year. At one point, things had gotten so contentious that Dr. Knafo told me she may have run out of options and could no longer help me. I could see she was at her wits' end (which is exactly what I wanted), but it gave me pause. I knew she could help me, despite my being hellbent on destroying her. Luckily, the healthy part of me woke up, and I implored, "Don't give up on me." Once again, she bravely answered the call, and we got through it. Into the ninth month of the regression, I finally got tired of running to doctors. I decided if I was going to die, I would just die. About a month after that decision (September 9, 2013), a date I'll never forget, I woke up one morning and felt well for the first time in a year, and it's been that way ever since.

Looking back, I'm convinced the reason for the last regression was that I still had something to learn. It gave me perspective on the first two and brought things to a head because it revealed a lifelong script that was running in me—a script so powerful that (unbeknownst to me), it actually took precedence over my desire to get well! What I wanted was really impossible. I wanted Dr. Knafo to give me the unconditional love I never got from my mother, but at the same time wanted to destroy her in order to vent a lifetime of rage as well as exact my revenge for never getting what I wanted. I wanted my cake and to eat it too. I was stunned that I never saw this before and was equally shocked that after twelve years of analysis, I was clearly more loyal to my pathology than I was to my health. But juggling two Mommies is not the answer—those ships sailed a long time ago. It's clear that mourning the loss and learning to love myself will eventually heal me, but that doesn't happen overnight. Lasting change takes time.

Dr. Knafo once asked me my definition of health. I told her, "It's the ability to live in the present." Being unencumbered by your past, however, is no easy task—twenty years of therapy may seem like a lot, but it's not. It took at least that long to get screwed up, so it may take equally as long or longer to untangle all those emotional knots—and there are no shortcuts. We're working on it.

So, here's how I feel. The regressions were necessary. *I had to break down in order to break through.* Busting my defenses wide open, with all the drama, was the only way for me to get in touch with my feelings, especially considering my propensity to use my intellect as a defense mechanism. Although "outside circumstances" triggered the regressions, I've also entertained the idea that my subconscious may have selectively screened and used them as an opportunity to trigger the regressions, all in an attempt at self-healing.

Would it have been possible to chip away at my defenses gradually, without an overwhelming breakdown? Maybe. I'll never really know, but I doubt it. I certainly would've preferred it, but I had to play the cards I was dealt. In addition, there were no guarantees I would survive these regressions; it's possible I might've killed myself, died from compromising my immune system to the point of actually inducing a terminal illness, or maybe even committed murder—all of which were possible. Luckily, under the courageous and empathetic care of Dr. Knafo, I made it through without that happening.

Ultimately, however, even with the most skilled therapist, I've learned that no one can really save you but you. As much as these regressions exposed my weaknesses, they served an equally important function in exposing strengths I never knew I had (none of which I take credit for—I was just born that way). On the occasions when Dr. Knafo and I considered commitment, I felt if I gave in and allowed that to happen, my remaining life would be a nightmare. I fantasized about being locked away in an institution, friendless, alone, curled up in a fetal position on a cold bare floor, all after being drugged into oblivion so I wouldn't bother anyone… and so I rallied. And Dr. Knafo and I are still here to talk about it.

Finally, I would like to comment on the severe depression I had following the psychotic regressions. It went on for months. Every night, almost exactly at 3:00 a.m., the floodgates would open, and unbearable anxiety would run through my veins, lasting most of the day. Occasionally, it would let up for brief periods of time, but only to return again. I couldn't stop the cycle. As horrible as that was, I refused to take any drugs because I felt the key to getting well was to endure the torture in order to overcome it. It was a "do or die" situation.

Eventually, however, my stubbornness gradually started to wear me down, and just like before, I began to feel ill. I ate just enough to subsist, lost close to 40 pounds, and felt completely run down. I finally went to see my doctor, convinced that I had a serious degenerative disease. However, as before, I was told that all my tests were normal. As much as I was relieved to hear the news, the anxiety persisted.

After a while, when I just couldn't bear it anymore, I finally agreed to try a small dose of Klonopin at Dr. Knafo's urging. After I took the medication, the cycle broke, and I began to recover. So, the question was, was it really the medication that did it? It seemed that way at the time, but upon reflection, the fact that I agreed to take it likely meant that the cycle was ready to be broken, regardless. I never needed any medication after that.

What was uniquely different about the depression, unlike the psychotic episodes, was the fact that I felt a very strong emotional foundation under me, one that Dr. Knafo and I built together over the years. I never went out of contact throughout the entire ordeal, and it's been that way ever since. At the time, as crazy as it sounded to me, Dr. Knafo saw the "graduation" from psychotic regression to severe depression as a huge improvement. It took me a while to appreciate what she was talking about, but eventually I "got it" and embraced my "diploma."

As of this writing (November 2022), I'm still in therapy and plan to stay in it as long as I can afford to. It's not that I feel particularly ill anymore, nor do I depend on having my therapist make life decisions for me (she never did); it's just that I've really come to appreciate the subtleties of my defense mechanisms and how intertwined they are. I find that the more I untie these emotional knots, the better I feel. So why not continue to deepen and improve my quality of life?

What has all this taught me? If you want to get well, and you're motivated and lucky enough to have a great therapist, good things will happen.

# Chapter 11

# Endings

Although the word termination implies finality, terminations are inevitably incomplete. Artful termination involves transcending the need for the therapeutic relationship while continuing the work of insight and relational transformation. Termination is intrinsic to the entire therapeutic process, and time—or the lack of it—is always the elephant in the room. In life, we know that we will one day die; similarly, one begins treatment with the knowledge that it will end. As with death, we tend to deny the ending, yet no ending in life is like the ending of life, so when the therapeutic relationship is finished, we hope it initiates a new beginning.

As with beginnings, endings have their own singular character. The person with psychosis often begins the treatment out of touch with their sense of self, or they express the self as a persona—God, Jesus, Moses, Satan, or the like. As a result, at the beginning of treatment, the therapist is not always regarded as a separate person. As the patient begins to acknowledge the relationship, the treatment takes on a wider scope, which will inevitably include the recognition of separation and loss. True mourning must be preceded by the recognition of desire, a development that many with psychosis resist, which forms a barrier to engagement. Indeed, many psychotic symptoms can be understood as deriving from the fear of not being able to integrate affects, some of the most intense of which reside within desire.

In this chapter, we first review some of the literature on termination and then address particular challenges in ending treatment with persons who have experienced psychosis or other extreme states, or with those who are still in the throes of psychosis. In our discussion, we describe good enough terminations, countertransference issues, and regression at termination. In our view, termination is always with us in the room, even though

DOI: 10.4324/9781003441519-11

the psychoanalytic endeavor creates an illusion of timelessness and infinite possibilities (Bass, 2009; Slochower, 1998), particularly because of the timelessness of the unconscious (Freud, 1915/1978c) revealed in free associations, fantasies, dreams, and inscriptions of trauma. Adding to the illusion may be the patient's fantasy to never leave the analysis and/or the analyst's hold on the patient, or the need in either patient or clinician to confirm the illusion of a never-ending, boundless love. In truth, much of psychoanalysis involves the work of mourning and the understanding, sorting out, linking, and separating of past, present, and future (Craige, 2002).

Although many analysts have written about the termination phase in terms of mourning (Bonovitz, 2007; Loewald, 1962; Novick, 1976), loss and mourning are intrinsic parts of every treatment, from beginning to end. Every patient must learn to mourn what they did not have, what they are not, and what they never will be. Every therapist must mourn what they cannot accomplish in the treatment and must be willing to be left behind—allowing the loss of their presence to be mourned by their patients as they grow and let the therapist go. Every patient and every therapist must accept that one day they will part ways. LaPlanche (1998) wrote that "The aim of psychoanalysis is to end it so new life can begin" (p. 23), which does not simply mean getting rid of symptoms (Arieti, 1974b).

Leader (2011) said that with a successful analysis, the self is reinvented. Yet one can say that psychosis itself is a reinvention, in which a person, through psychotic symptomatology, replaces who they had been with someone barely identifiable to their previous injured self. For example, the former inadequate sense of self, through the magic of psychosis, can become the all-powerful ruler of the universe. A frequent lament heard by the patient's parents is, "Where did my child go?" Not surprisingly, when a patient gets well, it does seem like a rebirth. The patient is born again, seemingly with no relationship to their previous psychotic self, a testament to the pain they suffered prior to their transformation. But in fact, the ending of treatment with psychosis, rather than revealing a new, reinvented self (Leader, 2011), acknowledges one's past self, perhaps even recognizing that one's previous self in the throes of psychosis received a modicum of comfort from the illness that was also a deep source of pain.

Although the therapeutic process cannot be easily portioned out into distinct stages without compromising our understanding of the psychoanalytic journey, there is, nonetheless, something distinctive about the finality of the process of ending, and we prepare for and prefigure the ending in numerous ways. When we say to a patient, "Time is up," the ending is with us in the room. The ending is there, whenever we don't have enough time to fully analyze a dream, when a pause temporarily stops the dialogue, or when we inform the patient of our vacation schedule. All these moments suggest an ending and offer opportunities for rehearsal. When a patient says, "I don't want to talk about this," they are saying, "I don't want to get to the bottom of this," and by implication, "I don't want to get to the end." For patients who struggle with psychosis, the primary reason for not getting to the bottom of something is often a wish to not return to the beginning.

Termination is prefigured throughout the analytic encounter in the interruptions and breaks endured and during various enactments that pose a threat to the relationship. The separation–reunion cycle is manifested throughout the treatment and is rife with possibilities for the preparation of both parties to face the final goodbye. Early on, the therapist's primary task is to emphasize continuity—for example, the therapist ends a session by reminding the patient that they will meet again in three days. As the bond deepens, the therapist can, from time to time, refer to loss, beginning with issues not intimately connected to their own relationship yet meaningful to the patient.

For example, MS commented to his patient, who also grew up in the Bronx: "I know how much Joe DiMaggio meant to you, and now he's gone."

Eventually, depending on the strength of the relationship that has been established, the therapist can extend the discussion to the therapeutic bond, by saying, for example, "A month without seeing each other can seem like a very long time."

Timing is important in determining when to focus on loss within the dyad. Just because the opportunity to examine loss occurs early and often does not mean that the patient is ready to discuss it. The relationship needs to attain significance for the patient, and he or she must then feel safe enough to acknowledge the significance to themselves and eventually share that knowledge with the therapist. In addition, the relationship must be strong enough to bear examining the loss that is likely to occur one day. "You mean something to me" can feel life-threatening to many who suffer from psychosis. The therapist, too, must be able to tolerate separation and loss and be free of the need to be important to the patient and thus allow them to let go. Having other colleagues for support and peer or mentor consultation helps with this process.

A successful termination brings with it a sense of having transcended the need for the relationship, but with the important caveat that the analytic process will continue. The dynamic process, the therapeutic work, the internalization of the relationship—these aspects of the process all live on past the ending. Some have noted the capacity of the patient to replace the therapist with self-analysis (Bergmann, 1997; Craige, 2002; Ticho, 1967). With the relational turn in psychoanalysis, there has been increased emphasis not only on intrapsychic change but also changes in one's relational patterns (e.g., Davies, 2005; Salberg, 2010). Mitchell (1997) directed our attention to a paradox inherent in the termination of a relational analysis: "If the analytic relationship is understood as essentially interactive, termination must result in important internalizations of and identifications with the analyst as an internal object. But if the patient's autonomy is to be preserved, these identifications must allow and nourish personal freedom and creativity rather than binding the patient through unconscious loyalties" (p. 26).

## Termination and New Beginnings

Whether termination should be considered a distinct phase is debatable. Some have argued that analysis lacks a paradigm for termination (Blum, 1989; Hurn, 1971), while others, like Novick and Novick (2006), consider it to be a discrete phase with specific tasks. The first task is agreeing upon an ending date with the patient. Schlesinger (2014) reserves the use of the word "termination" for a planned and agreed-upon end date on which most therapeutic goals have been achieved, yet he uses a helix model to reflect the cyclical nature of therapeutic work. Still others (Gabbard, 2009; Hoffmann, 2001; Knafo, 2018) claim that a linear paradigm—beginning, middle, and end— does not adequately represent the messiness or idiosyncratic nature of the trajectories of individual therapies. Perhaps this is why termination has sometimes been thought of as an aesthetic concept (Bergmann, 1997; Levenson, 1976) co-created (Salberg, 2010) by both members of the therapeutic dyad.

Not all terminations end well, and many, if not most, treatments end prematurely and asymmetrically. Patients may leave precipitately out of fear, anger, or discouragement; some patients end when they move or start school or a new job. Therapists may decide they cannot treat a particular person or problem. Either the patient or therapist can become ill or die. Freud (1918/1978) forced a termination of the Wolf Man case because the analysis had reached a stalemate and could go no further. Ironically, he found that fixing a termination date resulted in the emergence from a stalemate during the time they had left. According to Saffron (2002), short-term dynamic treatment, due to its built-in time constraints, of necessity deals with issues of separation-individuation and loss.

We now turn to a case example to illustrate termination with a patient who suffered from an olfactory delusion. This case shows how one can and should adapt therapeutic goals to each particular patient and the circumstances of the treatment.

## A Case Example of "Good Enough" Termination

John's psychosis first emerged when he was 16, and he was now 46. His primary delusion was that he emitted an odor of such potency that he had to drop out of school. He had lived as a shut-in with his parents for 30 years and had been to six therapists before coming to see MS. His prior therapists had all ended treatment because they felt they could not do anything else for John. MS was able to speak to three of John's previous therapists and learned that two had relied on medication as their primary intervention while the third, who was analytically trained, had also given up on John. There was, however, a difference in the treatment goals of John's three therapists. The analytically oriented therapist, after abandoning his reliance on searching for meaning, revised his goal to help the patient reduce the toxicity of his symptomatology through supportive measures. The analyst hoped to convince John to accept himself as he was (with the odor John smelled on himself) and thus reduce his anxiety about his symptomatology. "People differ both in terms of how they smell and how they respond to other people's odors," counseled the analyst. The drug-oriented doctors' approach was to try to eliminate John's olfactory symptoms through medication. Once the olfactory symptom was eliminated, they had hoped John could explore his inner world and interpersonal dilemmas. John told

MS he did not share these goals; his only goal was to be able to leave the family home and live on his own.

MS wanted to know everything John could tell him about the odor. He was puzzled by how little the patient could say about the details of the smell compared to the central role it played in his life. John did volunteer that he was reluctant to know more about the smell because knowledge about it might make it worse. John was surprised when MS asked him how he knew this would happen. Encouraged by MS's persistent questions, John began to realize how little he really knew or thought about his odor, except for feeling its negative impact on his life. He was now willing to learn more. Over time an alliance developed around their mutual interest in learning as much as possible about the odor and the ways in which it affected his life.

At about the same time, John's father was promoted, which required the family to move to California. John's father could put off the move for a while but needed to know when MS thought his son could safely stop their work. MS was concerned that John's ability to internalize him was shaky, and he was uncertain about how termination would affect John. Consistent with MS's concern and several months before John's father got promoted, John had told MS that his faith in reaching his goal was strongest when he saw MS but diminished as soon as he left his office. All these facts together increased MS's worry.

A month after the move to California had been discussed, John began his session with MS with an announcement that he had found an otolaryngologist who, he hoped, would find a way to help him. What moved him to take this action was his realization of how little he had been able to say about the odor when MS had asked him about it. "I took for granted that there wasn't anything I could do about it and, therefore, knowing more would be of no help. I was stuck with it."

Dr. Ballast took John's concerns seriously and wanted to learn more, echoing MS's repeated statement that knowledge is power. The specialist hesitated in immediately prescribing a particular medication because each person is unique, and one size does not fit all. John felt encouraged that what Dr. Ballast said reminded him of what MS had told him. The odor was part of being human, the specialist said, but if John was concerned, he could prescribe the medication. No medicine could totally eliminate the smell, though he added that he detected no foul smell coming from John. Nonetheless, there were drugs that he could "guarantee" significantly reduced any odor's intensity. Much to his surprise, John immediately felt relieved, believing that it might even be possible that a reduction in the odor would be enough to allow him to interact with other people.

MS was pleased by what he heard. He and John had been engaged in a joint effort to better understand him which so far had been limited to the two of them. Now John had unilaterally sought out a new situation that would help him learn more about himself. MS heard John's statement as concrete evidence that he had begun to internalize his therapist, suggesting termination was possible. Of course, part of John's incentive may have been based on the recognition that, since MS would no longer be available, he had better get additional support. Even if that were part of his motivation, he could easily have ignored that reality and clung more tightly to MS. Knowledge of real-world consequences is rarely the sole explanation for the patient raising questions about their psychotic symptomatology. Appeals to reason pale in the face of primitive thinking.

The remaining sessions were spent examining the treatment relationship, addressing its loss, and linking John's action in seeking out an otolaryngologist with his internalizing the knowledge he had taken from MS. This case illustrates that there are instances where termination is appropriate without complete resolution of psychotic symptomatology. Consistent with John's own goal for his treatment, the impact of his delusion on his life was diminished, not eliminated.

The therapist may find that they need to modify their goals when psychotic symptoms have been present for years. John's chronicity, despite years of treatment, could not be ignored. That does not mean a therapist should capitulate to chronicity. Rather, after persistent efforts have yielded little or no evidence of change, the therapist should ask themselves, "What are my goals for this treatment and what, if anything, would I accept as a valid indication of the need to modify my ambitions?" An unwillingness to review the treatment plan and consider modification is often the result of therapeutic idealization. The therapist may idealize their own ability to engender change, the power of the analytic process, or both.

Therapeutic idealization in our view is when a therapist believes that they and/or the therapeutic process should be capable of conquering any clinical dilemma. If the therapist has idealized their own skills, they may blame the patient or themselves so that they can reinstate their idealization of the process and, ultimately, themselves. "Now that I've seen my errors, next time

I'll be perfect," they think. They may double down on their efforts, making it impossible for them to feel comfortable about considering termination, which is viewed as tantamount to defeat. Therapeutic idealization can also arise as a counterforce to therapeutic nihilism, providing an incentive for an otherwise disillusioned therapist to keep going, or it may occur in response to a patient's demand to cure him or her when the therapist feels they must achieve what has been asked of them.

MS's lack of idealization helped the therapy in two ways. First, his pragmatism allowed MS to accept John's goals, in recognition of the reality of decades of therapy that had attempted to "cure" him rather than attend to the realistic expectations of what could be achieved. Second, MS's non-idealization of his own capacities made it easier for him to consider that John, building on what they had already accomplished, could continue with a new therapist. Seeing their time together as transferable to a new relationship in no way minimized MS's appreciation of what he and John had accomplished together. They explored both the significance of their relationship and the attendant loss. At the same time, acknowledging what they had built together provided the base from which work could continue with another therapist. John was both losing MS and bringing him along to a new encounter. In parting, MS gave John a tape of him (MS) saying, "Knowledge is power," telling John he might never need to listen to it. But in case he wanted to hear MS saying what he now knew to be true, all he had to do was to press the "on" button on the cassette player, echoing Winnicott's concept of the efficacy of a transitional object.

The therapist working with a patient who is not on the psychotic spectrum might think twice before giving their patient something concrete to take with them, trusting the internalization of their relationship to be all that is necessary and perhaps fearing infantilizing the patient. But the therapist who works with someone diagnosed with psychosis respects the greater difficulty the patient might have sustaining a relationship that is no longer active. In such cases, one can provide something—a photo or voice recording—that can reinforce trust and continuity. The multiple meanings the memento may represent should be considered early enough in the termination process. Devoting sufficient time to such exploration underscores reflection as a lifelong process rather than something confined to a particular phase of the patient's life.

## The Special Challenge of Ending with Patients Diagnosed with Psychosis

Although there is a voluminous literature on termination, much less has been written about ending treatment with those who have experienced psychotic episodes or who continue to experience psychosis. What then are the caveats to consider in ending psychodynamic therapy with these special patients? Persons with psychosis are known to suffer from fear of intimacy, boundary problems, and difficulty containing affect, and they often use complex methods of protecting themselves from closeness. Clearly, these features can contribute to making it difficult to complete the therapy. We believe the single best predictor of readiness for termination is the degree of solidity of the patient-therapist bond.

As we have noted elsewhere, many with psychosis fear intimacy and at the same time wish to merge with another (Searles, 1965). The patient fears that the price for connecting with their therapist will be subordinating their own identity. The patient's struggle to not be swallowed results in the need to disavow any legitimate basis for others having played a significant role in their development. For example, many individuals with psychosis feel it is critical that they be their own person, entirely self-made, an identity frequently contradicted by psychotic symptoms pointing to an external force determining the person's fate (for example, a delusion of being chosen by God or of having one's mind controlled by aliens). Therefore, one crucial difference between psychosis and non-psychosis is in how the treatment alliance develops. For the most part, nonpsychotic individuals name some internal distress or conflict they wish to resolve within themselves. Common examples are: "I can't sleep," "I'm afraid I'm losing my grip," or "Will anyone ever love me?" By contrast, those experiencing psychosis rarely present themselves as being in conflict, instead projecting the conflict on the outside world as part of their delusion. Even when negative symptoms predominate, individuals rarely express dissatisfaction with how they are managing their lives. They are likely to express their apathy, emotional collapse, and indifference to everything around them in terms of the harshness or cruelty of the external world.

Both positive- and negative-symptom psychoses present with a seeming absence of acknowledgment of internal conflict. In fact, not all who experience psychosis seek help. There are two common exceptions. The first is when the patient asks for the therapist's help in reducing external pressures, such as "You're a doctor. Can you stop the demons from invading my bloodstream?" The second is when the patient exposes their need for the therapist to believe them, often couching the request as a condition for engaging in treatment. This second scenario, when handled properly, can be a gold mine for alliance formation. The patient's request—often a demand—to be believed can seem off-putting to therapists more accustomed to overt requests for help. A nonpsychotic patient might ask, "Why is it so hard for me to believe that other people trust me?" By contrast, a patient with psychosis is unlikely to be aware that their need to be believed originates in self-doubt. Rather, they are more likely to say, "You better believe me or else," rather than "I need your assurance that I'm not crazy."

To arrive at a point where the patient recognizes that doubt resides within themselves is a complex process. The first step is the recognition by the therapist that the patient, by demanding acceptance of their unusual perception, is asking something of them. The therapist might initially respond by simply acknowledging that being believed is very important. Depending on the degree of trust already established, the therapist might explore the complexity of the patient's request, searching for clues about the patient's internal conflict with regard to the validity of their symptoms, which might widen the scope to uncover a non-psychotic aspect of the patient's personality.

For example, the man who insists he is Jesus Christ may need to feel worshiped and adored. The therapist can empathize with the patient's yearnings without endorsing that a miraculous transformation has taken place, thereby making a distinction between "wouldn't it be lovely if" and "it's already happened." The therapist thus recognizes the patient's use of magical thinking. The Jesus Christ example illustrates how often magical thinking relates to grandiosity, which is not surprising because both derive from the same source: the wish to flee from emptiness and insignificance. The therapist's ability to hear the patient's statement not as fact but as a wish allows the clinician to appreciate the patient's longings and, over time, explore their underlying causes.

Another example is that of Maurice who warned Dr. Petra, MS's supervisee, that only if she recognized he had magical powers could she appreciate who he was. Otherwise, Maurice would feel unknown to her and, therefore, would remain hesitant about how much he could reveal. Dr. Petra's initial reaction was to let the patient know she had heard him but was unable to immediately accede to his wishes. "If I said I believed you before I understood what constitutes complete acceptance, I would be lying to you, and you would be right not to trust me. What I do believe is how important this is to you. As I learn more, I'll tell you how the new information registers with me, either as confirmation or refutation. I realize that without my full endorsement, you will feel the need to be guarded in what you consider safe to tell me."

Maurice hesitantly agreed to these terms. As the treatment progressed, his suspicion of Dr. Petra lessened to the point where she felt comfortable enough to ask Maurice why he felt so strongly that he needed her affirmation. Maurice was encouraged by the therapist's appreciation of how much was at stake for him, should he doubt his own powers, and the treatment gradually came to focus on the patient's uncertainty. After months of hesitation, Maurice announced that from the start he had doubts about his powers and had devised a "test" to prove he was correct. Renowned magician and illusionist, Uri Geller's ability to bend spoons through mind control became his yardstick. Maurice could never be sure of the results of this experiment regarding his own spoon-bending abilities; however, whenever family members scoffed at his assertions, he found it easy to believe in his own powers. Since his therapist neither endorsed nor scoffed at his claim, leaving him with no one to oppose, he was left with his doubts. What evolved was his willingness, with frequent retractions, to begin doubting his omnipotence. Once the treatment alliance has developed, trust is established, and it is easier for the therapist to make deeper interventions. Step-by-step, the dyad moves toward greater understanding until the patient sees reality for what it is, not only what they wish it to be.

Termination can take place at any juncture of the treatment—at the end of a successful therapeutic endeavor or at the end of an incomplete analysis. Under certain circumstances, psychodynamic work is discontinued and replaced with support and maintenance rather than growth. This last category is not included in a traditional discussion of termination—a most unfortunate omission. Not infrequently, a therapist unconsciously decides to give up psychodynamic treatment but cannot allow this thought to reach consciousness. To accomplish conflicting goals of giving up while appearing to remain involved, the therapist continues to show up while restricting their activities to not rocking the boat.

Maintaining the status quo is perfectly acceptable if the therapist is aware and accepting of the change in therapeutic stance, remaining open to the possibility of engaging in more exploratory work in the future. But unfortunately, therapists often cling to the belief that they are continuing to work toward change because they find participation in maintenance unacceptable. Not surprisingly, the outcome of such an endeavor is that the therapist begins to resent the patient, and the process, and/or ritualized behavior results in boredom. For the patient, whatever positive effects they experienced from a previous active process will eventually wane. The patient may initially feel relief followed by feelings of devitalization; finally, they may feel the need to leave.

Dr. Goldfarb, a conscientious third-year extern, had been encouraged by her supervisor to include at least one patient diagnosed with psychosis in her caseload. She was reluctant but relented because she admired her supervisor, who told her she would be missing out on a complete learning experience if she didn't follow his advice. Her patient, Xavier, exhibited significant negativity, which she found difficult to tolerate. Her supervisor counseled patience: "Just let him know you are listening to him." Although she was relatively inexperienced, Dr. Goldfarb had already shown herself to be an exceptionally gifted therapist who learned to trust her reactions to her patients as accurate guides to their communications. Based on her reactions to Xavier, she concluded that, despite his apparent indifference to her presence, his "negativity" was anything but indifference. Her unusual reaction of anger, she believed, reflected Xavier's effort to establish a strong object bond of a sadomasochistic nature. Her supervisor believed otherwise and continued to counsel her to be patient. The following year, she was assigned a new supervisor, MS, with the option of transferring any of her patients to a new third-year student. She chose to continue with all her patients, including Xavier, the only one she was hesitant about staying with.

Despite the fact that Xavier initially showed little change in therapy sessions, Dr. Goldfarb no longer felt angry toward him. Her initial curiosity about her patient and their relationship soon waned, replaced by a bland acceptance of his sullen, provocative behavior. Nothing about this treatment had been making sense, so she made a decision to "accept it as it is." Soon Xavier followed suit. His level of arousal became tamped down as he seemingly accepted the new status quo. Thus, the meetings between patient and therapist took on an air of polite nonengagement. Midway through her fourth year, without any notice, Xavier stopped coming.

Dr. Goldfarb was confused and didn't understand what had gone wrong. MS pointed out to Dr. Goldfarb that of her entire caseload, Xavier was the only patient she had not discussed in any depth with him. What did she make of that?

Dr. Goldfarb realized that she had avoided attaching much significance to her treatment effort to help Xavier, and she did not think her work with him could provide her with an opportunity to learn more through supervision. She had terminated both possibilities, rationalizing her withdrawal as "acceptance" of him. Was it common for her to accept the "status quo" as the end product of therapy? MS wanted to know. Only then did she consider the nature of her involvement with Xavier, his treatment, and the educational opportunities she had dismissed. Dr. Goldfarb could now see that letting go of her anger toward Xavier did not indicate acceptance, but, rather, was a behavioral statement of abandonment. She was no longer involved with him. And he had responded as one normally does to being left. He initially adapted to Dr. Goldfarb's moving away with his own style of indifference. Finally, the hollow ritual they established was not sufficiently bonding, so he turned the tables and terminated his therapist.

Leader (2011) states that the most common cause of failure in the treatment of psychosis is not due to the clinician making a poorly judged intervention but rather to their loss of interest in the continuation of the work when there is no change in the patient. For example, Dr. Valencia consulted with DK about her 20-year treatment of Stanley, a man diagnosed with psychosis. The treatment had been at a standstill for years; nothing was happening. Dr. Valencia wished to end the treatment, though she had ambivalent feelings about doing so since Stanley arrived at each session and seemed to want to continue despite the lack of progress. It was clear she was feeling discouraged and ineffectual, and these feelings were having an impact on her professional identity. DK advised her not to end the treatment since Stanley was arriving for sessions and seemed to be attached to her despite showing no progress. DK also asked Dr. Valencia to consider what changes, if any, had taken place in Stanley, which might perhaps uncover the therapist's discouragement and/or fear of identification with her patient. It appeared to DK that, like Dr. Goldfarb from the previous example, the therapist had given up—checked out—and that might be the reason for the stalemate. She encouraged Dr. Valencia to try to access a renewed interest in her patient and the relationship. The therapist returned to DK several months later, exclaiming excitedly, "You won't believe what happened!" Indeed, Stanley had come to life and exhibited a new curiosity in the therapy. It was clear that his therapist's renewed interest in him revitalized both him and the treatment.

## Terminations vs. Endings

Traditional psychodynamic treatment refers to termination (assuming it is not premature termination) as the final step of a process that has been preceded by the exploration of transference, the establishment of mutual trust, and, most relevant to this discussion, the development of a complex relationship—one that has stood the test of time, challenges, and interpretations. According to the traditional psychoanalytic view, only then can termination take place. Termination most often refers to relinquishment of the therapeutic relationship, such that what has been learned from the patient-therapist experience will not remain encapsulated in the therapeutic dyad but rather becomes something the patient takes with them into the wider world. Therefore, termination depends on the patient-therapist connection having been meaningful enough to require mourning.

However, the loss is not possible if the object to be relinquished previously has not been significant or even recognized (the emotional investment Freud called *cathexis*). Yet that is precisely the fundamental issue confronting any therapist working with psychosis. Namely, many patients dread perceived or imagined demands for closeness, and establishing a relationship and acknowledging its existence as meaningful can be extraordinarily difficult for them. Not uncommonly, in psychosis only a partial connection will have been established. Thus, if successful termination requires first having achieved a solid connection, only a subset of patients with psychosis will meet the criteria for successful termination. In a fully successful treatment of psychosis, termination would be both a goal and the end stage of the analysis. However, as we have said, the orthodox view of termination may not be appropriate when working with patients experiencing psychosis. At times, keeping a patient out of the hospital is a worthy goal in and of itself. At other times, the therapist and the patient might agree to end the treatment with the caveat that the patient could contact the therapist when feeling endangered, a state clarified and agreed upon by both parties in advance.

Arieti (1974b) claimed that termination with psychosis poses greater problems than termination with other patients. We agree with Arieti that the loss of symptoms is an insufficient indication that a patient is ready to terminate. He lists some signs that suggest a patient is ready: expansion of personality; an increased range of interest; the return to secondary process thinking; and the demonstration of a psychologically-enriched view or a spectrum of views wider than that of the average person. Patients ready for termination, according to Arieti, have a definable sense of self-identity and an increased awareness of inner worth. Reality is experienced as less frightening and less impinging. Thus, the patient feels ready to return to the world with greater understanding and less fear. They no longer experience a sense of enormous passivity. They no longer see themselves purely as the object of fate, chance, nature, persecutors, spouses, parents, children, and so forth, but as someone who thinks and acts as independently as other members of society. They have succeeded in maintaining an active and satisfactory role in their work, activities, interpersonal relations, and especially, intimate relations.

Arieti's list is so comprehensive that we doubt many—psychotic or nonpsychotic—persons reach such complete resolution of problems and evolution of personality and relationality. Terminations are never complete. They do not need to resolve all problems. Freud (1913/1978) cautioned analysts to be wary of their ambitions, which may exceed those of the patient. Most important is the sense in both parties that the patient can continue alone. As analysts, we need to be prepared to become unnecessary, de-idealized, and cast off (Orgel, 2000). We need to be internalized and transcended. What we once did for the patient that they were unable to do for themselves, they can now do alone.

## Countertransference

Several countertransference issues crop up when nearing endings with patients who have been diagnosed with psychosis. Perhaps more than any other psychoanalyst, Harold Searles (1965) described and warned about countertransference pitfalls. He wrote that it may be easier for both the therapist and nursing staff to recognize and at least partially gratify the patient's early infantile needs than help them deal with powerful adult desires, such as their wish to marry, have children, and bear adult responsibilities. He claimed that because the therapist may have seen the patient as a deeply fragmented person earlier in the therapy, he or she may have difficulty letting go of a lingering impression of the patient's fragility. This inability to recognize the patient as a stronger and more evolved person may cause the therapist to move at a slower pace than what the patient needs. This type of countertransference can also be fueled by the late recognition on the part of the patient of how fragile they once were. Searles designated phases in the analysis of psychosis, claiming that only in the late phase can the patient's psychosis become clarified due to their finally being able to experience and integrate the emotions that at a much earlier date had to be repressed and defended against by the advent of psychosis. We add the finding that many therapists are unable to see their patients' strengths because they are sometimes expressed as resistances to the treatment. A patient's tenacity, their holding firm to a position, can be a strength, which, in the end, might be applied to more constructive ends.

Many therapists who work with psychosis feel repeatedly tested by their patients, with love and hate being taken to their limits. Leader (2011) noted that the level of commitment required, which he compared to that expected of a caregiver, is so great that often "the only therapists who are willing enough to take it on are those starting their careers or saints" (p. 321). Burton (1961) has noted that therapy characterized by symbiotic entanglement is less like a medical intervention and more like a marriage. He commented that some therapists even neglect their marriages due to overinvolvement with patients with whom they are emotionally engaged. Along similar lines, Searles (1965) has written that the therapist who works with psychosis may enjoy the symbiosis too much, thereby potentially interfering with the termination process. Many therapists go back into therapy themselves during these times. Searles pointed out that the therapist must be sufficiently secure in their own humanness to endure for long periods the role, in the patient's transference experience, of an inanimate object, or of some other projection that has not yet become differentiated as a sentient human being. Though it may feel unpleasant and dehumanizing, the therapist might understand the patient's de-animation of the clinician as the patient's way of having an impact on their world and allowing the clinician to remain in the room with them. Burton (1961) observed that the intensity of the therapeutic relationship can match its estrangement. In sum, the therapist's emotional reactions to the patient's transference form an equally essential contribution to relatedness in the real world.

Arieti (1974b) believed that the therapist gradually changes their attitude toward the patient as the patient improves. In Arieti's view, the therapist moves from being nurturing and maternal to becoming more demanding and paternal. Later in the therapy, therapists can point out to the patient that the demands made on them are proof of their improvement and the faith put in them, and a recognition that they can now face the world with less fear. We believe that therapists usually begin treatment with psychosis with caution rather than nurturance, needing to establish safety and boundaries. Another reason to begin cautiously is that a nurturant attitude can frighten many with psychosis because it highlights their vulnerability and neediness. We believe that the hardest challenge for therapists, especially beginning therapists, in treating patients with psychosis, is the threat they may feel to their professional identity as they are confronted with situations in which they cannot be as effective as they had been previously with nonpsychotic patients.

Although it is true that some patients are eager to terminate treatment prematurely, it is also true that some therapists convince themselves that they will remain indispensable to patients who used to be very fragile or fragmented. Some therapists enjoy being benefactors. The therapist's narcissistic needs are gratified by associating with a person who has greatly benefited from the therapeutic relationship and the therapist's interventions. It might also be painful for the therapist to face the emotional deprivation caused by not seeing a person toward whom they felt very close and in whom they invested affection and devotion for an extended period of time. Losing income may also be an issue. Searles (1965) believed that the therapist needs to be alert to the fact that they may have become so used to treating the patient that they are not aware of the patient's improvement. The routine of the treatment has become such an important part of the therapist's life that they might not recognize that sessions need to be curtailed or that they need to begin working toward termination. Therapists must pay serious attention to any request on the part of the patient to decrease or end the treatment with the knowledge that transference and countertransference are never completely resolved.

## Regression

Some have written about ways in which patients regress as they near termination (Cooper, 2010; Miller, 1965; Schafer, 2002). As we demonstrated in the case of Josh (Chapter 10), regressions are not always signs that the treatment has failed. In fact, some patients who have developed the capacity to trust the therapeutic relationship and their own ego strength regress as a positive prognostic sign indicating their readiness to confront past traumas.

Apart from regression, we'd like to stress how new material often emerges during the final phase of treatment and is one of the ways patients let us know there is more work to be done. It is also safe to bring up new material when there is little or no time to work on it. For therapists, this period is a vulnerable time when defenses are down, allowing them to see what they have otherwise missed. Cooper (2010) notes that termination presents an opportunity to examine previously underappreciated aspects of the transference–countertransference relationship.

Several authors who have written on termination mention that the transference relationship—often spoken about in terms of a love relationship—must undergo a significant transformation at the end. Menninger (1958) noted, "The love sought from the analyst, he [the patient] is now ready to seek elsewhere" (p. 159). Davies (2005) compared Oedipal love and transference love:

> [Both] hold in common the potential for highly romanticized, deeply bewitching, all-consuming, and utterly impossible love—a love of mythic epic proportion, a love designed to be healing and compensatory on the one hand, but a love that must also be relinquished and transformed in order for the child or patient to move on to more realizable forms of romantic engagement
>
> (p. 785).

These authors believed that Oedipal and transference love are necessary and that both must be relinquished and mourned. This process must take place without killing the capacity to love and to find new objects. A deep truth about termination is that we end an analysis but never really terminate it.

Even in the most successful treatment, the patient remains vulnerable to regression and the unpredictability of forces beyond their control. The process of termination itself raises issues that can be as challenging as anything the patient is likely to encounter at a later date. Negotiating the termination, therefore, is a predictor of the patient's resilience and readiness to successfully navigate the world. Is the patient capable of maintaining gains while relinquishing regular physical contact with the therapist? How able is the patient to accept loss and regulate the affect it evokes? What often occurs when a bond has been established between patient and therapist is that, as termination approaches, the threat of loss results in regression, which, importantly, does not necessarily require the therapist to attempt to strengthen the relationship. Indeed, as a yardstick for evaluating the readiness for termination, the therapist might examine the patient's regression to determine how much further the patient is able to go by relying on what has already occurred and what they have learned. The therapist can ask themselves how similar or different this regression is to those that came before. The therapist can ask the patient if they feel the need to increase their sessions and may then explore the various factors making up the patient's position. Therapists should examine indicators on a regular basis to determine when it might be safe to terminate.

Perhaps the most important factor when considering termination is to search for evidence of the patient's internalizing aspects of the therapy—either specific content or identification with the process and/or its proponent, the therapist. In searching for this information, therapists often dismiss a major data source: the patient's psychotic symptoms. In fact, psychotic symptoms are often the first place where evidence of internalization emerges. For example, Zachary, a patient with auditory hallucinations, reported hearing a new voice as the termination date approached. He couldn't quite place the voice and feared he was being taken over by its influence. "It's been a long time since I heard a new voice. This one scares me more than the others because I find myself listening to it rather than putting my hands over my ears," the patient said to Dr. Fitzgerald. Zachary, when asked what the voice was saying, replied that the voice was telling him not to jump to conclusions but, rather, to question if there might be other ways to understand his situation. He wondered whether this might be a plot to induce him to drop his guard. He speculated, "Maybe the voice belongs to the same secret organization that is trying to get me to surrender. It could even be the same person, just disguising their voice."

Dr. Fitzgerald nearly mistakenly viewed her patient's comments as evidence of his becoming paranoid again. Supervision with MS helped Dr. Fitzgerald to discern that the content conveyed by the new voice was echoing what Zachary and the therapist had recently discussed in session and that the patient had struggled to consider. Had Zachary phrased his concern outside the arena of his auditory hallucinations, he might have said: "I've been thinking about what you said about considering alternative ways of understanding my world, and I'm still having some trouble with it." Had he expressed himself in that way, Dr. Fitzgerald would have instantly recognized that the patient was continuing to engage with her guidance. Now that voice was coming from within the patient, albeit in the form of an auditory hallucination. All symptomatology is communication. Nowhere is this truer than in psychotic symptomatology, so what appears to be regression may not in fact be regression.

DK was recently invited to participate in a case conference at a locked inpatient unit. The staff chose Harold as the patient to be discussed because he perplexed them with his intelligence and charisma on the one hand and his resistance to change and recidivism on the other. Indeed, Harold had been hospitalized at the unit 28 times! DK asked that Harold be present at the conference. Before the conference began, DK observed the warm camaraderie that existed between Harold and the staff members, including psychiatrists, psychologists, social workers, nurses, and occupational therapists. Harold, a 52-year-old man, seemed excited to be the center of attention and hopeful to have his situation examined. His psychologist began presenting Harold to the group but, after a few minutes, Harold interrupted and took over the telling of his own story. "God's flame entered my body and soul when I was 18, and ever since then I've been psychotic," he explained. He spoke nonstop for 20 minutes telling his life story, which was marked by high points (he was chosen by God) and low points (he repeatedly broke down and required hospitalization). His story was peppered with quotes from religious texts that DK was later told were verbatim from their sources. Harold possessed an impressive and comprehensive knowledge of the Bible and related texts, and could solicit germane quotes at a moment's need. Seeing that Harold could go on endlessly, DK interrupted him and asked him what he considered to be his greatest problem.

Without hesitating, he replied: "Loneliness … I have no wife, no family, no profession, no home."

DK mentioned that she noticed how many people in the room seemed to know him, connect with him, and care for him.

"Yes," he agreed instantly.

"This poses a dilemma," offered DK: "On the one hand, you wish to become independent and emotionally healthy; on the other hand, the hospital has become the closest thing you have to a family and a home."

Harold sadly agreed. He confessed that he sometimes did drugs, which triggered manic behavior that caused people to call the police who then brought him to the hospital. He longed for the human contact and care he received there.

DK explained to the staff that they needed to work simultaneously on Harold's progress while inside the hospital as well as to ensure that his life outside the hospital would become meaningful and provide him with a sense of belonging. If the hospital, or the therapy relationship, is the best part of a person's life, then they will be reluctant to leave it and even force a regression to not lose it. We must not neglect the external conditions of our patients' lives. Loneliness is a major factor in those who experience psychosis (see Chapter 8). A proper termination considers both internal progress and changes in the patient's external life. Life outside the treatment room or the hospital needs to be a place that provides safety, support, and opportunities for relationships to flourish. In this way, termination becomes easier, more realistic, and resilient to regression while it facilitates a smooth transition to post-therapy life.

Sometimes the ending of treatment comes suddenly. Michael Eigen (2011), who has been treating patients with psychosis for many decades, beautifully recounts a 12-year treatment with Kurt, a man who began his therapy with the words, "The simplest kind of proposition, an elementary proposition, asserts the existence of a state of affairs" (p. 85). Eigen instantly recognized this as a quote from Wittgenstein and said simply, "You are here," recognizing the patient's situation to be both threatening and relieving.

A month later, Kurt said, "How *here* I can be remains to be seen" (p. 86).

Eigen, a realist, thought, "Therapy with Kurt might end today or tomorrow or go on for years and years" (p. 87). He told his patient, "It's a challenge to stay in the same room together and a challenge to stay in the same room with oneself as well" (p. 87).

Kurt did end up staying in therapy for twelve years. Eigen wrote, "I didn't call attention to the fact that his world was growing. I didn't rub his nose in his growth" (p. 93). He saw himself as a background support and presence to Kurt's evolution.

Eventually, Kurt was able to acknowledge that he had created his own paranoia. He said, "Something is lifting. Breath is coming back … I am less afraid of what I fear, less afraid of being afraid" (p. 95). Rather than perceive the world as a dangerous place, he now saw that his mind had been the source of danger: "I saw that the danger was a figment of my imagination" (p. 96.

Kurt married and channeled his psychosis into his art. His wife was pregnant when, one day, he came to therapy and announced, "It's time to move on" (p. 101).

Rather than interpreting Kurt's announcement as his desire to deny the forthcoming pressures of fatherhood, Eigen understood his patient's acceptance of the role of midwife to his life: "It was time to meet his life, to live it" (p. 101).

## Summary

In discussing termination of psychodynamic psychotherapy with persons diagnosed with psychosis, we have noted that termination is always in the room and that we have numerous opportunities to engage with separation, loss, and mourning throughout the treatment. Successful termination with psychosis requires a strong therapeutic alliance. The stronger the bond, the greater the probability of tolerating the separation from the therapist. In a firmly connected dyad, the patient will have assimilated aspects of the relationship that they can then apply to new contexts and will be able to use what they have learned. By the same token, the therapist becomes better equipped to apply the knowledge they have acquired in working with each specific patient to new situations.

A patient with psychosis often resists the relationship offered by the therapist due to fear that they will be required to subordinate their own identity as the price of connection. (The therapist's analog is their fear of being overwhelmed by the patient.) The patient's yearning for an omnipotent, all-protective mother complicates their struggle to avoid domination.

Good enough terminations include internal progress (a strengthened ego, good reality testing, improved confidence, and the ability to enter and engage in a meaningful relationship) and external factors (a life situation that involves independent living and supportive relationships). Countertransference issues arise toward the end of the treatment, in particular, the therapist's reluctance to notice when someone has progressed and is ready to go it alone. Finally, regression can appear toward the end of therapy as a way of showing both parties that the work is not finished and as a way of denying the reality of endings. Regression can also illustrate trust in the relationship to confront realities that were heretofore experienced as too dangerous.

Every therapy is ultimately incomplete, but one hopes the patient has internalized the therapist and the therapeutic process sufficiently to face life's challenges on their own.

# Chapter 12

# Supervision

Supervision is a complex process that involves two mutually influential dyads: the supervisor and the therapist and the therapist and their patient (Frawley-O'Dea, 2003). When the therapist is in treatment themselves, as is often the case, their relationship with their therapist forms a third dyad. Thus, psychodynamic supervision is a "complicated web of transferences and countertransferences" (Werbart, 2007) and parallel processes (Baudry, 1993; Gediman and Wolkenfeld, 1980). Some of the many roles and tasks of the supervisor include:

- sharing their experience and knowledge with the novice therapist and providing an opportunity for identification;
- providing a safe space for the therapist to express a multitude of emotions that come along with the responsibilities of clinical work;
- nurturing positive aspects in the therapy and supervision while also noting interfering aspects;
- negotiating the dual loyalties of caring for the therapist while also making sure the patient receives the best possible treatment;
- maintaining vigilance when it comes to the boundaries between supervision and personal analysis/therapy;
- remaining zealous in avoiding the temptation to adopt an omniscient role, which could create a false analytic self in the supervisee.

The supervisor who expresses their own confusion about what is happening in the treatment under consideration models for the supervisee that it is all right to not know everything and remain open to uncertainty and further exploration. Indeed, the supervisory relationship involves interactions that reflect authority, power, gender roles, race, and class. Yet, despite their

DOI: 10.4324/9781003441519-12

greater knowledge and experience, supervisors must be open to their own learning process and alert to their own blind spots (Berman, 2004).

The work of supervision becomes even more challenging when a beginning therapist initiates therapy with a patient undergoing a psychotic episode. Therapists often become frightened by the patient's bizarre symptoms and apparent lack of control and can become annoyed by the patient's lack of cooperation. The novice clinician may feel the patient poses a danger—either physical danger or danger of contagion—and often feels lost and unable to comprehend the patient's behavior and communication. A patient with psychosis leaves the therapist feeling confused and convinced that working with people who have a severe mental illness is "out of their league." Adding to this pessimistic view may be what the new therapist has heard about people with psychosis: that they do not benefit from therapy and that their condition is strictly biological, requiring medication and not therapy. On the other end of the spectrum, some therapists cast themselves in the savior role and believe they can accomplish what no one else has been able to do with the patient. For all these reasons, a supervisor working with clinicians who are seeing patients with psychosis must be highly sensitive and create a warm and safe environment in which the therapist can feel comfortable expressing their most uncomfortable feelings—omnipotence, fear, dependency, inadequacy, confusion, guilt, and anger.

This chapter discusses the role of clinical supervision with therapists who are learning to treat patients diagnosed with psychosis. Many assume that such patients are the most difficult to treat therapeutically. Although we agree that patients experiencing psychosis present challenges in therapy, so do severe borderline patients and ritually fixated obsessive-compulsive patients, as well as persons with perversions and addictions. In fact, any type of patient is easier to treat when one is prepared for what to expect. The supervisor's role is crucial in this preparation. The supervisor is critical, too, in dispelling the many myths regarding the treatment of psychosis— the major one being that people with serious mental illness are untreatable.

We refer to the supervision relationship as a *learning alliance*, akin to the therapeutic alliance that takes place in therapy. In both types of relationships, an *alliance* is the keystone that maintains the human bond. However well-versed in theory the therapist may be, he or she will find that the healing core of the encounter with psychosis is in the relationship itself because in most cases, one or more trauma-inducing relationships have played a central role in the onset of psychosis. And not surprisingly, the therapeutic relationship can potentially provide a corrective experience. When patients, or those who have been patients, are questioned about what they found most helpful in their journey, they nearly always name a relationship (Bordin, 1979; Horvath and Symonds, 1991; Luborsky, 1976; Sawyer, 2015). Thus, it is imperative for a supervisor to convey respect, careful listening, curiosity, empathy, and hope to supervisees and, at a remove, to the patients of those novices. Nothing is more important than showing someone you see their humanity and treating that person as a subject whose voice matters. Some therapists on inpatient units complain that they have very little time to apply dynamic techniques designed for long-term treatments. Supervision can help these therapists appreciate the importance of making a human connection, even if it is brief. Such connections can remain with a patient and offer them hope for more connections in the future. Moreover, making an authentic connection can encourage them to seek treatment after discharge. Fromm-Reichmann noted that patients need to have at least one person in their lives who can imagine the possibility of their getting well (Hornstein, 2002).

Since supervision is often conducted with professionals in the early stages of their training, supervisors frequently encounter rigidity in their supervisees who are trying hard to adhere to the theories and techniques they have been taught. But when encountering patients with psychosis, trying to work "by the book" often results in disastrous consequences. The most important message to convey to these new therapists is to be present, to be authentic, and to show an interest in the patient. Insights and interpretations can come later, if at all. The supervisor often needs to help therapists trust their intuition, feel free to be creative, and think outside of the box. Such a flexible approach might mean seeing some patients for five minutes per day rather than 45 minutes per week if that is all the patient can tolerate. It might mean meeting in the hallway, with the door open, or going to the patient's room in a facility rather than having them come to one's office. It might mean having sessions outdoors while going for a walk together. For example, MS sat in a quiet room with a patient, and DK listened to Bob Dylan tapes with a patient because that was all he wished to talk about. DK saw a patient who didn't show up occasionally. At some point, she learned that he skipped appointments when he felt he might physically hurt her. Had she insisted he come to session or interpreted his behavior as resistance or an enactment, she would have missed the fact that he was being protective toward her. The therapist must begin where the patient stands and show them that the clinician is there, ready to connect, while not imposing the connection.

Because of the way they manifest, psychotic symptoms often mask the patient's nonpsychotic parts as well as their strengths and talents. As we've already mentioned, appreciating the nonpsychotic aspects of a patient is very helpful to the treatment, as these parts can become allies and even co-therapists (Podvoll, 2003). Supervision can help focus the supervisee's attention on the whole person, not merely their symptoms. We have encountered many stories of very talented individuals who, while hospitalized due to a psychotic episode, were unknown to staff as possessing exceptional skills. (Among these real-life examples were a well-known author, a concert pianist, an artist, and a professor.) Moreover, supervision can help the therapist discern the creative, intellectual, and adaptive nature of their patients' seemingly bizarre symptoms. Unless the therapist can appreciate what we all have in common, they can easily fall prey to the vicious cycle of the unknowing therapist and the unknowable patient. Hence, the supervisory challenge is to help therapists move from experiencing their patients solely through the lens of their eccentric symptom picture to becoming aware that these individuals share the human desire for safety, meaning, and the wish to be known. Symptoms, however bizarre, can reveal the patient's underlying conflicts, and some may even match the therapist's own struggles. When symptoms are perceived as efforts at adaptation, they shorten the distance between therapist and patient.

When supervisees cannot see any similarity between themselves and their patients, DK finds it helpful to compare an encounter with psychosis to that of traveling to a foreign land. One can look for the familiar, or, better yet, one can enjoy learning about a new culture and language. We do not expect the French to speak English when we are in France. Similarly, we should not expect the person diagnosed with psychosis to speak in a logical manner using conventional symbols. We can begin understanding a foreign culture by noting its customs, ways people communicate with one another, what they find humorous, and so forth. The same can apply to one's encounter with someone experiencing psychosis. One can observe patterns: words or phrases the patient repeats, ways they greet and separate from others, and ways they express needs and frustrations. The same excitement one has when traveling to another land and encountering a different culture can occur in one's encounters with the world of psychosis.

## Safety and Parallel Processes

The bedrock of any supervision, regardless of patient diagnosis, is to make sure that the patient, supervisee, and supervisor all feel safe enough to explore any issues that might arise. Creating a sense of security requires examining the factors that contribute to feeling safe or endangered and considering the degree of danger each participant is willing to tolerate. Completely removing the sense of danger and discomfort is unrealistic and can cover up important aspects of the treatment and supervision. However, a degree of safety must be met for people to feel free to open themselves up to the analytic process—whether in therapy or supervision.

In addition, participants must also trust in the process itself. The supervisor trusts that the dominant treatment issues will eventually appear in the supervisory experience, either directly (i.e., content) or in a modified or disguised form (i.e., transference, enactments). When the therapist fails to recognize what is happening in the treatment (i.e., there is some unacknowledged difficulty with the patient), that failure often resurfaces in the interaction with the supervisor (i.e., parallel process). The novice therapist unconsciously enacts with their supervisor the very problems they are experiencing with their patient. The supervisor, by responding empathically to the supervisee, frees the therapist to empathize with their patient. Here is an example:

Bart, a 52-year-old office worker, had, for the past 30 years, done all he could to avoid human interaction. When not at work or watching television, his only contacts were visual hallucinations of multiple, ghostlike persecutory creatures. MS's supervisee, Dr. Quinones, was both confused and irritated by her patient's acceptance of his hallucinations, and she became increasingly irritated with what she labeled his "passivity." She exclaimed, "Why doesn't he let me help him get rid of them? If it were me, I would do anything to get rid of them!" As MS and Dr. Quinones approached six months of supervision, the time allotted in the curriculum for working together, she expressed the fear of beginning again with a different supervisor. This usually composed supervisee started to fidget and her voice trembled: "Please tell me if we can continue."

MS thought that what was happening between them related to her work with her patient but wasn't clear how to use this information to help her. He said that she may have just provided them with the key to making sense of her struggle with Bart. MS asked if she were willing to share what she was experiencing now.

She replied that ending the supervision left her feeling so alone, adding she would now be all alone with her patient as well. She knew it would be good for her training to work with a new supervisor who would offer her a fresh point of view, but she regretted not videotaping her sessions with MS because, if she had, she could simply play the old tapes and maybe not need a new supervisor. She knew it sounded crazy, but that was what she'd been thinking.

"What did she make of her "crazy" thought?" MS wanted to know.

Dr. Quinones identified Bart as the force driving her to experience her own loneliness, leading her to recognize the extremes each of them was willing to go to in an effort to alleviate their pain. Dr. Quinones's videotape and Bart's ghosts illustrated not only what the patient and therapist had in common but also illuminated their differences. Each was trying to quell their pain, but Bart was doing so at the expense of forgoing conventional reality.

Through interaction with MS, Dr. Quinones made her unconscious identification with her patient conscious, facilitating her ability to empathize with him. This example also illustrates how psychotic symptomatology can dominate the clinical picture in a way that obscures what patients and therapists are going through relationally, including which emotions they share. Dr. Quinones may have been threatened by Bart's hallucinations. Her question, "Why doesn't he want to rid himself of his hallucinations?" indicates a threat to her so dangerous that she needed to reassure herself that she would never allow her own psyche to fall into similar disarray.

## Lack of Knowledge and Lack of Identification

Therapists who conduct therapy with psychosis often begin with one or two convictions about themselves that can impede the therapeutic project. Either they feel lacking in even the most modest skills needed to work with patients and/or cannot identify a shred of similarity between themselves and the individuals they are attempting to treat. Let us address the lack of knowledge first. As we've already noted, there is a deficiency of training in the psychotherapy of psychosis. Therefore, it is the responsibility of the supervisor to prepare their supervisee with didactic material that includes a general orientation for understanding psychosis, including addressing misinformation (Harding and Zagniser, 1994). New therapists must be schooled in what to expect (in the patient and in themselves) when first encountering psychosis and must familiarize themselves with the literature on the treatment of psychosis. Rendering the person with psychosis in human terms and assuring the supervisee that psychosis is treatable by psychodynamic methods help alleviate some of the anxiety a beginning therapist might have (Karon, 2008). Therapists are more likely to be open to the supervisor's inquiries if that person first makes clear that they appreciate the difficulty of working with psychosis. That recognition, coming early in the supervisory process, makes it easier for supervisees to consider that they may be distancing themselves both from their patients and their own unease.

Here are some points that supervisors can make at the beginning of supervision:

- Fear (more likely, terror) is a given in psychosis; therefore, tread carefully, and try to create a safe space and a therapeutic alliance.
- Much of the communication during the session takes place on a nonverbal level. Therefore, pay attention to body language, facial expressions, and tone of voice, and do not rely on verbal interpretations alone.
- It is normal to feel discomfort, confusion, frustration, and/or anger.
- Patients use primitive defenses, like regression, splitting, projection, and projective identification. In response, therapists often also engage in similar defenses.
- Pay attention to the patient's personal language and symbols, usually manifest in their repetitive verbalizations, symptoms, and dreams.
- Transference and countertransference are key to understanding what is happening in the room.
- When the patient is being seen in an institutional setting, recognize that both patient and therapist develop a transference to that setting as well as to each other.
- The notes you bring to supervision may be scant on patient verbalizations. Therefore, try to record patient behavior and mannerisms. Share any comments you can about your own reactions both during and after sessions.

With or without such an orientation, many new therapists continue to pro-
fess that neither their formal training nor life experiences have prepared
them for this work. One therapist exclaimed, "I feel like I've been dropped
on Mars." The supervisory experience can counter such protestations of
unfamiliarity by offering multiple opportunities for therapists to reveal
resistance to engaging with their patients. Hearing oneself present a case
provides a therapist with an occasion to observe that they are withdrawing from their patient. If the therapist remains unaware, the supervisor can
gently help identify the emotional flatness in the case presentation and then
raise the question as to what this might mean.

Lack of knowledge is rarely the sole factor at play when therapists are
resistant. Even when the supervisor provides the technical information the
supervisee professes to lack, they often resist applying it in the treatment
situation. One supervisee, after spending weeks discussing therapeutic
action with psychosis, said, "I'm usually eager to get this kind of
information, but I find myself not wanting to take in what you're saying."
Such supervisees may insist that they have nothing in common with their
patients; their complaint is less about technical inexperience than what they
deem to be profound unfamiliarity with their patient's struggles or, more
commonly, ways to deal with them. They might say something like, "Even
if I knew what to do with his symptoms, I could never feel connected to
him." Thus, they convince themselves that their patients will always remain
a mystery. Ironically, the therapist's appreciation that they share some
degree of similarity with their patient can free them to then identify their
differences. They thus experience a demystifying familiarity while, at the
same time, creating a boundary that promotes feeling safer and encourages
curiosity and desire for exploration.

## Feeling Deskilled

Supervisors may discern a therapist's resistance when an otherwise
articulate supervisee finds themselves without words to describe their
experience. Interacting with a patient experiencing psychosis has made
them feel incompetent, unable to connect with what they had previously
known, and therefore paralyzed about taking meaningful action or even
accurately describing what they are trying to do. Frequently therapists
will point to their efforts to make contact as the main factor in their
dilemma—for example, "No matter what I do I can't reach this patient."

The "failed" encounter arouses intense affect, and the defeated therapist feels "deskilled."

Deskilling is a consequence of the patient–therapist interaction, promoted by the patient's confusing, inaccessible, aggressive, or bizarre presentation. The sense of being deskilled is exacerbated when the therapist fears their own irrationality surfacing. The therapist becomes perplexed, and their customary belief in their own proficiency is shaken, which results in hesitancy. The patient's anxiety is then likely to increase, culminating in an escalation of their psychotic symptomatology, which further increases the therapist's doubts about how to proceed. Soon a vicious cycle is spinning.

It is important to clarify that deskilling is different from lack of knowledge. Deskilling, prompted by the therapist's response to a bewildering or aggressive patient, results in the therapist feeling that they are incompetent and/or unable to retrieve what they have previously known. Or they may believe that what once worked no longer does. The end result is that the therapist feels reluctance to engage with their patient. Supervision addresses this problem by conducting a collaborative examination of the stressors that have led to the therapist's withdrawal.

Both "I haven't a clue how to help the patient" and "There is absolutely nothing about the patient that is like me" limit a therapist's ability to freely interact with their patient or apply their own life experiences to understand the patient. Supervisees who feel deskilled are concerned with their professional identities, whereas therapists who fear their own psychotic core emerging are preoccupied with their personal identities. However, considerable overlap exists between these two positions.

## Transference and Countertransference

Transference, the return in the present of a form of past object relations, exists in every human interaction to a greater or lesser degree. Nonpsychotic transference has an "as if" quality to it: for example, "It is *as if* the therapist is the patient's mother." Such a distinction is lacking in psychotic transference, which tends to take on a literal meaning. To reach the transference and countertransference layers of the therapeutic dyad, normally a supervisor can ask the therapist: "Who are you to the patient?" and "Who is the patient to you?" In one of DK's supervisions, she asked her supervisee the first question, and Dr. Canto responded without hesitation: "I am his mother." She was ashamed to confess to DK that she was entertaining fantasies about adopting her patient after her rotation on the unit.

Indeed, the patient waited impatiently for Dr. Canto every morning, and he greeted her enthusiastically, yelling out "Mommy!" as soon as he caught a glimpse of her. Having had a painful childhood herself, Dr. Canto empathized with her patient's traumatic background with neglectful caretakers. But it wasn't until she was asked to speak about the transference and countertransference to DK that she realized the role she had been playing. She had become the good mother to her patient, one who would, in her mind, make up for the abuse and neglect his own mother had caused him. Projective identification was alive in the dyad, and both therapist and patient enjoyed the shared fantasy of a benevolent and unbreakable mother–son dyad. Once Dr. Canto realized what was happening in the treatment, she took note of the ways she and her patient had colluded to avoid his mourning his losses and her own avoidance of the impending ending of their treatment.

## Contagion

Many therapists beginning to work with psychosis fear that engaging with their patients can endanger their sense of self through emotional contagion and symptom transmission. It is true that working with psychosis can pose an emotional risk for therapists. Factors contributing to this heightened risk include the intensity of the encounter, the wall of isolation erected by some patients, the obscure nature of many of the patient's communications, boundary disturbances, the incongruity between what the patient is saying and what they appear to be feeling, acceptance of one's own illogicality, and, perhaps most of all, the threat that the patient's psychosis will unmask and activate a similar psychosis within the therapist.

It is thus essential for the supervisor to not treat psychopathology simply as one individual's problem but, rather, as an interpersonal engagement that includes shared experience. The thought of partaking in a patient's psychosis can be terrifying to the therapist, who will try mightily to avoid this fate. Unfortunately, these avoidance mechanisms create distance between the therapist and patient and can result in the patient feeling abandoned and misunderstood. Supervision helps by elucidating the unconscious mechanisms at play as well as firming up the boundaries between therapist and patient.

For example, Dr. Angle exhibited confusion and fear in supervision as he recounted a session with a manic patient. Jeremy told his therapist: "Let's say I was you, and you came up to me, and you were me, and you were an inconsistent person and a person who could not see themselves and could not help themselves at all." Upon hearing this, Dr. Angle felt his identity slipping into the patient and no longer felt he knew who he was. He questioned what the patient was telling him. Was he saying the therapist and the patient were alike in their inconsistency and in their lack of ability to help themselves? The momentary blurring of boundaries can create a *folie à deux* (shared delusion) which can be quite frightening to the therapist. In this case, it was important for DK to help Dr. Angle differentiate himself from Jeremy but also to see how Jeremy had brought him to a place of dedifferentiation. Searles (1959) insightfully wrote about how patients with psychosis need a sense of symbiotic belonging and enmeshment, and that such patients can drive their therapists mad in the way they themselves were once driven to insanity. DK's supervision with Dr. Angle involved helping him organize Jeremy's disorganized thoughts. Both patient and therapist found a path toward clarity and a sense of groundedness. Indeed, Jeremy had repeated throughout the session his need to be grounded— i.e., brought down from his manic high. Despite understanding what had happened between him and Jeremy, Dr. Angle decided to leave his training in psychology to study law.

Another example took place when Dr. Gabaldon met Peter, a man diagnosed with paranoid schizophrenia. Peter, who had a history of several assault convictions, was transferred from jail after having struck a bus driver for "looking at me like I was queer. I knew he was a Nazi." In therapy, Peter repeatedly questioned Dr. Gabaldon's way of looking at him. His tone became more strident, and, in one session, Peter rose from his chair while making a menacing gesture. That evening, Dr. Gabaldon was waiting for the elevator in his apartment building when he became convinced that when the elevator door opened, Peter would emerge and assault him. This felt true despite the fact that the therapist knew Peter was in a locked ward several miles away. The following day, in supervision with MS, Dr. Gabaldon insisted on ending his involvement with Peter. The reason he gave was not that he was afraid of his patient, or that he couldn't understand or help him, but that interacting with Peter had revealed to him his own psychotic self. He rejected the plausible hypothesis that there was a connection between his legitimate fear of being assaulted and having imagined Peter emerging from the elevator. Instead, he insisted that he already was or about to become psychotic: "I should never have chosen a residency in psychiatry. Maybe I was just trying to prove that my suspicions were incorrect."

It is rare that the fear of a psychotic part of the self emerges so easily and so early in one's training. Customarily, supervisees' fears are buried, surfacing gradually and with considerable resistance. Whether therapists suspect a psychotic core in themselves or believe their patients are currently driving them mad, the impact on the treatment is the same. These therapists will need to assure themselves that they and their patients have almost nothing in common, an adaptation that will, in the end, make their work more difficult and their professional selves less competent.

When facing such powerful convictions in a supervisee, one of the most challenging tasks is to walk the fine line between being a supervisor and acting as a therapist. Certainly, supervision can be therapeutic in and of itself. Moreover, a hard and fast distinction between therapy and supervision is difficult at times, and perhaps impossible and even undesirable. Although being in treatment can serve as a helpful adjunct to supervision while a novice therapist learns to work with psychosis (and any other form of psychopathology, for that matter), it might also be beneficial to limit the number of patients with psychosis one treats at any given time.

One aspect of supervision that can be helpful with therapists who fear being similar to a patient with psychosis, or being contaminated by them, is the supervisor's pointing out the universal struggles that preoccupy such persons: fear, yearning, frustration, the terror associated with the desire to love and be loved, lack of certainty, and chaos. All these states, though expressed with differing intensity, are intrinsic to the human condition.

## Withdrawal and Normalization

Two adaptive approaches to the disorientation novice therapists feel when first encountering psychosis are withdrawal and normalization. To avoid feeling "out of their depth," the therapist may regress to a state of illusory safety, toggling between their wish for immunity ("Nothing that's happening here can get to me") and defensively feeling that, since they have nothing to offer their patient, they do not belong with the patient or that the treatment is meaningless. On the surface, withdrawal from one's patient may not appear to be abandonment. The therapist may show up for appointments, hear what the patient is saying, take notes, etc., and still not be engaged. It is likely that, after a while, the therapist will ask themselves, "What, if anything, am I able to accomplish here?" If unable to arrive at an acceptable answer, the psychodynamic therapist may abandon exploration in favor of a strictly supportive approach.

Normalization, as we are using the term, refers to a process by which the therapist, threatened by a patient's intensity, sanitizes psychopathology. Normalization can be difficult to distinguish from empathic understanding, and telling them apart depends on understanding the therapist's underlying motivation. On the one hand, a therapist who is empathically connected understands the patient's sense of themselves and their world, which makes the patient's thoughts and actions predictable and grants the therapist perspective. On the other hand, a therapist who is threatened by the patient's irrationality may convince themselves that what the patient is describing makes sense to them when, in fact, they do not comprehend the patient's perspective. For example, one supervisee emphatically exclaimed that her patient was "normal" despite the patient's floridly psychotic symptoms; she insisted that the patient's normality had "eluded" the supervisor.

The following is an example of how supervision might address the therapist's flight from psychosis. Dr. Aziri felt "frozen in place" when her patient Oscar insisted that his word salad made perfect sense to anyone who "truly" wanted to understand him. "That includes you!" he declared accusingly to his therapist. Despite the fact that Oscar's words seemed like gibberish, Dr. Aziri was unable to reassure herself that her perception was correct. Perhaps she should be able to make sense of what he was saying, she mused. What was wrong with her? She felt unable to think.

MS, as her supervisor, simply asked, "Why don't you tell him that you're two different people, that you see things differently? What makes sense to him might not make sense to you." She seemed shocked by MS's suggestion.

"You mean I can just say that to him?" She then said that what was most helpful wasn't *what* MS said, but *how* he said it. "You were so matter-of-fact," she announced with surprise. The therapist found herself unable to think freely because she feared what her inability to comprehend her patient's communication signified that she might act out her frustration. Even if she had previously known what to do, she was no longer able to access that information. She had convinced herself that she needed to use a different set of rules when working with a person diagnosed with psychosis. These patients are different, she reasoned, and she had to discover an entirely new way of being with them. She could no longer rely on her previous expertise or even trust her motivation. Assumptions about a diagnostic label and all that goes with it had deskilled her and interfered with what she already knew about interacting with patients.

The more a therapist insists that nothing they have been taught nor anything they have experienced sheds light on how to work with patients with psychosis, the more likely they are to eventually realize that their adamancy conceals an underlying concern about themselves. Supervisors should intervene only if the therapist fails to reach that understanding by themselves. The supervisor's ability to be forbearing depends upon their appreciation that any obstacle within the treatment experience will eventually make its appearance in the supervisor's office. There is no need to rush.

## Omnipotence and the Savior Complex

Therapists who work with psychosis sometimes try to avoid supervision or do not mention challenging cases to their supervisor, usually because they fear revealing their own craziness to the supervisor, or because they do not want to acknowledge their angry feelings toward a recalcitrant patient. Sometimes they are ashamed of the lack of progress in the treatment. Less frequently, but by no means rare, a therapist becomes convinced that they are the only one who can save a patient. In these cases, the therapist believes that retaining an exclusive bond with their patient requires avoiding exposure to the outside world, including supervision. The patient is often the original architect of this position, inviting the therapist to join them in an "us against the world" stance. However, if the therapist accepts this invitation, the patient will have surrendered their strategy of seeking safety by avoiding human contact, the classic need-fear dilemma that Burnham and his colleagues (1969) wrote about. Allowing the patient to act on their need for the therapist has created the very situation in which the patient fears the therapist will abandon them. To counteract this fear, the patient struggles to make their therapist feel even more special, insisting that they are the only one who can help them and, therefore, must never leave. Soon a vicious cycle ensues, further enhancing the therapist's wish to avoid supervision. Following is an example of supervision (narrated by MS) addressing the problem of the "special" patient–therapist relationship as well as a more general example of the role of supervision for a therapist working with psychosis.

Joann was creating havoc on her inpatient unit. She would not speak to any staff member except her psychiatrist, Dr. Sachdev, who compounded the problem by doing almost nothing to explain Joann to the frustrated staff. The impasse became so difficult that the head of service mandated that Dr. Sachdev be assigned an additional supervisor for the express purpose of reviewing his work with Joann, an unusual move in an environment in which a therapist had one supervisor for all his or her inpatients.

I (MS) was assigned as Dr. Sachdev's second supervisor, and we worked together for 18 often turbulent but ultimately rewarding months.

Dr. Sachdev did not consider that being assigned an additional supervisor reflected concern about his competence. Rather, additional supervision confirmed for him the uniqueness of his relationship with Joann, which would be difficult for any outsider to grasp. He seemed to feel that others envied and resented his closeness with Joann, and that was the reason he was assigned an additional supervisor.

I told Dr. Sachdev that I was having difficulty getting a clear picture of Joann and what the treatment was like. My confusion pleased him. I wondered aloud whether my failure to understand Joann meant that their special relationship transcended conventional understanding.

"Maybe," he replied. I took his response as hopeful, suggesting that their interaction might be something we could discuss later.

During our first six months together, Dr. Sachdev, almost as an aside, told me that when he began his work with Joann (our supervision started several months after their therapy had begun), she had bombarded him with frightening delusions of a world bent on destroying her. Her persecutors were relentless, spreading such negative propaganda that people were afraid to be seen with her, which solidified her aloneness. As he recounted these events, I was impressed by how little importance he now gave them, even though at the time he had felt stymied about how to help her and, at times, felt angry with her. It was as if all that history belonged to someone else, having nothing to do with the current Joann or their interaction. Instead, Dr. Sachdev focused on how involved Joann was in their relationship.

I frequently asked Dr. Sachdev how he understood his work with Joann. Rather than respond to my question, he detailed the many ways Joann's previous therapists had disappointed her. While uncertain about how this had happened, he was pleased that she found him different from the others. He politely but firmly resisted any effort to explore their relationship, subtly requesting that I stop asking about their interaction. Thinking he might be less guarded talking about the supervisory relationship, I shifted the focus to our interaction. Did he have any thoughts about my difficulty under-standing what went on in their therapy?

My question did not surprise him. On the contrary, he reminded me how difficult it had been for him to make contact with Joann. "The only way to get the real sense of Joann is to know her the way I do," he insisted.

Since he understood her so completely, I wondered aloud, "What prevented you from making Joann clear to me?"

He had no answer. It was obvious that his priority was to protect their relationship from my prying eyes and ears.

Rather than enter a head-on confrontation over what his relationship with Joann meant to him, I decided to use a hypothetical, "what if" approach, hoping that would give him enough emotional distance to talk more freely. "If I were to become the second person in the world who came to know the real Joann, albeit through your revealing her to me, what might the consequences be? Would they be the same for both you and her?"

My hypothetical question opened an access point into their relationship. Dr. Sachdev was uncertain about Joann's reaction. She might be annoyed that he had violated the sanctity of their private space, but she might also think that I would be so impressed by their unique accomplishment that I would tell the staff to leave them alone. With regard to his own reaction, Dr. Sachdev wondered if I might be jealous of their bond and wish to destroy it.

Over time, Dr. Sachdev came to understand that his reluctance to examine his unique relationship with Joann, or, more accurately, his fear of losing it, had two sources. One involved his concern about returning to the struggles he experienced at the onset of therapy—his patient's wall of paranoid rage and despair, a subject he had shown no interest in earlier. The other was the threat of losing the specialness Joann had conferred on him. She told him that he was the only therapist who had been able to provide her with a feeling of safety, and he believed her. She repeatedly let him know that he was the only one who had dared to accept the challenge of joining her to face down the evil persecutors, despite the fact that, in the earliest sessions, she had accused him of being "one of them" and often refused to meet with him. Dr. Sachdev described the impact of Joann's alternating views of him as persecutor and savior as "being in hell versus being in heaven."

It was clear to me that Dr. Sachdev viewed me as the enemy, an agent of the inpatient service, either wanting to break up his special relationship with Joann or challenge its legitimacy. He had to test me before he could trust me. He laid traps for me. Instead of asking me whether I believed his relationship with Joann was real, he claimed he had begun to doubt the relationship to see whether I would encourage him to drop it completely. He was shocked when, instead, I showed curiosity about their relationship.

"You always wanted to know more about us," he later told me. "I had expected you to try to convince me to let her go," he said, puzzled. Instead of responding as he had feared, I demonstrated that our supervision was meant to aid him in his work with Joann. The result, over time, was establishing a sufficient learning alliance that allowed us to work together to understand the role their relationship played in initially obscuring, and then serving, as the point of entry for understanding Joann.

How can we understand Dr. Sachdev's gradual willingness to examine his relationship with Joann? Therapists working with patients experiencing psychosis are likely to experience a mixture of intense feelings, and it takes considerable trust to acknowledge these issues in supervision. Repeated contact is crucial, and regular meetings with Dr. Sachdev provided me with a clearer picture of his struggles and, equally important, his strengths, which allowed me to begin asking more of him. His resilience in fending off my inquiries, his intelligence—as demonstrated in the traps he laid for me—and his capacity for dedication and loyalty exemplified by his year-long allegiance to Joann were all strengths that I could rely on as we pursued the complexity of their relationship. For Dr. Sachdev, the time we spent together gave him the breathing space to surface his concerns, including his suspicions about me.

The more Dr. Sachdev became involved in the supervision, the freer he felt to consider suggestions made by the staff about how he might encourage Joann to allow the staff a role in her treatment. He began to feel like a "real therapist" again. By the same token, the less special his relationship with Joann became, the more she clung to him. She made it difficult for him to end their sessions, insisting that her life would be over if he were to leave her. Over time, as their symbiotic bond was replaced with a clear patient–therapist boundary, Joann also began including staff in her interactions.

Dr. Sachdev attributed his new-found ability to establish boundaries to increased collaboration with other members of the treatment team as well as the pride he felt in the re-emergence of his professional identity. "Now I am doing what I am supposed to do rather than trying to be a savior," he said with confidence.

I wondered about his categorical characterization of himself. What are therapists "supposed" to do? Hadn't he first needed to develop a bond with Joann to later examine her desperation and the psychotic defenses she employed to protect herself? I reminded him that something similar had happened in our work. I had waited until our alliance strengthened before confronting him about his relationship with Joann. Until that point, my interest in what he was describing fostered our working relationship, just as his interest in Joann had created a zone of safety, both resulting in the provision of a place for exploratory work. Not surprisingly, Dr. Sachdev recognized the parallel. Therapists are better able to appreciate countertransference issues when these same issues emerge in supervision.

Our final sessions centered on the special bond Dr. Sachdev had developed with Joann. He insisted that, whatever else was true about their interaction, his relationship with Joann had indeed been special. I readily agreed, pointing to the totality of their work together, which included their special bonding, the tearing apart of that connection, and the subsequent pain involved. With all that, their collaboration survived. They were able to explore the nature of that specialness, and so were we.

Dr. Sachdev wanted to talk more about his feeling that he had betrayed Joann. When she accused him of "going over to the other side" and abandoning her, was she onto something?

I responded to his inquiry with a series of questions of my own. Might she have another side too? If she did, and her therapist ignored it, could that constitute betrayal? Was Joann accurate in her assessment that she would never be able to face being alone? Hadn't Dr. Sachdev seen examples of her resilience prior to the weakening of their symbiotic bond? Could he simply walk away from her capacity for autonomy? Wasn't it possible that what allowed Joann to survive their rupture was her identification with the strength he had witnessed in her? Loewald (1960) wrote that the patient identifies not only with whom the therapist sees in the present but also with whom they can become—their unrecognized developmental potential.

This case illustrates several important points. First, it shows one way in which therapists (especially beginners) cope with feelings of inadequacy: they launch into savior mode, replete with rescue fantasies. Patients and therapists collude in believing that they have a unique and special bond. A supervisor in these cases is viewed as an interloper, merely there to remind the therapist of their vulnerability and to destroy the special oneness that exists between therapist and patient. Second, even though the therapist is defensively dealing with their own vulnerability, the supervisor must keep in mind that beginning therapists bring enthusiasm and optimism to difficult cases. Their fresh outlook can sometimes help in ways a seasoned professional's experience and more temperate attitude might not (Berman, 2004). MS worked with Dr. Sachdev on both levels. He did not challenge or try to dismantle the therapist's special bond with Joann, which allowed Dr. Sachdev to eventually share what would have otherwise been "highly classified material." Slowly introducing curiosity into the supervisory frame, including curiosity about the (parallel) relationship with MS, allowed Dr. Sachdev to be ready to look beyond his rescue fantasies and continue the treatment with Joann within clearer therapeutic boundaries.

## Summary

The central supervisory task is to assist supervisees in becoming aware that their patients are struggling with issues like those they themselves have experienced, though likely in a form and degree to which the therapists have not seen before. Therapists may resist conscious awareness of similarity, fearing that identifying any commonality between themselves and their patients would be tantamount to entering a psychotic world without a secure exit pass. In that scenario, the therapist feels that safety demands absolute discontinuity between therapist and patient. Alternatively, the therapist might bolt the door when they find themselves frightened by how much they enjoy the primitive aspects of interactions with their patient.

A learning alliance analogous to the therapeutic alliance develops when supervisees and supervisors can work together to facilitate the therapist's involvement with their patients, their impact on patients, and the possible bases for clinician vulnerability. Within the context of the learning alliance, the therapist/supervisee, as participant observer (Sullivan, 1947), is able to live out and reflect on their experience with their patient. Issues that the therapist had previously considered as belonging exclusively to the patient can then reappear in the supervisor's office, reflecting the therapist's identification with their patient. A frequent consequence is that therapists recognize areas they and their patients share, and they find their belief in their own competence reinforced. No longer fearful of discovering what they do share while retaining an awareness of their differences allows therapists more freedom to engage with their patients through the totality of their being.

Both supervision and therapy involve the therapist's increasing self-awareness. Learning about oneself is not restricted exclusively to supervisees and their patients. Searles (1965) emphasized that the therapist's openness to being shown aspects of themselves by their patient is an essential ingredient—and we would add an essential benefit—of the psychodynamic treatment of psychosis. The joint supervisory journey is likely to move in fits and starts, but all participants are on the same road, sometimes separated, but never losing complete sight of each other.

# References

Alanen, Y. O. (1997). *Schizophrenia: Its origins and need-adapted treatment*. Karnac Books.

Allen, M. (1995). Sullivan's closet: A reappraisal of H.S. Sullivan's life and his pioneering role in American psychiatry. *Journal of Homosexuality, 29*(1), 1–18.

American Psychiatric Association. (2013). *Diagnostic and statistical manual of mental disorders* (5th ed.). https://doi.org/10.1176/appi.books.9780890425596

Amir, I., & Shefler, G. (2020). The "Lechol Nefesh" project: Intensive and long term psychoanalytic psychotherapy in public mental health centers. *Psychoanalytic Inquiry, 40*(7), 536–549.

Andersen, T. (1991). *The reflecting team: Dialogues and dialogues about the dialogues*. W. W. Norton & Co.

Arango, C., Buchanan, R. W., Kirkpatrick, B., & Carpenter, W. T., Jr. (2004). The deficit syndrome in schizophrenia: Implications for the treatment of negative symptoms. *European Psychiatry, 19*, 21–26.

Arieti, S. (1974a). An overview of schizophrenia from a predominantly psychological approach. *Journal of Psychiatry, 131*(3), 241–249.

Arieti, S. (1974b). *Interpretation of schizophrenia* (2nd ed.). Basic Books.

Aron, L., & Lieberman, A. (2017). In memory of Harold Searles: 1918–2015. *Psychoanalytic Dialogues, 27*(2), 182–191.

Auchincloss, E. L., & Weiss, R. W. (1992). Paranoid character and the intolerance of indifference. *Journal of the American Psychoanalytic Association, 40*(4), 1013–1037.

Aulagnier, P. (2001). *The violence of interpretation: From pictogram to statement* (A. Sheridan, Trans.). Taylor and Francis Group (Original work published 1975).

Ayaya, S. & Kitanaka, J. (2023, June 12). Japan's radical alternative to psychiatric diagnosis. *Aeon*. Retrieved from https://aeon.co/essays/japans-radical-alternative-to-psychiatric-diagnosis

Bach, S. (1985). *Narcissistic states and the therapeutic process*. Rowman & Littlefield.

Badcock, J., Shah, S., Mackinnon, A., Stain, H., Galletly, C., Jablensky, A., & Morgan, V. (2015). Loneliness in psychotic disorders and its association with cognitive function and symptom profile. *Schizophrenia Research, 169*, 268–273.

Baird, A., & Forde Thomson, W. (2018). The impact of music on the self in dementia. *Journal of Alzheimer's Disease, 61*, 827–841.

Bakhtin, M. (1984). *Dostoevsky's poetics* (C. Emerson, Trans.). University of Texas Press.

Balint, M. (1968). *The basic fault: Therapeutic aspects of regression*. Brunner/Mazel.

Balsam, P., & Tomie, A. (2014). *Context and learning*. Psychology Press.

Bass, A. (2008). It takes one to know one; or, whose unconscious is it anyway? *Psychoanalytic Dialogues, 11*(5), 683–702.

Bass, A. (2009). "It ain't over till it's over:" Infinite conversations, imperfect endings, and the elusive nature of termination. *Psychoanalytic Dialogues, 19*(6), 744–759.

Bauby, J. D. (1998). *The diving bell and the butterfly*. Knopf-Doubleday.

Baudelaire, C. (1995). *The painter of modern life and other essays* (J. Maine, Ed. & Trans.) Phaidon Press (Originally work published 1863).

Baudry, F. D. (1993). The personal dimension and management of the supervisory situation with a special note on the parallel process. *Psychoanalytic Quarterly, 62*, 588–561.

Bayley, R. (1996). First person account: Schizophrenia. *Schizophrenia Bulletin, 22*(4), 727–729.

Bebbington, P., Wilkins, S., Jones, P., Foerster, A., Murray, R., Toone, B., & Lewis, S. (1993). Life events and psychosis. Initial results from the Camberwell collaborative psychosis study. *British Journal of Psychiatry, 162*, 72–79.

Beck, A., Grant, P., Huh, G., Perivoliatis, D., & Chang, N. (2013). Dysfunctional attitudes and expectancies in deficit syndrome schizophrenia. *Schizophrenia Bulletin, 39*(1), 43–51. https://doi.org/10.1093/schbul/sbr040

Beck, A., Himelstein, R., & Grant, P. (2019). In and out of schizophrenia: Activation and deactivation of the negative and positive schemas. *Schizophrenia Research, 203*, 55–61.

Becker, E. (1973). *The denial of death*. The Free Press.

Beckett, S. (1975). *The unnamable*. Calder & Boyars.

Beecher, B. (2009). The medical model, mental health practitioners, and individuals with schizophrenia and their families. *Journal of Social Work Practice, 23*(1), 9–20. https://doi.org/10.1080/02650530902723282

Belin, S. (1993). *The power of madness: Parallel processes when working with early disturbed and psychotic patients*. Nature and Culture.

Benatar, M. (2008). A Reconsideration of the clinical work of Harold Searles. *Journal of Trauma & Dissociation, 9*(4), 563–577.

Benedetti, G. (1987). *Psychotherapy of schizophrenia*. New York University Press.

Bentall, R. P. (2003). *Madness explained: Psychosis and human nature*. Penguin.

Bentall, R. P., & Fernyhough, C. (2008). Social predictors of psychotic experiences: Specificity and psychological mechanisms. *Schizophrenia Bulletin, 34*(6), 1012–1020.

Berenson, A. (2019). *Tell your children: The truth about marijuana, mental illness, and violence*. Free Press.

Bergmann, M. (1997). Termination: The Achilles heel of psychoanalytic technique. *Psychoanalytic Psychology, 14*, 163–174.

Bergner, D. (2022). *The mind and the moon: My brother's story, the science of our brains, and the search for our psyches*. Ecco.

Bergström, T., Seikkula, J., Alakare, B., Mäki, P., Köngäs-Saviaro, P., Taskila, J. J., Tolvanen, A., & Aaltonen, J. (2018). The family-oriented Open Dialogue approach in the treatment of first-episode psychosis: Nineteen-year outcomes. *Psychiatry Research, 270*, 168–175. https://doi.org/10.1016/j.psychres.2018.09.039

Berman, E. (2004). *Impossible Training: A relational view of psychoanalytic education*. Analytic Press.

Bion, W. (1957). Differentiation of the psychotic from the non-psychotic personalities. *International Journal of Psychoanalysis, 38*, 266–275.

Bion, W. (1959). Attacks on linking. *International Journal of Psychoanalysis, 40*, 308–315.

Bion, W. (1967). *Second thoughts: Selected papers on psychoanalysis*. Heinemann.

Bion, W. (1970). *Attention and interpretation*. Tavistock.

Bion, W. (1978). *Seven servants: Four works by Wilfred Bion*. Jason Aronson.

Bion, W. (1990). *Brazilian lectures*. Karnac Books.

Bion, W. (1992) *Cogitations*. Karnac Books.

Birchwood, M., Meaden, A., Trower, P., Gilbert, P., & Plaistow, J. (2000). The power and omnipotence of voices: Subordination and entrapment by voices and significant others. *Psychological Medicine, 30*(2), 337–344.

Blechner, M. (1995). Schizophrenia. In M. Lionells, J. Fiscalini, C. Mann & D. Stern, (Eds.) *Handbook of interpersonal psychoanalysis*. (pp. 375–496) Analytic Press.

Blechner, M. (2019). Aspects of clinical work with psychotic patients. *Psychoanalysis of the psychoses* (pp. 107–119). Routledge.

Bleuler, E. (1950). *Dementia Praecox or the group of schizophrenias* (J. Zinkin, Trans.). International Universities Press. (Original work published 1911).

Blum, H. (1989). The concept of termination and the evolution of psychoanalytic technique. *Journal of the American Psychoanalytic Association, 37*, 275–295.

Bollas, C. (1987). *The shadow of the object: Psychoanalysis of the unthought known*. Free Association Books.

Bollas, C. (2013). *Catch them before they fall: The psychoanalysis of breakdown*. Routledge.

Bollas, C. (2015). *When the sun bursts: The enigma of schizophrenia*. Yale University Press.

Bonovitz, C. (2007). Termination never ends: The inevitable incompleteness of psychoanalysis. *Contemporary Psychoanalysis, 43*(2), 229–246.

Bordin, E. (1979). The generalizability of the psychoanalytic concept of the working alliance. *Psychotherapy: Theory, Research and Practice, 16*, 252–260.

Bott Spillius, E. (1983). Some developments from the work of Melanie Klein. *International Journal of Psychoanalysis, 64*, 321–332.

Boulanger, G. (2007). *Wounded by reality: Understanding and treating adult onset trauma*. Routledge.

Breuer, J., & Freud, S. (1957) Studies on hysteria. In J. Strachey (Ed. & Trans.), *The standard edition of the complete psychological works of Sigmund Freud* (Vol. 2). Hogarth Press (Original work published 1893–5).

Brousse, M. H. (2008). Ordinary psychosis in the light of Lacan's theory of discourse. *Psychoanalytical Notebooks, 19*, 7–20.

Burnham, D. L., Gladstone, A. I., & Gibson, R. W. (1969). *Schizophrenia and the need-fear dilemma*. International Universities Press.

Burton, A. (Ed.). (1961). *Psychotherapy of the psychoses*. Basic Books.

Cacioppo, J. T., & Patrick, W. (2008). *Loneliness: Human nature and the need for social connection*. W.W. Norton & Co.

Carlat, D. (2010). *Unhinged: The trouble with psychiatry—A doctor's revelations about a profession in crisis*. Free Press.

Carpenter, W. T., Jr., Heinrichs, D. W., & Alphs, L. (1985). Treatment of negative symptoms. *Schizophrenia Bulletin, 11*(3), 440–452.

Carpenter, W. T., Jr., Heinrichs, D. W., & Wagman, A. M. (1988). Deficit and nondeficit forms of schizophrenia: The concept. *American Journal of Psychiatry, 145*, 578–583.

Chrostek, P., Grygiel, M., Anczewska, M., & Switaj, P. (2016). The intensity and correlates of the feeling of loneliness in people with psychosis. *Comprehensive Psychiatry, 70*, 190–199.

Clarkson, P., & Pokorny, M. (Eds.). (1994). *The handbook of psychotherapy*. Routledge.

Conan, N. (Host). (2012, October 22). Psychiatrists shift focus to drugs, not talk therapy [Audio podcast episode]. In *Talk of the nation*. NPR Washington DC https://www.npr.org/2012/10/22/163409863/psychiatrists-shift-focus-to-drugs-not-talk-therapy

Conci, M. (2010). *Sullivan revisited—Life and work: Harry Stack Sullivan's relevance for contemporary psychiatry, psychotherapy and psychoanalysis*. Tangram Edizioni Sceintifiche.

Conti, A. (2019, February 17). When "going outside is prison": The world of American hikikomori. *New York Magazine*. https://nymag.com/intelligencer/2019/02/the-world-of-american-hikikomori.html

Cooperi, S. (2010). The changing firmament: Familiar and unfamiliar forms of engagement during termination. In J. Salberg (Ed.), *Good enough endings: Breaks, interruptions, and terminations from contemporary relational perspectives* (pp. 145–166). Routledge.

Corradi, R. (2004). Medical psychotherapy of schizophrenia. A dynamic supportive approach. *Journal of the American Academy of Psychoanalysis, 32*(4), 633–644.

Craig, T. J. K., Rus-Calafell, M., Ward, T., Leff, J. P., Huckvale, M., Howarth, E., & Garety, P. A. (2018). Avatar therapy for auditory verbal hallucinations in people with psychosis: A single-blind randomized controlled trial. *The Lancet Psychiatry, 5*(1), 31–40.

Craige, H. (2002). Mourning analysis: The post-termination phase. *Journal of the American Psychoanalytic Association, 50*(2), 507–550.

Cullberg, J. 2006. *Psychoses: An integrative perspective*. Routledge.

Davies, J. (2005). Transformations of desire and despair: Reflections on the termination process from a relational perspective. *Psychoanalytic Dialogues, 15*(6), 779–806.

Davoine, F., & Gaudillière, J. M. (2004). *History beyond trauma*. Other Press.

Davoine, F., & Gaudillière, J. M. (2009). France: The contribution of some French psychoanalysts to the clinical and theoretical approaches to transference in the psychodynamic treatment of psychosis. In Y. O. Alanen (Ed.), *Psychotherapeutic approaches to schizophrenic psychoses* (pp. 137–144). Routledge.

Davoine, F., & Gaudillière, J. M. (2016). Stoppage of time in schizophrenia: Similarities to the field of war trauma. *International Forum of Psychoanalysis, 25*, 104–109.

Davoine, F., & Gaudillière, J. M. (2017). The psychoanalysis of psychosis at the crossroads of individual stories and of history. In D. Laub & A. Hamburger (Eds.), *Psychoanalysis and Holocaust testimony: Unwanted memories of social trauma.* (pp. 92–103). Routledge.

DeLeo, M. (Director). (2001). *Bellevue: Inside out* [film]. HBO Home Video.

De Masi, F. (2009). *Vulnerability to psychosis: A psychoanalytic study of the nature and therapy of the psychotic state*. Karnac Books.

Dillon, J., Moncrieff, A., & Rapley, M. (2011). Carving nature at its joints? DSM and the medicalization of everyday life. In M. Rapley, A. Moncrieff, & J. Dillon (Eds.), *De-medicalizing misery: Psychiatry, psychology and the human condition* (pp. 1–9). Palgrave MacMillan.

Docherty, J. P., & Feister, S. J. (1985). The therapeutic alliance and compliance in psychopharmacology. In R. E. Hales & A. J. Frances (Eds.), *Annual Review of Psychiatry* (Vol. 4, pp. 607–632). American Psychiatric Press.

Dolder, C. R., Dunn, L. B., Leckband, S. G., Lacro, J. P., Leckband. S. G., & Jeste, D. V. (2002). Prevalence of and risk factors for medication nonadherence in patients with schizophrenia: A comprehensive review of recent literature. *Journal of Clinical Psychiatry, 63*(10), 892–909. https://doi.org/10.4088/jcp.v63n1007

El Bouhaddani, S., Veling, W., Schaefer, B., Doreleijers, T., & van Domburgh, L. (2018, November 26). *Transdiagnostic school-based intervention for adolescents with early persistent psychiatric symptoms: An initial single-group effect study.* Wiley Online Library. https://doi.org/10.1111/eip.12755

Eigen, M. (1986). *The psychotic core.* Jason Aronson.

Eigen, M. (2011). *Contact with the depths.* Routledge.

Eshel, O. (1998). 'Black holes', deadness and existing analytically. *International Journal of Psychoanalysis, 79*(6), 1115–1130.

Eshel, O. (2013). Patient-analyst "withness": On analytic "presencing," passion, and compassion in states of breakdown, despair, and deadness. *Psychoanalytic Quarterly, 82*(4), 925–963.

Evans, F. B. (1996). *Harry Stack Sullivan: Interpersonal theory and psychotherapy.* Routledge.

Fairbairn, R. (1952). *Psychoanalytic studies of personality.* Routledge and Kegan Paul.

Falloon, I. H., Held, T., Roncone, R., Coverdale, J. H., & Laidlaw, T. M. (1998). Optimal treatment strategies to enhance recovery from schizophrenia. *Australian and New Zealand Journal of Psychiatry, 32*(1), 43–47.

Falloon, I. R., & Talbot, R. E. (1981). Persistent auditory hallucination: Coping mechanisms and implications for management. *Psychological Medicine, 11*(2), 329–339.

Farber, L. (1958). The therapeutic despair. *Psychiatry, 21*(1), 7–20.

Federn, P. (1952). *Ego psychology and the psychoses* (E. Weiss, Ed.). Basic Books.

Fenton, W. S., Bleyer, C. R., & Heinssen, R. K. (1997). Determinants of medication compliance in schizophrenia: Empirical and clinical findings. *Schizophrenia Bulletin, 23*, 637–651.

Fleischhacker, W. W. (2004). Compliance in schizophrenia: Psychopathology, side effects, and patients' attitudes toward the illness and medication. *The Journal of Clinical Psychiatry, 65*(9), 1211–1218.

Fleischhacker, W. W., Meise, U., Günther, V., & Kurz, M. (1994). Compliance with antipsychotic drug treatment: Influence of side effects. *Acta Psychiatrica Scandinavica, 89*(s382), 11–15.

Frances, A. (2013). *Saving normal: An insider's revolt against out-of-control psychiatric diagnosis, DSM-5, big pharma and the medicalization of ordinary life.* William Morrow.

Frank, A. F., & Gunderson, J. G. (1990). The role of the therapeutic alliance in the treatment of schizophrenia: Relationship to course and outcome. *Archives of General Psychiatry, 47*(3), 228–236.

Frawley-O'Dea, M. G. (2003). Supervision is a relationship too. *Psychoanalytic Dialogues, 13*, 355–366.

Freud, S. (1953). On Psychotherapy. In J. Strachey (Ed. & Trans.), *The standard edition of the complete psychological works of Sigmund Freud* (Vol. 7, pp. 255–268) (Original work published 1905).

Freud, S. (1958). Psychoanalytic notes on an autobiographical account of a case of paranoia. In J. Strachey (Ed. & Trans.), *The standard edition of the complete psychological works of Sigmund Freud* (Vol. 7, pp. 1–82). Hogarth Press (Original work published 1911).

Freud, S. (1961). Neurosis and psychosis. In J. Strachey (Ed. & Trans.), *The standard edition of the complete psychological works of Sigmund Freud* (Vol. 19, pp. 147–154). Hogarth Press (Original work published 1924).

Freud, S. (1962a). The neuro-psychoses of defence. In J. Strachey (Ed. & Trans.), *The standard edition of the complete psychological works of Sigmund Freud* (Vol. 3, pp. 45–62). Hogarth Press (Original work published 1894).

Freud, S. (1962b). Further remarks on the neuro-psychoses of defence. In J. Strachey (Ed. & Trans.), *The standard edition of the complete psychological works of Sigmund Freud* (Vol. 3, pp. 157–185). Hogarth Press. Original work published 1896).

Freud, S. (1964). Constructions in analysis. In J. Strachey (Ed. & Trans.), *The standard edition of the complete psychological works of Sigmund Freud* (Vol. 23, pp. 255–270). Hogarth Press (Original work published 1937).

Freud, S. (1978a). Recommendations to physicians practicing psychoanalysis. In J. Strachey (Ed. & Trans.), *The standard edition of the complete psychological works of Sigmund Freud* (Vol. 12, pp. 111–120). Hogarth Press (Original work published 1912).

Freud, S. (1978b). On beginning the treatment (Further recommendations on the technique of psycho-analysis). In J. Strachey (Ed. & Trans.), *The standard edition of the complete psychological works of Sigmund Freud* (Vol. 12, pp. 123–144). Hogarth Press (Original work published 1913).

Freud, S. (1978c). The unconscious. In J. Strachey (Ed. & Trans.), *The standard edition of the complete psychological works of Sigmund Freud* (Vol. 14, pp. 159–215). Hogarth Press (Original work published 1915).

Freud, S. (1978d). From the history of an infantile neurosis. In J. Strachey (Ed. & Trans.), *The standard edition of the complete psychological works of Sigmund Freud* (Vol. 17, pp. 7–122). Hogarth Press (Original work published 1918).

Fromm, E. (1941). *Escape from freedom*. Farrar & Rinehart.

Fromm-Reichmann, F. (1948). Notes on the development of treatment of schizophrenics by psychoanalytic psychotherapy. *Psychiatry, 11*(3), 263–273.

Fromm-Reichmann, F. (1952). Some aspects of psychoanalysis and schizophrenics. In E. R. Brody & F. C. Redlich (Eds.), *Psychotherapy with schizophrenics* (pp. 89–111). International University Press.

Fromm Reichmann, F. (1959). Loneliness. *Psychiatry, 22*, 1–15.

Fuller, P. (2012). *Surviving, existing, or living: Phase-specific therapy for severe psychosis*. Routledge.

Furlan, F., & Benedetti, G. (1985). The individual psychoanalytic psychotherapy of schizophrenia: Scientific and clinical approach through a clinical discussion group. *Yale Journal of Biology and Medicine, 58*, 337–348.

Gabbard, G. (2009). What is a "good enough" termination? *Journal of the American Psychoanalytic Association, 57*(3), 575–594.

Gaebel, W., & Ücok, A. (2008). Side effects of atypical antipsychotics: A brief overview. *World Psychiatry, 7*(1), 58–62. https://doi.org/10.1002/j.2051-5545.2008.tb00154.x

Garfield, D., & Steinman, I. (2018). *Self psychology and psychosis: The development of the self during intensive psychotherapy of schizophrenia and other psychoses*. Karnac Books.

Garrett, M. (2019). *Psychotherapy for psychosis: Integrating cognitive-behavioral and psychodynamic treatment*. Guilford Publications.

Garrett, M., & Turkington, D. (2011). CBT for psychosis in a psychoanalytic frame. *Psychosis: Psychological, Social and Integrative Approaches, 3*(1), 2–13.

Gay, P. (1988). *Freud: A life for our time*. W.W. Norton & Co.

Gediman, H., & Wolkenfeld, F. (1980). The parallelism phenomenon in psychoanalysis and supervision: Its reconsideration as a triadic system. *Psychoanalytic Quarterly*, *49*, 234–255.

George, T. & Vaccarino, F. (2018). Cannabis legalization and psychiatric disorders: Caveat "Hemp-tor". *Canadian journal of psychiatry*, 63(7), 447–450.

Gerlach, J., Koret, B., Gereš, N., Matiü, K., Prskalo-ýule, D., Vrbanc, T. Z., Lovretiü, V., Skopljak, K., Matoš, T., Filipþiü, I. S., & Filipþiü, I. (2019). Clinical challenges in patients with first episode psychosis and cannabis use: Mini-review and a case study. *Psychiatria Danubina*, *31*(2), 162–170.

Ghelani, A., Armstrong, G., & Haywood, A. (2023). Motivations for cannabis use in youth with first episode psychosis: a scoping review. *Psychosis*, 15(1), 17–27.

Grassian, S. (2006)    Psychiatric effects of solitary confinement. *Washington University Journal of Law and Policy*, *22*(24), 325–380.

Greenberg, J. (1964). *I never promised you a rose garden*. Signet.

Grossmark, R. (2012). The unobtrusive relational analyst. *Psychoanalytic Dialogues*, *22*(6), 629–646.

Grossmark, R. (2016). Psychoanalytic companioning. *Psychoanalytic Dialogues*, *26*(6), 698–712.

Grotstein, J. (2001). A rationale for the psychoanalytically informed psychotherapy of schizophrenia and other psychoses: Towards the concept of "rehabilitative psychoanalysis." In P. Williams (Ed.), *A language for psychosis* (pp. 9–26). Wiley.

Hamer, A. M., & Meunch J. (2010). Adverse effects of antipsychotic medications. *American Family Physician*, *81*(5), 617–622.

Hamilton, I. (2017). Cannabis, psychosis and schizophrenia: Unravelling a complex interaction. *Addiction*, *112*(9), 1653–1657.

Hamilton, N. G. (1990). The containing function and the analyst's projective identification. *International Journal of Psychoanalysis*, *71*, 445–453.

Hammersley, P., Langshaw, B., Bullimore, P., Dillon, J., Romme, M., & Escher, S. (2008). Schizophrenia at the tipping point. *Mental Health Practice*, *12*(1), 14–19.

Hanly, C. (1990). The concept of truth in psychoanalysis. *International Journal of Psychoanalysis*, *71*, 375–383.

Harding, C. M., & Zahniser, J. H. (1994). Empirical correction of seven myths about schizophrenia with implications for treatment. *Acta Psychiatrica Scandinavica*, *90*, 140–146.

Harding, C., Brooks, G., Ashikaga, T., Strauss, J., & Breier, A. (1987). The Vermont longitudinal study of persons with severe mental illness, I: Methodology, study sample, and overall status 32 years later. *American Journal of Psychiatry*, *144*(6), 718–726.

Harrow, M., Jobe, T., Faull, R., & Yang, J. (2017). A 20-year multi-followup longitudinal study assessing whether antipsychotic medications contribute to work functioning in schizophrenia. *Psychiatry Research*, *256*, 267–274.

Harrow, M., Jobe, T., & Thomas, H. (2007). Factors involved in outcome and recovery in schizophrenia patients not on antipsychotic medications: A 15-year multifollow-up study. *The Journal of Nervous and Mental Disease*, *195*(5), 406–414.

Hearing Voices Network USA. (n.d.). *About us*. http://www.hearingvoicesusa.org/about-us

Hedrick, M. (2014, September 4). Living with schizophrenia: The importance of routine. *The New York Times*.

Herz, M. I. (2012). Review of CBT for psychosis: A symptom-based approach. *Journal of Clinical Psychiatry, 73*(7), 1037.

Hoffman, I. (2001). *Ritual and spontaneity in the psychoanalytic process: A dialectical-constructivist view*. Analytic Press.

Hollister, L. E. (1974). Clinical differences among phenothiazines in schizophrenics. Introduction: Specific indications for antipsychotics: Elusive end of the rainbow. *Advances in Biochemical Psychopharmacology, 9*, 667–673.

Hornstein, G. A. (2000). *To redeem one person is to redeem the world: The life of Frieda Fromm-Reichmann*. Other Press.

Horvath, A. O., & Symonds, B. D. (1991). Relation between working alliance and outcome in psychotherapy: A meta-analysis. *Journal of Counseling Psychology, 38*, 139–149.

Hurn, H. (1971). Towards a paradigm of the termination phase. *Journal of the American Psychoanalytic Association, 19*, 3323–48.

Hurvich, M. (1989). Traumatic moment, basic dangers and annihilation anxiety. *Psychoanalytic Psychology, 6*(3), 309–323.

Hurvich, M. (2003). The place of annihilation anxieties in psychoanalytic theory. *Journal of the American Psychoanalytic Association, 51*(2), 579–616.

Jackson, M. (2001). *Weathering the storms: Psychotherapy for psychosis*. Routledge.

Jones, E. G., & Mendell, L. M. (1999). Assessing the decade of the brain. *Science, 284*(5415), 739–739.

Joseph, B. (1982). Addiction to near death. *International Journal of Psychoanalysis, 63*, 449–456.

Jung, C. G. (1939). On the psychogenesis of schizophrenia. *Journal of Mental Science, 85*(358), 999–1011.

Jung, C. G. (1960). The psychogenesis of mental disease. In G. Adler & H. Read (Eds.), R. F. C. Hull (Trans.). *Collected works of C.G. Jung* (Vol. 3). Princeton University Press (Original work published 1907).

Jung, C. G. (1961). *Memories, dreams, reflections*. Vintage.

Kafka, J. (2010). Chestnut lodge and the psychoanalytic approach to psychosis. *Journal of the American Psychoanalytic Association, 59*(1), 27–47.

Kahr, B. (2007). The infanticidal attachment. *New Directions in relational psychoanalysis and psychotherapy, 1*(2), 117–132.

Kallert, T., & Leisse, M. (2000). Schizophrenic patients' subjective needs for care during community-based treatment. *Psychiatria Danubina, 12*(3–4), 253–265.

Kamali, M., Kelly, L., Gervin, M., Browne, S., Larkin, C., & O'Callaghan, E. (2001). Psychopharmacology: Insight and comorbid substance misuse and medication compliance among patients with schizophrenia. *Psychiatric Services, 52*, 161–163.

Karon, B. (2008). Supervising therapists treating the severely mentally ill. In A. K. Hess, K. D. Hess, & T. H. Hess (Eds.), *Psychotherapy supervision: Theory, research, and practice* (pp. 359–379). Wiley.

Karon, B., & VandenBos, G. (1981). *Psychotherapy of schizophrenia: The treatment of choice*. Jason Aronson.

Kasanin, J. (Ed.). (1944). *Language and thought in schizophrenia*. University of California Press.

Kimhy, D., Delespaul, P., Corcoran, C., Ahn, H., Yale, S., & Malaspina, D. (2006). Computerized experience sampling method (ESMc): Assessing feasibility and validity among individuals with schizophrenia. *Journal of Psychiatric Research, 40*(3), 221–230.

Kimhy, D., Tarrier, N., Essock, S., Malaspina, D., Cabannis, D., & Beck, A. T. (2013). Cognitive behavioral therapy for psychosis—Training practices and dissemination in the United States. *Psychosis: Psychological, social and Integrative Approaches, 5*(3), 296–305.

Kirkpatrick, B., Buchanan, R., Ross, D., & Carpenter, W. (2001). A separate disease within the syndrome of schizophrenia. *Archives of General Psychiatry, 58,* 165–171.

Kirshner, L. A. (2015). Trauma and psychosis: A review and framework for psychoanalytic understanding. *International Forum of Psychoanalysis, 24*(4), 216–224. https://doi.org/10.1080/0803706X.2013.778422

Klein, M. (1963). *Envy and gratitude & other works 1946–1963.* Delta.

Klein, M. (1975). *Love, guilt, and reparation & other works, 1921–1945.* Delacorte Press (Original work published 1945).

Knafo, D. (2012a). Alone together: Solitude and the creative encounter in art and psychoanalysis. *Psychoanalytic Dialogues, 22,* 54–71.

Knafo, D. (2012b). Working at the limits of human experience. *The American Psychoanalyst, 46*(2), 17–18, 20.

Knafo, D. (2013). Artists' solitude and the creative process. In A. Kramer Richards, L. Spira, & A. A. Lynch (Eds.), *Encounters with loneliness* (pp. 153–156). IPBooks.

Knafo, D. (2016). Going blind to see: The psychoanalytic treatment of trauma, regression and psychosis. *American Journal of Psychotherapy, 70*(1), 79–100.

Knafo, D. (2018). Beginnings and endings: Time and termination in psychoanalysis. *Psychoanalytic Psychology, 35,* 8–14.

Knafo, D. (2020). Alone in a crowded mind: When psychosis masks loneliness. *Psychoanalytic Psychology, 37*(2), 108–116.

Knafo, D., & Selzer, M. (2015). "Don't step on Tony!" The importance of symptoms when working with psychosis. *Psychoanalytic Psychology, 32*(1), 159–172.

Knafo, D., & Selzer, M. (2017). Outpatient psychodynamic psychotherapy with psychotics: Managing isolation and creating safety. In D. L. Downing & J. Mills (Eds.), *Outpatient treatment of psychosis: Psychodynamic approaches to evidence-based practice* (pp. 29–52). Karnac Books.

Kohut, H. (1971). *The analysis of the self: A systematic approach to the psychoanalytic treatment of narcissistic personality disorders.* International Universities Press.

Kohut, H. (1977). *The restoration of the self.* International Universities Press.

Krabbendam, J., Bak, M., Vollebergh, W., de Graaf, R., & Van Os, J. (2004). Childhood abuse as a risk factor for psychotic experience. *Acta Psychiatry Scandinavia, 109*(1), 38–45.

Kraeplin, E. (1919). *Dementia Praecox and paraphrenia.* E. & S. Livingstone.

Kris, E. (1952). *Psychoanalytic explorations in art.* International Universities Press.

Kroeze, W., Hufeisen, S., & Popadak, B. (2003). H1-histamine receptor affinity predicts short-term weight gain for typical and atypical antipsychotic drugs. *Neuropsychopharmacology, 28,* 519–526. https://doi.org/10.1038/sj.npp.1300027

Kvarnes, R., & Parloff, G. (Eds.). (1976). *A Harry Stack Sullivan case seminar: Treatment of a young male schizophrenic.* W. W. Norton & Company.

Kyziridis, T. C. (2005). Notes on the history of schizophrenia. *German Journal of Psychiatry, 8*(3), 42–48.

Lacan, J. (1975). *De la psychose paranoïaque dans ses rapports avec la personnalité [Paranoid psychosis in its relationship with the personality].* Editions du Seuil (Original work published 1932).

Lacan, J. (1981). *The Seminar of Jacques Lacan. Book III: The psychoses 1955–1956* (J. A. Miller, Ed., R. Grigg, Trans.). W. W. Norton & Co.

Lacan, J. (2005). *Le Séminaire. Livre XXIII: Le sinthome* [*The seminar of Jacques Lacan. Book XXIII: The sinthome*]. Éditions du Seuil (Original work published 1975–1976).

Lader, M. (1999). Some adverse effects of antipsychotics: Prevention and treatment. *The Journal of Clinical Psychiatry, 60*(Suppl. 12), 18–21.

LaPlanche, J. (1998). *Essays on otherness.* Routledge.

Lasky, R. (1984). Dynamics and problems in the treatment of the "Oedipal Winner." *Psychoanalytic Review, 71*(3), 351–374.

Laub, D., & Lee, S. (2003). Thanatos and massive psychic trauma: The impact of the death instinct on knowing, remembering, and forgetting. *Journal of the American Psychoanalytic Association, 51*(2), 433–463.

Lavretsky, H. (2008). History of schizophrenia as a psychiatric disorder. In K. T. Mueser & D. V. Jeste (Eds.), *Clinical handbook of schizophrenia* (pp. 3–13). Guilford Press.

Lazar, S. G. (Ed.). (2010). *Psychotherapy is worth it: A comprehensive review of its cost-effectiveness.* American Psychiatric Publishing.

Leader, D. (2011). *What is madness?* Penguin.

LeDoux, J. (2002). *The synaptic self.* Viking.

Lee, T. (2006). *Hermeneutics and phenomenology of delusions: Paranoid delusion narratives as relational allegories* [Unpublished doctoral dissertation]. LIU Post.

Lehmann, H. & Ban, T. (1997). The history of the psychopharmacology of schizophrenia. *The Canadian Journal of Psychiatry, 42*(2), 152–162.

Lemaire, A. (1977). *Jacques Lacan.* Routledge.

Levenson, E. A. (1976). Problems in terminating psychoanalysis (a symposium): The aesthetics of termination. *Contemporary Psychoanalysis, 12*(3), 338–342.

Levy, A. (2008). The therapeutic action of play in the psychodynamic treatment of children: A critical analysis. *Clinical Social Work Journal, 36*(3), 281–291.

Levy, S., McGlashan, T., & Carpenter, W. (1975). Integration and sealing over as recovery styles from acute psychosis. *Journal of Nervous and Mental Diseases, 161*(5), 307–312.

Lichtenberg, J. (1963). Untreating—Its necessity in the therapy of certain schizophrenic patients. *British Journal of Medical Psychology, 36*(4), 311–317.

Little, M. (1990). *Psychotic anxieties and containment: A personal record of an analysis with Winnicott.* Jason Aronson.

Loewald, H. W. (1962). Internalization, separation, mourning and the superego. *Psychoanalytic Quarterly, 31*, 483–504.

Loewald, H. W. (1960). On the therapeutic action of psychoanalysis. *International journal of psychoanalysis, 41*, 16–33.

London, N. J. (1973a). An essay on psychoanalytic theory: Two theories of schizophrenia. Part I: Review and critical assessment of the development of the two theories. *International Journal of Psychoanalysis, 54*, 169–178.

London, N. J. (1973b). An essay on psychoanalytic theory: Two theories of schizophrenia. Part II: Discussion and restatement of the specific theory of schizophrenia. *International Journal of Psychoanalysis, 54*, 179–194.

Luborsky, L. (1976). Helping alliance in psychotherapy. In J. L. Cleghorn (Ed.), *Successful psychotherapy* (pp. 92–116). Brunner/Mazel Publishers.

Lucas, R. (2009). *The psychotic wavelength: A psychoanalytic perspective for psychiatry.* Routledge.

Lutgens, D., Gariepy, G., & Malla, A. (2017). Psychological and psychosocial interventions for negative symptoms in psychosis: Systemic review and meta-analysis. *British Journal of Psychiatry, 210*, 324–332.

Lynn, D. J. (1993). Freud's analysis of A.B., a psychotic man, 1925–1930. *Journal of the American Academy of Psychoanalysis, 21*(1), 63–78.

Magliano, L. (2014). "Social dangerousness and incurability in schizophrenia": Results of an educational intervention for medical and psychology students. *Psychiatry Research, 219* (3), 457–463.

Mäkinen, J., Miettunen, J., Isohanni, M., & Koponen, H. (2008). Negative symptoms in schizophrenia—A review. *Nordic Journal of Psychiatry, 62*(5), 334–341.

Mander, H., & Kingdon, D. (2015). The evolution of cognitive-behavioral therapy for psychosis. *Psychology Research and Behavior Management, 8*, 63–69. https://doi.org /10.2147/PRBM.S52267

Martindale, B. (2015). Widening the dialogue: Psychoanalysis and open dialogue. *Context, 138*, 41–44.

Medco Health Solutions. (2011, November 16). *America's state of mind: New report finds Americans increasingly turn to medications to ease their mental woes; women lead the trend* [Press release]. https://www.prnewswire.com/news-releases/americas-state -of-mind-new-report-finds-americans-increasingly-turn-to-medications-to-ease-their -mental-woes-women-lead-the-trend-133939038.html

Meltzer, D. (1968). Terror, persecution and dread. *International Journal of Psychoanalysis, 49*, 396–400.

Meltzer, H., Bebbington, P., Dennis, M., Jenkins, R., McManus, S., & Brugha, T. (2013). Feelings of loneliness among adults with mental disorder. *Social Psychiatry and Psychiatric Epidemiology, 48*(1), 5–13.

Menninger, K. (1958). *Theory of psychoanalytic technique*. Basic Books.

Mentzos, S. (1993). The psychotic symptom as a substitute for an object relationship. In G. Benedetti & P. M. Furlan (Eds.), *The psychotherapy of schizophrenia: Effective clinical approaches—Controversies, critiques and recommendations* (pp. 107–113). Hogrefe and Huber Publishers.

Merleau-Ponty, M. (1945). *Phénoménologie de la Perception* [*Phenomenology of perception*]. Éditions Gallimard.

Michels, R. (2003). The relationship between psychoanalysis and schizophrenia by Richard Lucas—A commentary. *International Journal of Psychoanalysis, 84*(1), 9–12.

Miller, I. (1965). On the return of symptoms in the terminal phase of psycho-analysis. *International Journal of Psychoanalysis, 46*, 487–501.

Miller, J.-A. (2013). Ordinary psychosis revisited. *Psychoanalytical Notebooks, 26*, 34–35.

Mitchell, S. (1997). *Influence and autonomy in psychoanalysis*. The Analytic Press.

Moffic, H. S., & Kinzie, J. D. (1996). The history and future of cross-cultural psychiatric services. *Community Mental Health Journal, 32*(6), 581–592.

Moller, H. J. (2003). Management of the negative symptoms of schizophrenia: New treatment options. *CNS Drugs, 17*, 793–823.

Moncrieff, J. (2007). *The myth of the chemical cure: A critique of psychiatric drug treatment*. Palgrave Macmillan.

Morken, G., Widen, J. H., & Grawe, R. W. (2008). Non-adherence to antipsychotic medication, relapse and rehospitalisation in recent-onset schizophrenia. *BMC Psychiatry, 8*(1), 32.

Moscovitz, A., Dorahy, M., & Schafer, I. (2019). *Psychosis, trauma and dissociation: Evolving perspectives on severe psychopathology.* Wiley.

Moskowitz, A. (2011). Schizophrenia, trauma, dissociation, and scientific revolutions. *Journal of Trauma and Dissociation, 12,* 347–357.

Mote, J., Grant, P., & Silverstein, S. (2018, August 20). Treatment implications of situational variability in cognitive and negative Symptoms of schizophrenia. *Psychiatric Services Online.* https://ps.psychiatryonline.org/doi/10.1176/appi.ps.201800073

Narimanidze, M. (2015). *Who's talking to whom? A qualitative study of voice hearers* [Unpublished doctoral dissertation]. LIU Post.

Nass, M. (1984). The development of creative imagination in composers. *International Review of Psycho-Analysis, 11,* 481–491.

Nayani, T. H., & David, A. S. (1996). The auditory hallucination: A phenomenological survey. *Psychological Medicine, 26*(1), 177–189.

Novick, J. (1976). Termination of treatment in adolescence. *Psychoanalytic Study of the Child, 35,* 299–320.

Novick, J., & Novick, K. (2006). *Good goodbyes: Knowing how to end in psychotherapy and psychoanalysis.* Jason Aronson.

Ogden, T. H. (1979). On Projective Identification. *International Journal of Psychoanalysis, 60,* 357–373.

Ogden, T. H. (1989). *The primitive edge of experience.* Jason Aronson.

Ogden T. H. (1995). Analysing forms of aliveness and deadness of the transference-countertransference. *The International Journal of Psychoanalysis, 76*(4), 695–709.

Ogden, T. H. (2003). On not being able to dream. *The International Journal of Psychoanalysis.* https://onlinelibrary.wiley.com/toc/17458315/2003/84/1 *84*(1), 17–30.

Ogden, T. H. (2009). *Rediscovering psychoanalysis: Thinking and dreaming, learning and forgetting.* The New Library of Psychoanalysis.

Olfson, M., Mechanic, D., Hansell, S., Boyer, C. A., Walkup, J., & Weiden, P. J. (2000). Predicting medication noncompliance after hospital discharge among patients with schizophrenia. *Psychiatric Services, 51*(2), 216–222.

Ophir, O. (2015). *Psychosis, psychoanalysis and psychiatry in postwar USA: On the borderland of madness.* Routledge.

Orgel, S. (2000). Letting go: Some thoughts about termination. *Journal of the American Psychoanalytic Association, 48*(3), 719–739.

Os, J., & Bentall, R. (2012). Childhood adversities increase the risk of psychosis: A meta-analysis of patient-control, prospective- and cross-sectional cohort studies. *Schizophrenia Bulletin, 38*(4), 661–671.

Palmer, B. A., Pankratz, V. S., & Bostwick, J. M. (2005). The lifetime risk of suicide in schizophrenia: A reexamination. *Archives of General Psychiatry, 62*(3), 247.

Pao, P. N. (1979). *Schizophrenic disorders.* International Universities Press.

Perkins, D. O. (2002). Predictors of noncompliance in patients with schizophrenia. *Journal of Clinical Psychiatry, 63*(12), 1121–1128.

Pestalozzi, J., Frisch, S., Hinshelwood, R. D., & Houzel, D. (Eds.). (1998). *Psychoanalytic psychotherapy in institutional settings.* Karnac Books.

Pine, F. (1990). *Drive, ego, object, and self: A synthesis for clinical work.* Basic Books.

Podvoll, E. (1979). Psychosis and the mystic path. *Psychoanalytic Review, 66*(4), 571–590.

Podvoll, E. (2003). *Recovering sanity: A compassionate approach to understanding and treating psychosis.* Shambala Publications (Original work published 1990).

Poland, W. (2000). The analyst's witnessing of otherness. *Journal of the American Psychoanalytic Association, 48*(1), 17–35.

Putman, N., & Martindale, B. (Eds.). (2021). *Open dialogue for psychosis: Organising mental health services to prioritise dialogue, relationship and meaning.* Routledge.

Rabkin, J. G. (1980). Stressful life events and schizophrenia: A review of recent literature. *Psychological Bulletin, 87*, 408–425.

Räkköläinen, V. (1977). *Onset of psychosis. A clinical study of 68 cases* [Ph.D. thesis, University of Turku]. Annales Universitatis Turkuensis (Turku, Finland), Series D, Vol. 7 Turun yliopisto/Google Books. https://www.google.com/books/edition/Onset_of_Psychosis/WcM7vQEACAAJ?hl=en

Read, J. (2004). *Models of madness: Psychological, social and biological approaches to schizophrenia.* Brunner-Routledge.

Read, J., Fosse, R., Moskowitz, A., & Perry, B. (2014). The traumagenic neurodevelopmental model of psychosis revisited. *Neuropsychiatry, 4*, 65–79. https://doi.org/10.2217/NPY.13.89

Read, J., & Ross, C. A. (2003). Psychological trauma and psychosis: Another reason why people diagnosed schizophrenic must be offered psychological therapies. *Journal of the American Academy of Psychoanalysis, 31*(1), 247–268.

Read, J., Van Os, J., Morrison, A. P., & Ross, C. A. (2005). Childhood trauma, psychosis and schizophrenia: A literature review with theoretical and clinical implications. *Acta Psychiatrica Scandinavica, 112*, 330–350. https://doi.org/10.1111/j.1600-0447.2005.00634.x

Rector, N. A., & Beck, A. T. (2001). Cognitive behavioral therapy for schizophrenia: An empirical review. *The Journal of Nervous and Mental Disease, 189*, 278–287. https://doi.org/10.1097/00005053-200105000-0000210.1016/j.schres.2005.02.018.

Rettenbacher, M. A., Hofer, A., Eder, U., Hummer, M., Kemmler, G., Weiss, E. M., & Fleischhacker, W. W. (2004). Compliance in schizophrenia: Psychopathology, side effects, and patients' attitudes toward the illness and medication. *The Journal of Clinical Psychiatry, 65*(9), 3557.

Riviere, J. (1936). A contribution to the analysis of the negative therapeutic reaction. *International Journal of Psychoanalysis, 17*, 304–320.

Robinson, S., & Rollings, L. (2011). The effect of mood-context on visual recognition and recall memory. *Journal of General Psychology, 138*(1), 66–79.

Romme, M. A., & Escher, S. (1989). Hearing voices. *Schizophrenia Bulletin, 15*(2), 209–216.

Romme, M. A., & Escher, S. (1993). *Accepting voices.* Mind Publications.

Romme, M., Escher, S., Dillon, J., Corstens, D., & Morris, M. (2009). *Living with voices: 50 stories of recovery.* PCCS Books, Ltd.

Rosen, J. (1947). The treatment of schizophrenic psychosis by direct analytic therapy. *Psychiatric Quarterly, 21*, 3–37. https://doi.org/10.1007/BF01674766

Rosenbaum, B. (2015). Psychodynamic psychotherapy for persons in states of psychosis: Some research perspectives. *British Journal of Psychotherapy, 31*(4), 476–491. https://doi.org/10.1111/bjp.12187

Rosenbaum, B., & Harder, S. (2007). Psychosis and the dynamics of the psychotherapy process. *International Review of Psychiatry, 19*(1), 13–23. https://doi.org/10.1080/09540260601080854

Rosenbaum, B., Harder, S., Knudsen, P., Køster, A., Lindhardt, A., Lajer, M., Valbak, K., & Winther, G. (2012). Supportive psychodynamic psychotherapy versus treatment as usual for first-episode psychosis: Two-Year outcome. *Psychiatry: Interpersonal and Biological Processes, 75*(4), 331–341. https://doi.org/10.1521/psyc.2012.75.4.331

Rosenbaum, B., Valbak, K., Harder, S., Knudsen, P., Køster, A., Lajer, M., Lindhardt, A., Winther, G., Petersen, L., Jørgensen, P., Nordentoft, M., & Andreasen, A. H. (2005). The Danish National Schizophrenia Project: Prospective, comparative longitudinal treatment study of first-episode psychosis. *British Journal of Psychiatry, 186*(5), 394–399. https://doi.org/10.1192/bjp.186.5.394

Rosenbaum, B., Valbak, K., Harder, S., Knudsen, P., Køster, A, Lajer, M., Lindhardt, A., Winther, G., Petersen, L., Jørgensen, P., Nordentoft, M., & Andreasen, A. H. (2006). Treatment of patients with first-episode psychosis: Two-year outcome data from the Danish National Schizophrenia Project. *World Psychiatry, 5*(2), 100–103.

Rosenfeld, H. (1971). A clinical approach to the psychoanalytic theory of the life and death instincts: An investigation into the aggressive aspects of narcissism. *International Journal of Psychoanalysis, 52*, 169–178.

Rossi, G., & Beck, M. (2020, September). A little dab will do: A case of cannabis-induced psychosis. *Cureus, 12*(9). https://www.ncbi.nlm.nih.gov/pmc/articles/PMC7544610/

Rowan, A. (2014). "Ordinary psychosis" – A clinic of our time? Lacunae. *Lacanian Journal of Psychoanalysis, 3*(2), 166.

Rüsch, N., Corrigan, P. W., Todd, A. R., & Bodenhausen, G. V. (2011). Automatic stereotyping against people with schizophrenia, schizoaffective and affective disorders. *Psychiatry Research, 186*(1), 34–39.

Saffron, J. (2002). Brief relational psychoanalytic treatment. *Psychoanalytic Dialogues, 12*(2), 171–195.

Salberg, J. (Ed.). (2010). *Good enough endings: Breaks, interruptions, and terminations from contemporary relational perspectives*. Routledge.

Sawyer, A. (2015). *Smoking cigarettes, eating glass: A psychologist's memoir*. Santa Fe Writer's Project.

Schafer, R. (1968). The mechanisms of defence. *International Journal of Psychoanalysis, 49*, 49–62.

Schafer, R. (1992). *Retelling a life: Narration and dialogue in psychoanalysis*. Basic Books.

Schafer, R. (2002). Experiencing termination: Authentic and false depressive positions. *Psychoanalytic Psychology, 19*, 235–253.

Schlesinger, H. (2014). *Endings and beginnings: On terminating psychotherapy and psychoanalysis*. Routledge.

Searles, H. (1959). The effort to drive the other person crazy – An element in the aetiology and psychotherapy of schizophrenia. *British Journal of Medical Psychology, 32*, 1–18.

Searles, H. (1960). *The nonhuman environment*. International Universities Press.

Searles, H. (1961). Schizophrenic communication. *Psychoanalytic Review, 48*(1), 3–50.

Searles, H. (1965). *Collected papers on schizophrenia and related subjects*. International Universities Press.

Searles, H. (1979). *Countertransference and related subjects: Selected papers*. International Universities Press.

Searles, H. (2017). Concerning transference and countertransference. *Psychoanalytic Dialogues, 27*(2), 192–210. https://doi.org/10.1080/10481885.2017.1285167

Sedler, M. J. (2016). Medicalization in psychiatry: The medical model, descriptive diagnosis, and lost knowledge. *Medicine, Health Care and Philosophy, 19*(2), 247–252. https://doi.org/10.1007/s11019-015-9670-5

Segal, H. (1991). *Dreams, phantasy and art*. Tavistock/Routledge.

Seikkula, J. (2011). Becoming dialogical: Psychotherapy or a way of life? *Australian and New Zealand Journal of Family Therapy (ANZJFT), 32*(3), 179–193. https://doi.org/10.1375/anft.32.3.179

Seikkula, J., Aaltonen, J., Alakare, B., Haarakangas, K., Keränen, J., & Lehtinen, K. (2006). Five-year experience of first-episode nonaffective psychosis in open-dialogue approach: Principles, follow-up outcomes, and two case studies. *Psychotherapy Research, 16*(2), 214–228. https://doi.org/10.1080/10503300500268490

Seikkula, J., Aaltonen, J., Rasinkangas, A., Alakare, B., Holma, J., & Lehtinen, V. (2003). Open dialogue approach: Treatment principles and preliminary results of a two-year follow-up on first episode schizophrenia. *Ethical and Human Sciences and Services, 5*(3), 163–182.

Seikkula, J., & Alakare, B. (2013). *Psychosis as a personal crisis*. Routledge.

Selzer, M. (1983). Preparing the chronic schizophrenic for exploratory psychotherapy: The role of hospitalization. *Psychiatry, 46*, 303–310.

Selzer, M., Carsky, M., Gilbert, B., Weiss, W., Klein, M., & Wagner, S. (1984). The shared field: A precursor stage in the development of a psychotherapeutic alliance with the hospitalized chronic schizophrenic patient. *Psychiatry, 47*(4), 324–332.

Selzer, M., & Schwartz, F. (1994). The continuity of personality in schizophrenia. *Journal of Psychotherapy Practice and Research, 3*, 313–324.

Selzer, M., Sullivan, T. B., Carsky, M., & Terkelsen, K. G. (1989). *Working with the person with schizophrenia*. New York University Press.

Sérieux, P., & Capgras, J. (1909). *Les folies raisonnantes, le délire de l'interprétation* [*Reasoning follies, the delirium of interpretation*]. J-F Alcan.

Shevlin, M., Houston, J., Dorahy, M., & Adamson, G. (2008). Cumulative traumas and psychosis: An analysis of the national comorbidity survey and the British psychiatric survey. *Schizophrenia Bulletin, 34*(1), 193–199.

Slochower, J. (1998). Clinical controversies: Ending an analysis. *Psychologist-Psychoanalyst, 18*, 24–25.

Smith, R. C., & Bartholomew, T. (2006). Will hospitals recover?: The implications of a recovery-orientation. *American Journal of Psychiatric Rehabilitation, 9*(2), 85–100.

Smith, S. M. (1979). Remembering in and out of context. *Journal of Experimental Psychology: Human Learning and Memory, 5*(5), 460–471.

Smith, S. M., & Vela, E. (2001). Environmental context-dependent memory: A review and meta-analysis. *Psychonomic Bulletin & Review, 8*(2), 203–220.

Sommer, I., De Kort, G., Meijering, A. L., Dazzan, P., Hulshoff, P., Kahn, R., & Van Haren, N. (2013). How frequent are radiological abnormalities in patients with psychosis? A review of 1379 MRI scans. *Schizophrenia Bulletin, 39*(4), 815–819.

Stanton, M. (1992). Harold Searles talks to Martin Stanton. *Free Associations, 3*(3), 323–339.

Steiner, J. (1982). Perverse relationships between parts of the self: A clinical illustration. *International Journal of Psychoanalysis, 63*, 241–251.

Steiner, J. (1993). *Psychic Retreats: Pathological organizations in psychotic, neurotic and borderline patients*. Routledge.

Stern, D. B. (1997). *Unformulated experience: From dissociation to imagination in psychoanalysis*. Analytic Press.

Stierlin, H. (1959). The adaptation to the "stronger person's" reality. *Interpersonal and Biological Processes, 22*(2), 143–152.

Sullivan, H. S. (1947). Therapeutic investigations in schizophrenia. *Psychiatry, 10*(2), 121–126.

Sullivan, H. S. (1953). *The interpersonal theory of psychiatry*. W. W. Norton & Co.

Sullivan, H. S. (1956). *Clinical studies in psychiatry*. W. W. Norton & Co.

Sullivan, H. S. (1962). *Schizophrenia as a human process*. W. W. Norton & Co.

Sullivan, H. S. (2006). *Conceptions of modern psychiatry*. Kessinger Publishing (Original work published in 1940).

Switaj, P., Grygiel, P., Anczewska, M., & Wciorka, J. (2014). Loneliness mediates the relationship between internalized stigma and depression among patients with psychotic disorders. *International Journal of Social Psychiatry, 60*(8), 733–740.

Symington, N., & Symington, J. (1996). *The clinical thinking of Wilfred Bion*. Routledge.

Taleb, N. (2012). *Antifragile: Things that gain from disorder*. Random House.

Tasman, A. (2002). Lost in the DSM-IV checklist: Empathy, meaning and doctor–patient relationship. *Academic Psychiatry, 26*, 38–44.

Thompson, M. G., & Thompson, S. (1998). Interview with Dr. Otto Allen Will, Jr. *Contemporary Psychoanalysis, 34*(2), 289–304.

Ticho, G. R. (1967). On self-analysis. *International Journal of Psychoanalysis, 48*, 308–318.

Tolpin, P., & Tolpin, M. (Eds.). (1996). *Heinz Kohut: The Chicago Institute lectures*. Routledge.

Turkington, D., Wright, N. P., & Tai, S. (2013). Advances in cognitive behavior therapy for psychosis. *International Journal of Cognitive Therapy, 6*(2), 150–170.

Tutter, A. (2006). Medication as object. *Journal of the American Psychoanalytic Association, 54*(3), 781–804.

Valenstein, E. (2004). *Blaming the brain: The truth about drugs and mental health*. Simon and Schuster.

Van Os, J., Bak, M., Hanssen, M., Bijl, R., de Graaf, R., & Verdoux, H. R. (2002). Cannabis use and psychosis: A longitudinal population-based study. *American Journal of Epidemiology, 156*(4), 319–327.

Varese, F., Smeets, F., Drukker, M., Lieverse, R., Lataster, T., Viechtbauer, W., Read J., van Os, J., & Bentall, R. P. (2012). Childhood adversities increase the risk of psychosis: A meta-analysis of patient-control, prospective-and cross-sectional cohort studies. *Schizophrenia Bulletin, 38*, 661–671.

Werbart, A. (2007). Utopic ideas of cure and joint exploration in psychoanalytic supervision. *International Journal of Psychoanalysis, 88*, 1391–1408.

Whitaker, L. C. (2007). Forces pushing prescription psychotropic drugs in college mental health. *Journal of College Student Psychotherapy, 21*(3–4), 1–25.

Whitaker, R., & Cosgrove, L. (2015). *Psychiatry under the influence: Institutional corruption, social injury, and prescriptions for reform*. Palgrave McMillan.

Will, O. (1958). Psychotherapeutics and the schizophrenic reaction. *Journal of Nervous and Mental Disease, 126*(2), 109–140.

Wing, J., & Brown, G. (1970). *Institutionalism and schizophrenia*. Cambridge University Press.

Winnicott, D. W. (1953). Transitional objects and transitional phenomena—A study of the first not-me possession. *International Journal of Psychoanalysis, 34*, 89–97.

Winnicott, D. W. (1960). The theory of the parent–child relationship. *International Journal of Psychoanalysis, 41*, 585–595.

Winnicott, D. W. (1965). *The maturational processes and the facilitating environment: Studies in the theory of emotional development.* International Universities Press.

Winnicott, D. W. (1971). *Playing and reality.* Tavistock Publications.

Winnicott, D. W. (1974). Fear of breakdown. *International Review of Psycho-analysis, 1,* 103–107.

Winnicott, D. W. (1975). *Through pediatrics to psycho-analysis.* Basic Books.

Wykes, T., Steel, C., Everitt, B., & Tarrier, N. (2008). Cognitive behavior therapy for schizophrenia: Effect sizes, clinical models, and methodological rigor. *Schizophrenia Bulletin, 34*, 523–537.

Yanof, J. (2013). Play technique in psychodynamic psychotherapy. *Child and Adolescent Psychiatric Clinics of North America, 22*(2), 261–282.

Young, J. L., Zonana, H. V., & Shepler, K. (1986). Medication noncompliance in schizophrenia: Codification and update. *Bulletin of the American Academy of Psychiatry & the Law, 14*(2), 105–122.

Young, R. M. (1995). The vicissitudes of transference and countertransference: The work of Harold Searles. *Free Associations, 5B*(2), 171–195.

Zimmermann, G., Favrod, J., Trieu, V. H., & Pomini, V. (2005). The effect of cognitive behavioral treatment on the positive symptoms of schizophrenia spectrum disorders: A meta-analysis. *Schizophrenia Research, 77*(1), 1–9.

# Index

Milton Keynes UK
Ingram Content Group UK Ltd.
UKHW021848011123
431753UK00022B/170